Introduction to
Operations & Information Management Systems

KENNETH A. KOZAR
TOMASZ MIASKIEWICZ
UNIVERSITY OF
COLORADO—BOULDER

Kendall Hunt
publishing company

Cover image © Shutterstock, Inc.

Kendall Hunt
publishing company

www.kendallhunt.com
Send all inquiries to:
4050 Westmark Drive
Dubuque, IA 52004-1840

CONTENTS

chapter 1

Introduction to Operations and Information Management

A SYSTEMS VIEW

Systems exist everywhere. But we need to know precisely the meaning of the word "systems" to understand Operations and Information Management from a systems perspective. This chapter introduces the topic of viewing complex things as systems and why systems thinking is important in a business or an organizational setting. It explains how viewing an organization from an information systems perspective goes hand in hand with information systems and operations management.

What Are Systems?

The word "systems" has many definitions and may mean different things to different people. In the context of this book, systems are a set of interrelated and interdependent parts that exist for a purpose. When we study a system, or conduct systems thinking, we not only must understand each of the parts of a system, but how the parts work together and interrelate. Since the parts can work together synergistically and add up to more than the sum of the parts, it is important to understand the overall purpose of the system and how the "whole" of the system works together. Peter Senge in his bestselling book *The Fifth Discipline* considered systems thinking the fifth discipline that considers seeing the parts versus seeing the wholes.

Systems can be both physical and conceptual. There are business systems, computer systems, solar systems, environmental systems, communication systems, transportation systems, entertainment systems and many other kinds of systems. The important thing to remember is that systems have a set of interrelated parts that exist for a purpose. To understand, improve and even to "beat" systems, we must understand some basic system concepts. These concepts include system goals/purpose, how

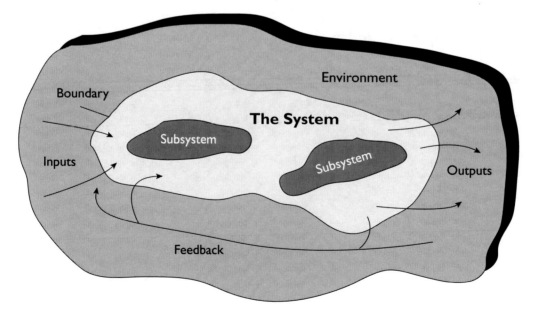

FIGURE 1.1—*A Pictorial View of a System*

inputs/processes/outputs define a system, subsystems, supra-systems, feedback loops and boundaries. Once we understand these concepts, we can begin to practice systems thinking.

Systems exist in an environment. Let us think of a car as a system. It exists in an environment that includes resources outside the boundary of the car. These resources include such things as fuel, tires and even a driver. The car as a system accepts resources as inputs from the environment to keep it running and meeting its objective or purpose of providing the ability to get from point A to point B. The car consists of various subsystems, such as the fuel subsystem, the electrical subsystem, the suspension subsystem and the exhaust subsystem. These subsystems accept the inputs either from the environment or another subsystem and process them by interacting with one another to produce outputs. We call this interaction at the boundary of a system or subsystem an interface. For example, the fuel system and the electrical system interact or interface when a spark that powers the engine ignites the fuel mixture. The output is power that can interface with the drive train subsystem to provide movement. The car exists in and operates on the highway system, which we could consider a supra-system or a system more encompassing than just a car. The car and the highway systems are part of an even larger transportation system that also includes airplanes, trains and bicycles.

All systems, subsystems and supra-systems accept inputs, process them and produce some type of output. Depending on whether the output is acceptable or not, a change in inputs or processing must take place. This is called a *feedback* or *control loop*. The feedback loop helps to keep the system on target toward its purpose or goal. This control mechanism keeps the system in constant adjustment. For example, the driver of a car receives feedback on the output of speed from the speedometer and makes adjustments based on the desired speed. The driver may speed up or slow down based on the set standard. This is the control mechanism in the system. We can even automate the speed feedback control mechanism in a car through the use of a "cruise control." The same is true of steering the car with the driver constantly making adjustments based on observing whether the car is between the lines in the lane in which it is traveling. Someday steering systems may become automated by sensing whether the car is "between the lines;" if not, it would make adjustments.

Managers of organizations keep the organization heading toward its goal or purpose by acquiring people, materials, machines, technology, capital, energy and other resources from the environment. They then supervise processing those resources into goods and services that then become output to the environment. Figure 1.2 shows an organization in an environment ready to receive inputs. The manager is attempting to achieve the greatest efficiency in the use of the resources and uses feedback in the form of information to determine if the organization is in control and heading toward its goals. We call the consideration of all the interacting parts and the assurance that they are working together in the best way systems thinking. The manager must focus

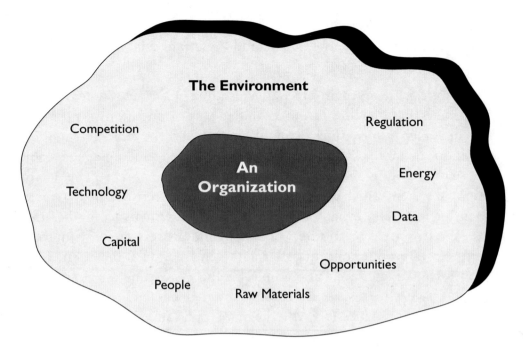

FIGURE 1.2—*The Environment in Which Organizations Exist Is of Concern to a System*

on determining whether the forces in the environment, namely the customers, desire the outputs in the form of products and services.

Depending on the manager's perspective and scope, he or she may see a subsystem as a system or vice-versa. For example, the chief executive officer (CEO) might be viewing the entire organization as within his or her system scope and the marketing function as a subsystem, while a chief marketing executive might see the marketing system as his or her system. Each of these systems and subsystems has a conceptual boundary. The environment outside the boundary of the system often is beyond the control of the manager. The CEO cannot control what the organization's competition will do, and the marketing executive often will not have control over capital acquisition or finance functions. In any case, all the organizational systems must work together to survive in an industry that exists in the economic supra-system.

Many people perform systems thinking without consciously calling it systems thinking. One could see a car or motorcycle mechanic as a systems thinker. In fact, one of the books that best describes systems thinking is Robert Pirsig's *Zen and the Art of Motorcycle Maintenance*. Pirsig describes how a good mechanic examines the interacting subsystems and methodically determines if there is fuel from the fuel subsystem, spark from the ignition system, and transfer of engine power through the drive train to propel the motorcycle. Not only does one have to tune each subsystem to perfection, all the subsystems must interface and work together to have a smoothly running vehicle.

Organizational Systems

Organizational systems often are conceptual rather than physical. The inputs and outputs can be physical, but the mind of the manager creates the perception and coordination of all the subsystems. One can't see the motivation of the people in the system and their desire for high performance, but the results are visible in the system outputs and the efficiency based on the worker productivity or the amount of output produced compared to the amount and cost of the inputs and processing. To examine this productivity and efficiency, the manager must examine and measure by using data processed into information.

Based on our definition of systems, organizational managers must consider all the inputs, processes, outputs and control/feedback mechanisms. People sometimes will say they have a system when they really mean to say that they have a method. A method is narrow in the sense that it really is a set of steps to accomplish something or what we refer to as a process. We like to think wider and attempt to understand the entire scope of the system, including the inputs and outputs and the interaction with the environment. We may even attempt to expand our system boundary by controlling or bringing into the system boundary inputs that currently exist in the environment. For example, if we are a restaurant, we may bring our vegetable supplier into our system boundary and into our control by acquiring the supplier or even growing our own vegetables. Often this will result in more control over quality and may provide a lower cost solution. Thus, system boundaries can change.

A System of Systems

Systems thinking is part of putting a building in the environment. We can see the building as a system. Texas Instruments built a new wafer production plant in Richardson, Texas, in 2006. The manager in charge, Paul Westbrook, started with a blank sheet of paper and took a systems approach in coming up with a new design. He said that the designers needed to rethink every process and the connections between the processes. For example, he examined how they could use waste heat from one system to power another, much like a Toyota Prius uses braking to generate electricity to charge the batteries. He said, "You have to think of a house or building not just as walls, windows and floors, with lights, heating and cooling, but as a system of systems, and then rethink how they interact." He believed that the heating and air-conditioning could "talk" to the windows and the windows could talk to the "lighting." "Smart" windows could let in more light and heat when it was cold and tell the lights to dim, and the heater could get some help from the windows and lights depending on the detected conditions. Westbrook said tests had determined that this "system of systems" would result in a 20 percent savings in electricity and a 35 percent savings in water.

(From Friedman, Thomas L. *Hot, Flat, and Crowded.* New York: Farrar, Straus, and Giroux, 2008, pages 282–283.)

Another system boundary that has changed over time is how data is inputed and by whom. The movement of customer self-service has caused this. The customer places many orders directly (usually by using a web site). He or she is responsible for the time taken to enter an order and to assure that it is correct. The customer may even take a larger role, as in self-service gas stations, and provide inputs on payment as well as pumping the fuel. The age of the station attendant who pumps gas and takes your money and even provides minor service such as washing a windshield is long gone. Businesses have expanded the systems boundary to include the customer within the system.

The Value of Systems Understanding

If we understand a system, we can more easily manage it. Systems diagrams allow us to see the composition of complex things and how they interact. We can draw a picture of a system with its inputs, processes and outputs and have a better view of what inputs and processes we can change as well as what is outside the system boundary and often beyond our control. We also can evaluate the impact on people's behavior if we have a better picture of a system. When we have a picture of a system, we help clarify our thinking and see the interactions between subsystems. This will allow us to ask "what if . . ." kinds of questions that can help us avoid unintended consequences.

Systems thinking can assist our thinking and help us look for loopholes or weaknesses. This is important in both problem solving and opportunity finding. Lawmakers and politicians need to take a systems view to avoid unintended consequences. One example of not thinking broadly enough was a law passed in Nebraska where parents could "drop off an unwanted child" at a fire station to protect the child and ease the strife of stressed out parents. The lawmakers did not think broadly enough by clarifying the law and precisely stating who parents could drop off. They presumed the drop offs would occur only on a local or regional level and would be infants. The law had the unintended consequence of parents dropping off "troubled" teenagers from around the country at fire stations just as the law allowed. Thinking through the law, diagramming and understanding the system and determining what could happen would have prevented the need for further legislation to clarify the law.

There are many examples of suggested changes to a system that did not have the intended results. One of the best sources of unintended consequences caused by inappropriate systems thinking is a book by John Gall. Gall's book entitled *The Systems Bible* was formerly called *Systemantics*. "Systemantics" really refers to "System" "Antics" or unintended consequences of not thinking through how a system might really perform and react. These "antics" could be as simple as believing that increasing product prices could increase revenues since each sale would bring in more money. But, increased prices could reduce demand and cut the number of items sold. Total revenue could decrease. Gall provides many of these types of examples.

Systems in a Business Organization

Although systems exist in all organizations, we will focus on taking a business systems view of the functions in an organization. Businesses require the performance of different functions. Often, these functions align with popular majors in a university's business school, such as accounting, finance, human resources, information systems, management and marketing. No matter what your major, you will encounter systems in an organization. From our basic understanding of systems, we can create a systems view of an organization and determine why certain business functions are necessary:

- **Operations systems**—raw material procurement, logistics and production systems

- **Human resource systems**—people procurement, compensation and people management systems

- **Financial systems**—capital acquisition and allocation systems, credit approval systems

- **Accounting systems**—general ledger, accounts payable, accounts receivable, payroll systems

- **Marketing and sales systems**—customer relationship, sales management and reporting systems

- **Information management systems**—data management and reporting systems

Professor Stephen Lawrence of the University of Colorado/Boulder Leeds School of Business compared the business functions in an organization with systems in the human body. He compared marketing to the eyes, ears and mouth of the organization because it listens to and observes customers and then "speaks" to them through advertising. He compared finance to the gastrointestinal tract that feeds the organization with capital needed to keep it nourished. Human resources could play a similar role obtaining labor that keeps the organization fulfilled with workers. Accounting is similar to the circulatory system that allocates, distributes and assures the organization's balance. Operations management is the muscle and bone that holds the organization together and provides the production processes that keep the organization moving and operating. Finally, the information system is the nervous system that provides key performance indicators and needed intelligence to keep all the other systems coordinated. This anatomical analogy can help us view the organization as a system similar to our human bodies.

The focus of this book is on the operations and information management systems in an organization—the muscle, bone and nervous systems in Dr. Lawrence's analogy. As shown in Figure 1.3, an organization survives by generating revenue from selling products and services. Marketing may be responsible for promoting and selling products and services, but operations management acquires the needed raw materials and

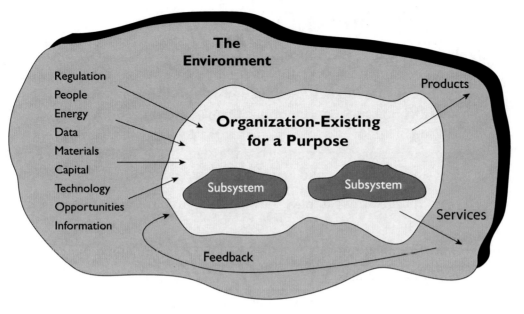

FIGURE 1.3—*An Organization in the Environment*

manages the processes to convert these raw materials into finished goods. Business people often call this the production function or operations management. Without operations management, marketing and sales would not have anything to sell to the customers in the environment. Within operations management, production management also works with human resource managers to assure there are people necessary to perform the production processes. In a purely service production firm, production management schedules and manages the persons needed to provide the services. Thus, we can see that operations management plays a key role in the thriving of an organization, as well as with other activities that provide support for the production of goods and services, such as in accounting and finance.

One other area that supports the entire organization is the information systems function, or what Dr. Lawrence referred to as the nervous system. We can call this group by many different names. Often, people call it information management systems, but we would like to shorten that phrase. Others might call it information technology, but the people portion of information systems is just as important as the technology, and our definition should include it. Thus, we will refer to it as information systems. A major role of information systems is to collect, store and maintain all the data from both inside and outside the organization so it can become processed into information.

The information systems team in an organization serves all managers in the organization. It stores internally processed data and external data from the environment in a data warehouse to allow all managers to analyze the best solutions to management problems and to take advantage of opportunities. The information systems group also provides analytic tools, such as regularly scheduled reports, and answers ad hoc inquires. The entire organization needs information to manage wisely.

Information allows managers to manage because it takes the pulse of the organization through measurement. Some even claim that if you cannot measure something, you cannot manage it. The reason this is true is that managers establish plans and then have metrics or measures that determine if the organization's results align with the plan. If not, they have to make adjustments. The measurements are the feedback to the managers. Typical measures from a systems perspective include an examination of the system outputs and the amount of resources that are input or consumed to process the inputs into the outputs.

Managers also examine the efficiency of processes for all business functions. Managers of human resources need information about people who have needed skills and how much it would cost to hire and retain them, as well as the cost of labor per unit of production. Managers of marketing need to know about existing and potential customers and what products and services they might be interested in purchasing, as well as the effectiveness of advertising and promotions. Finance needs to know the cost of capital. We often refer to these measures as key performance indicators. We will delve into them later in the book under the topic of business intelligence. Managerial decisions must take place utilizing business intelligence or data that has been analyzed to produce information that leads to knowledge. As Chapter 3 will explain, management should take place by utilizing information, not by guessing.

As we will see, operations management also needs measures to determine if all is well. When procuring raw materials, operations managers need to know whether any of the raw materials do not meet the quality standards of the organization. It needs to know whether suppliers are delivering the materials when needed. It needs to know whether there are any price increases from suppliers, and, if so, whether the company should evaluate and consider other suppliers. Once the raw materials and human resources are available, the operations manager must schedule the production of finished goods or the delivery of services. The operations managers must examine alternative production schedules and whether or not more people or machines are needed. The manager must determine if it would be beneficial to the organization to have someone else do the production, and even consider outsourcing to other firms or offshoring by having production done in another country with lower labor costs. As you can see, there are many decisions to make. This should take place with information, as informed decisions lead to effectiveness, doing the right things and efficiency.

Operations and information management must work together since the operations managers can create and utilize models of the organization that evaluate alternatives in order to make wise decisions. These models can be mathematical representations of the many interdependencies in a system. They can utilize data as model inputs to assist the manager in scheduling people and machines, in routing trucks and other means of transportation to assure appropriate pick up and delivery, and in simulating processes to choose the most efficient means of production. The models need clean and accurate data as an input. This is the responsibility of the information systems group. As we can see, operations and information management need to work together closely to assure efficiency and reduced costs. We can analyze all of these interactions using a systems perspective that utilizes systems thinking.

How Might Students View This Topic?

When they designed a class on operations and information management, the authors determined that they wanted to meet the needs of their students. They wanted to do their design with information, not guesswork. To do that, they created a persona or a fictional, but realistic, representation of a potential student. This persona was the result of conducting focus groups and interviews with past, present and future students in the class. This helped the authors understand how students might view the topic of operations and information management and resulted in the persona of Molly shown on the next page. Molly was the ideal student that the teachers of the class desired.

The class designers and authors of this book shared this persona with some future class recitation leaders. They pointed out that this was the type of student the teachers desired but that the class also would have to have some students who needed convincing of the relevancy of this topic. This led to the persona of Dave. See Dave's persona on page 12.

We are presenting these two personas for you to review so you can determine your own agenda and interest in the subject. Hopefully, doing this will allow you to gain a greater appreciation for the subject matter and to express your own concerns about learning operations and information management.

Chapter Summary

Systems are important when examining organizations. Understanding systems and subsystems, as well as their inputs, processes and outputs and how one uses feedback to keep the system in control, can assist in managing organizations. This ability to conduct systems thinking and to understand how systems link together will assist you in gaining a greater appreciation for others in an organization. Systems thinking can help clarify where problems may be occurring and where opportunities may exist to gain efficiency and effectiveness. Business students can gain a competitive advantage by having this knowledge. It also could affect career choice since many jobs exist in the area of operations and information management.

MOLLY GORDON

AGE: 20
MAJOR: Marketing
YEAR: Junior
PRIMARY GOALS

- To be challenged to think!
- To see the value of putting forth extra effort
- To learn why systems are important in the marketing field
- To not be burdened with definitions and "techy talk"
- To be engaged with and involved in the class

"I want the class to become more relevant to my interests in marketing."

Molly Gordon is about to start her 3rd year at the Leeds School. From the day she first entered the halls of the business school, she knew that she wanted to be a Marketing major. Since high school, she has envisioned herself working at an advertising agency, and she has already successfully completed an internship at an ad firm in New York.

She is a driven student who has excelled in all of her classes at the business school thus far. She does not mind putting in the extra effort to get an A in a class as long as she sees the value of doing so.

However, she is not looking forward to attending the Introduction to Operations and Information Management class. Her friends that have taken the class warned Molly about the class. They told her that the class has nothing to do with marketing, is filled with "techy" talk that most students do not understand, and to do well you just have to memorize definitions. Molly's friends thought the class was a waste of time and money.

Molly recently heard from her undergraduate advisor that the class is going to be completely changed this upcoming semester. First of all, she despises classes that simply ask the students to memorize facts, definitions, and slides. She feels that her intellect, knowl-

edge, and effort is underutilized in such classes. Molly wants to THINK in the class! She wants to analyze a particular situation or real-world case and apply her knowledge. She feels that it is particularly absurd to be asked to memorize definitions and features of specific technologies. She has grown up with the Internet and technology. She does not need to know the definition or features of a certain technology because she already knows how to use it!

Also, Molly wants the new class to become more relevant to her own interests in marketing. She hopes to learn how systems interact with, help, and influence the work that marketers do in the real world. She hopes the skills and knowledge that she learns through the class will set her apart when she interviews for her first job after college.

Finally, Molly hopes that the professor of the class will engage the students and encourage them to be personally involved in the class. She does not want to come to class, sit in a large auditorium, and just take notes every day. Molly wants to share her knowledge, opinions, and perspectives with her fellow classmates. She wants to get deeper into the material, to discuss it's real world impacts, and to learn from not only the professor but also from the perspectives of her classmates.

DAVID KING

AGE: 19
MAJOR: Undecided
YEAR: Sophomore
PRIMARY GOALS
- To see the real-world impacts of the class
- To not be burdened with learning complex technologies
- To understand how systems and technology affect managers and CEOs
- To see the value of putting forth an effort in the class
- To have fun!

"I think that systems have nothing to do with the business world."

David King is about to start his sophomore year at the Leeds School. David's father is a partner at Accenture (a Fortune 500 consulting company), and he hopes to follow in his father's footsteps and one day become a manager in the business world. However, he is currently undecided about his major, and has found only a few classes that were even remotely interesting to him at the business school.

David is willing to work hard, but only when he enjoys the class and sees the value of him putting forth an effort. However, he is dreading attending the Introduction to Operations and Information Management class during the upcoming semester because he believes that the class will be teaching him only about complex technologies. He commonly thinks of systems majors as computer science majors without the quantitative skills for an engineering degree. He feels comfortable using his iPhone and other devices that are essential to communication and getting his school work done, but has had trouble even doing complex operations with numbers in Excel. In the systems class, David is afraid of being exposed as someone without technical savvy.

David also aspires to become a well-known CEO one day, and doesn't think that CEOs need systems to do their jobs effectively. He thinks that systems are some-thing that only techies work with. Personally, he only uses technologies when he has to, and has no interest in simply learning about new technologies or systems.

David has heard a rumor from his friends that the Introduction to Operations and Information Management will be going through a complete overhaul before the start of the upcoming semester. While he is very skeptical that the new version of the class will be of any interest to him, he hopes that the professor can make an effective case to him for how systems impact the work that businesspeople do every day.

Additionally, David hopes that the value of even offering this class at the business school becomes apparent. Currently, he has trouble even understanding why the Operations and Information Management department is part of the business school—marketing, finance, accounting, and management make sense to him, systems do not. So, he hopes that the professor can clearly illustrate how businesses depend on systems, and why business school students need a systems education.

Finally, David hopes that the class presents the material in a fun and interactive manner. Classes that simply feed students with Powerpoint slides tend to "lose" David. He stops paying attention and develops a very cynical view of the class.

Food for Thought/Systems

☞ What systems have you seen around you this week?

☞ Why are systems important when you try to understand why something happens or doesn't happen?

☞ Do functional areas such as accounting, finance, human resources, marketing, etc. all have systems? Why would it be to your advantage to understand these systems in your area of interest?

References

Gall, John. 2002. *The systems bible: The beginner's guide to systems large and small.* Walker, MN: General Systemantics Press, Third Edition.

Haines, Stephen G. 1998. *The manager's guide to systems thinking and learning.* Amherst, MA: HRD Press.

Kozar, Kenneth A. 1989. *Humanized information systems analysis and design: People building systems for people.* New York: McGraw-Hill Book Company.

O'Connor, Joseph, and Ian McDermott. 1997. *The art of systems thinking.* London: Thorsons.

Pirsig, Robert M. 1974. *Zen and the art of motorcycle maintenance: An inquiry into values.* New York: William Morrow and Company.

Senge, Peter M. 1994. *The fifth discipline.* New York: Doubleday Business.

Weinberg, Gerald M. 2001. *An introduction to general systems thinking.* New York; Dorset House Publishing.

Exercise

Some say the human body could be viewed as a system composed of many subsystems and that a physician is a systems analyst. What would you say to defend this view? What are the subsystems in a human body? How do these subsystems interact? Are there interdependencies between the subsystems? What are the inputs to the human body? Are there things in the environment that the human body would need to survive? What sub-systems process the inputs into outputs? Give some examples of a feedback loop to keep the human body functioning. Consider some things like hunger, thirst and body temperature.

Exercise

Perform a systems scan and draw a diagram of an organizational unit. This could be a club or even a fraternity or sorority, or one segment of such an organization. Specify the system boundaries to state what the system includes and excludes. Specify the inputs and outputs from the system. What people are involved with the organization? What processes do they perform? What information is necessary to keep this organizational unit functioning? How do feedback loops keep the organizational unit on track and heading toward its goal?

chapter 2

Aligning Systems and Business Strategy

Both business and information systems units within organizations have strategies. The business strategy defines what needs to be done to enable the organization to excel in the marketplace, and the information systems strategy indicates where to use resources to utilize technology to assist in running and managing the business. These strategies must support each other. In fact, they must be carefully linked so that resources are not wasted. History shows that business managers have felt their information needs lacking. The managers have often felt that the information systems organization is a group of technical people who do not understand the business. This has been a problem. Some of the problem stems from the management and lack of leadership in the information systems area. Some of the problem stems from the assumption by business management that the technology people understand the business needs of the organization.

The Chief Information Officer

The highest ranking information systems manager in a business organization is the chief information officer or the CIO. The CIO is responsible for all technological support for the organization, including computing and telecommunications. The technology could range from cell phones to personal computers to networks of computers and storage units to private telephone systems. This is a very difficult job because it requires interaction and communication with all other company managers, which all have information needs. Most chief information officers spend a short time span in the position before they either leave or become released from their duties. This has caused some cynics to state that CIO really stands for Career Is Over.

The number one issue that surveys of the cause of loss of sleep for chief information officers in the mid-1990s revealed was how to align business and information systems strategy. This issue continued as the top concern of corporate managers through the 1990s and into the next century. In 2006, *CIO Magazine* published an article on "The State of the Chief Information Officer." Many things have changed over the years, but the issue that has not gone away is that of aligning information systems and business strategy. Researchers have not yet met the challenge of this problem. But, some study of the challenge may be helpful in understanding how information systems can ripple through the organization. A better understanding can provide a competitive advantage for those organizations that take a broader view of their organization and include information systems as an integral part of its business strategy.

Ernst and Young, an information systems consulting company, was curious about why the CIO job was so difficult. They surveyed CIOs, the bosses of the CIOs, including Chief Executive Officers, and peers of the CIO, including Chief Financial Officers and Chief Marketing Officers. The surveys investigated the views of each of the three groups within an organization with regard to what they thought needed doing in regard to information systems. The number one "to-do" for all three groups was to "Align IS and Corporate Goals." Further investigation revealed what corporate business managers felt was the number one best way for the CIO to get fired. It was not lacking knowledge about technology as many had suspected but "Failing to

Communicate with Senior Management." Other issues with the CIO included "Not fitting in with corporate culture," "Not being a team player" and "Failing to deliver functionality required by the business." The CIOs seemed to be failing to be managers and were focusing on technology.

All of these discoveries give some clues why the alignment of information systems and corporate goals may be difficult. Many CIOs came through the technical ranks of the company and focused on technical, not business, issues. But the business managers did not want to participate in "tech talk"; they wanted to know how technology could assist them in meeting their business objectives. Senior business managers wanted to communicate with information systems managers about business matters, not the latest technology. The corporate culture was one of business, even for companies that specialized in providing technology for others. The business managers did not feel that the CIO was a team player unless he or she could sit in the boardroom and communicate about business issues. Functionality required by the business was processing transactions and providing information to allow the rest of the management team to make better decisions. The CIO needed to be part of the business team and communicate about the business strategy and how better business intelligence could improve it.

So, the challenge is for the business managers and information systems managers to communicate. But, what do they say to each other? What questions should they be asking each other? This chapter addresses this issue with a set of questions that could lead to a dialog about linking business to technology. These simple questions assist in moving beyond technology talk to business talk.

Communicate About What?

The business of business is making quality products and delivering valued services at a price that will encourage customers to purchase them. Of course, we cannot spend more to make these products and to deliver these services than we can sell them for. The difference between the revenues generated from sales and the cost of the goods and services is our profit.

Our business is NOT to purchase the latest machines or computers or support staff unless they help us increase our revenues or reduce our costs. In some cases, technology managers, including the CIO, have forgotten this simple truth. Managers in the rest of the organization have not forgotten that the bottom line calculation (revenues – expenses) is critical to organizational survival. The CIO will become a valued business team member when he or she realizes that technology is a tool that provides leverage to attract and retain customers and to reduce the cost of providing the customers with products and services. Technology per se that exists without aiding the organization results in costs without adding value. Businesses must use the technology to provide benefit to other organization members and not just to provide great calculating speed, storage capability and communication capacity. "Feeds and speeds" should be left for technology salespeople, not business managers. And to align the business strategy with information systems strategy, the CIO must be a business manager.

Key Elements in Linking the Business to IS

A phrase often heard is that business needs "technology savvy business managers" and "business savvy technology managers." This can happen if all of the organization's managers can communicate about four entities. These four entities are business objectives, business tactics, information system objectives and information system tactics. We often shorten the terms for information system objectives and tactics and refer to them as system objectives and tactics. We will briefly describe each of the entities, present a model for linking the entities together with an interactive dialog and then explore each in more detail.

The measure of a company's bottom line is profits. Companies calculate profits by subtracting costs from revenues. The challenge of business managers is to increase revenues or to reduce costs. They refer to these achievements or ends as business objectives. The means to reach these ends or objectives are called *business tactics,* tasks performed to meet the business objectives. The information system must meet its objectives by providing results in the form of information that helps organizational members perform the business tactics. They must perform information system tactics to meet the information system objectives. As with the business systems, the system objectives are the ends or achievements, and the system tactics are the means to achieve the ends. Combining the business tactics leads to a business strategy. Likewise, combining system tactics can lead to an information systems strategy. A challenge is to link or align the business and system strategies so that the systems strategy supports the business strategies. Only then will information systems add value to the organization.

In one summary sentence, we can say that a problem or an opportunity creates a need to avoid some business costs or to increase some revenues (business objectives), which require changed employee behaviors (business tactics) supported by information system achievements (system objectives) that require changed information system behavior (system tactics). An example of such a sequence is the following:

> *Increased seasonal demand resulting in high overtime payments creates a need to reduce overtime costs by 15 percent over the next quarter (business objective). The means to reduce these costs is to hire more temporary people during times of great demand (business tactic). The information system could help by providing reports or screens of predicted labor demand two days in advance of the potential for overtime (system objective). The means of generating the reports is a database of labor availability, predicted labor needs and product demand cycles, along with computer programs to analyze the database (system tactics).*

Communication between the business managers and the information system managers is necessary to specify and solve such business problems. Figure 2.1 provides a set of questions to assist such communication.

Note that the arrows flowing in the diagram indicate that the managers can progress through the diagram in both directions. They can either start with the business objectives on the upper left (called the *business need approach*) or with the system tactics on the lower right (called the *technology push approach*).

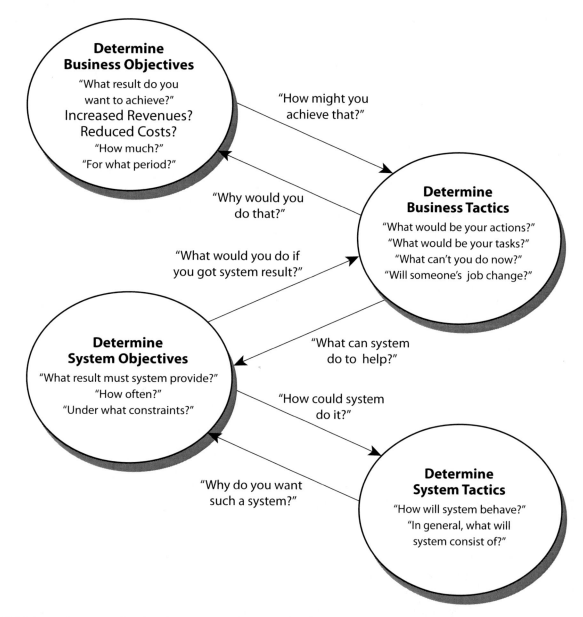

FIGURE 2.1—*Communication between Business and Information System Managers*

Business Need Approach

Starting in the upper left corner of Figure 2.1, the first question a business manager or team of managers must answer is "What result do you want to achieve?" This will help specify the business objectives. The statement of the desired result is in terms of increased revenues or reduced costs to ensure a "bottom line" or profitability focus. The manager(s) should attempt to estimate the size of the impact of the achievement by stating the actual dollar impact or the anticipated percentage increase for a specific time period. These amounts will be the estimated dollar benefits from the system that should offset any costs to make the project feasible.

The next point of discussion is to answer the question "How might you achieve that?" The answer will lead to the business tactics or the actions needed by the business managers to achieve the business objectives. Specific details of the business tactics include: "What would be your actions?" "What would be your tasks?" "What can't you do now?" "Will someone's job change?" At this point, there should be some clarity about why something is occurring (business objectives) and what should be done from a business perspective. Now we need to see if information can help the business persons when they are performing the business tactics.

To link to the information system, we must address the question, "What can the system do to help?" "Are there reports or screens or alerts that could help to perform the business tactics?" "How often must the company provide these results?" "How fresh or current must they be?" Answers to these questions will assist in defining how information will assist the business managers.

Finally, we get the to the area where previous CIOs spent most of their time, the system tactics. The question to address is, "How could the system do it?" The business manager may not even care to know the details of the solution, only whether whatever needs doing is possible and at what cost.

Both the system tactics and the business tactics will consume organization resources and have a cost associated with them. The company must offset these costs with the benefits received by achieving the increased revenues and reduced costs. If not, it is difficult to justify the expenditures economically for the tactics. In a financial sense, we could see this balance from a risk/reward perspective. Performing the tactics is a risk with the reward coming with the achievement of the business objectives.

Technology Push Approach

Often, a new technology in the form of hardware or software will appear on the market that could be useful for some special purpose in the organization. An example of this was the use of wireless printing calculators by rental car companies. The devices allowed rental car returns at the point where the renter stopped the car when returning it. An agent could check mileage, fuel amount and condition of the car and print a receipt right at the car. This reduced the need for check-in counters, saved time for both the rental car company and the customer, and gave renters the convenience of loading luggage from the car onto a bus where the car returns were taking place.

In such a case, the first questions to address appear in the system tactics circle in Figure 2.1. These are: "How will system behave?" and, "In general, what will system consist of?" The movement through Figure 2.1 results in answering the question of "Why do you want such a system?" moving to the systems objectives circle where the questions: "What result must system provide?" "How often?" "Under what constraints?" are answered. Now both the business persons and the systems persons will understand the components of, and the results from, the information system.

Once you have the results defined, the next question to answer is, "What would you do if you got the system result?" This leads to specifying the business tactics or what the business people have to do to use the information provided by meeting the system objectives. Of course, the business manager must consider whether the employees assigned the business tactics are capable of performing them.

Finally, in the technology push approach, we must address the question of "Why would you do that?" that refers to the business tactics. This leads to the business objectives and a specification of the potential increased revenues and reduced costs that would impact the company's bottom line. Again, this is where the benefits must occur that will offset the costs of performing the changed business tactics and instituting the system tactics.

There are a few things that you should notice about Figure 2.1. First, the questions to address are not complex, yet they stimulate communication between the business and information systems managers. The technical people must move closer to the business people, and the business people must attempt to utilize the leverage of technology. A spirit of cooperation and team work is necessary. Second, just meeting the information system objectives will provide NO DIRECT value to the organization. The business people must use the results from the system to perform the business tactics better. There is no direct link from the system objectives to the business objectives. The company must use the information to provide real benefits. If not used, then the cost of the system tactics remains without any offsetting benefits from achieving the business objectives.

To fully understand the components of the model shown in Figure 2.1, we will examine each of the four major entities more closely.

A Closer Look at Business Objectives

Business objectives ultimately must focus on increased revenues or reduced costs. This is what will impact the bottom line or the profitability. Suggestions may be made to include items such as social responsibility as a business objective. Social responsibility is an extremely important value that ultimately could increase revenues or reduce costs due to improved customer perceptions. This could take place particularly if a need existed to spend money to convince customers that the company considered their impacts on society important. But without profitability the firm cannot continue to exist in the marketplace. Ultimately, the company should make attempts to convert all intangibles to quantifiable increased revenues or reduced costs.

The vision and mission of the organization are the basis of its business objectives. The leaders of any business organization must determine what kinds of business the firm will engage in and what it will not do. This includes determining what products and services it will offer and what it will avoid. Leaders must attempt to visualize what the organization will look like in the future, including its size, location and values, as well as any indicators that the organization is truly succeeding. All of this analysis will lead to a determination of problems to solve and opportunities to pursue. Brainstorming and idea generation often is necessary to set the company's direction. Once these strategic views and general goals are clear, business managers can attempt to detail specific objectives.

Clues may aid managers in defining business objectives. They should view these clues in terms of their potential for increasing revenues or for reducing costs. The evaluation of existing product lines may lead to questions of whether the lines need reduction or expansion. They can evaluate product quality to determine if they are meeting customer needs or if poor quality is hindering sales and generating product returns. Examining existing markets can lead to changes in terms of both reductions and expansions of market areas where the organization will participate. Product and services prices may lead to clues with regard to either increases or decreases. Good managers will examine all aspects of the business with an eye to change that could improve the bottom line.

With all of these clues in mind, managers should look specifically at revenue enhancement. Increased sales could come from new markets, retaining existing customers, increasing sales to existing customers who currently buy one product or service but not another, adding to product or service lines, avoiding inventory outages that prevent sales, forming alliances with other companies with complementary products or services, and any other factors that could increase the overall revenues.

Classic cost reduction could come from avoiding overtime costs, reducing waste or spoilage, reducing loan charges by improving cash flow, reducing employee turnover and hiring costs, reducing absenteeism, reducing just-in-case inventory costs including storage or reducing uncollected debts. The list could go on and on, but, again, good managers will see the problems or opportunities to reduce overall costs. Business managers also might have to conduct more detailed analysis, such as evaluating whether production should take place within the company or whether they should outsource it, allowing other companies to take on the production responsibilities.

After reading these long lists, it should be clear that we are just scratching the surface of stating business objectives. In any case, a good business manager must be proactive in pursuing strategies for improving the bottom line.

A Closer Look at Business Tactics

Business tactics provide the means for achieving business objectives. Business tactics provide an important link between the information received when system objectives are met and the business objectives where benefits to the organization are achieved. As mentioned earlier, the company must use the information to provide real value.

Business tactics specify how the company should use the information provided for the greatest benefit. This means that the information must be in a usable form and that the employees should know how to use it. Procedures may need changing or directives clarified for the persons intended to receive the information. Training may be necessary about how to perform the business tactics and how to use provided information. The company cannot assume that employees will know what to do. They need to inform them and then provide some actual testing with the procedures and information. Besides training, it may be necessary to change job descriptions, job entry qualifications, compensation and even union contracts for unionized employees.

Making changes in the workplace can be complex, and the company should think them out carefully.

A Closer Look at System Objectives

System objectives are what the information systems must achieve so that the employees who must perform business tactics receive the necessary information. From a systems viewpoint, system objectives are the outputs from the information system. They include both scheduled and ad hoc or requested reports, screens of information that allow different levels of detail and summarization, and alerts or alarms sent to business persons indicating a need for action. One could also state the system objectives in terms of additional communication capabilities, such as Websites or access to certain information using retrieval software.

Specification of system objectives needs to include a high level of detail. It is not sufficient to just say "give me a report." There must be a clear and precise statement of content, order, format, time period, circulation or restricted availability, currency or freshness, and any other detail that could cause confusion or debate. The mediums or devices that need support also need specification along with the level of protection or security required.

A Closer Look at System Tactics

As mentioned earlier in this chapter, system tactics historically have existed where technologists focused. This focus got many CIOs in trouble with other business managers and labeled as "techies." The system tactics are the means of achieving the system objectives. They often involve great complexity and require the CIO to surround her or himself with experts in many technologies. It is just too difficult for one person to keep current, since much of the technologic knowledge is perishable with all the rapid changes going on. The CIO often struggles with loyalty to the business strategy while at the same time remaining loyal to all of the persons specializing in addressing the technical complexities.

The system tactics include a preliminary technology strategy when all of the necessary technology needs are combined. Some persons refer to this as systems architecture. Hardware and software vendors often get involved in assisting technology managers since they will be providing the equipment, computer programs and communication support needed to satisfy system objectives.

Challenges in Aligning Business and Systems Strategy

Bridging the gap between technologists and business persons is a necessary but difficult endeavor. It would be easy for each of these groups to go its own way and not to communicate with each other. But both the CIO and his or her team and the business management team owe it to themselves and the organization to work together to leverage the advantages of technology to assist business management. Experience has indicated some areas where special attention may be necessary to meet the challenges of alignment.

In specifying business objectives, companies should take care to clearly state and quantify increased revenues or reduced costs. They should closely scrutinize and convert to "increased revenues" terms such as "improved service." This could happen if the better service impresses customers enough to buy more products or services. As mentioned earlier, we can say the same for "improved social responsibility." Conversion to either reduced costs or increased revenues will more clearly indicate real organizational benefits, not some undefined "intangible."

A phrase often heard in business is "if you can't measure it, you can't manage it." The phrase indicates that to truly determine if you are on target or winning in the game, you need to keep score. Words such as "better," "faster," "fresher," "more" and so forth do not allow you to keep score. Quantification is necessary so you can have a benchmark to measure against. You should specify objectives in clear, precise, measureable statements that state when, how many, to whom, by whom and for what time period. Debatable items will be debated.

All affected persons must review and accept any statements of business objectives and tactics and system objectives and tactics. This includes not only managers but those who must perform business tactics as well. Workers whose jobs, training or entry qualifications may change, as well as representatives such as labor union officials, must review how work will change.

In some cases, a clear statement of benefits and costs may not be appropriate. If the government requires a new tax reporting system, the company will have little choice whether or not to do it. The change is compulsory. Of course, one could measure the cost of not changing in terms of fines or other punishments for non-compliance.

Setting business objectives is not an exact science. It is difficult to set objectives so they motivate people and do not make them give up. Some art and opinion is involved. Managers are similar to coaches of athletic teams in that they want their teams to work together with will and determination. If the objective is too easy to achieve, people may not have the motivation to achieve it. If people see the objective as impossible to achieve, they may become discouraged and not even try to achieve it. Stating business objectives in public and listing them puts up a banner for all to see. Thus, companies should take care in setting goals or objectives to assure they are reasonable and motivating.

Chapter Summary

Entry level employees might argue that all of the above is academic and will not affect them. However, an understanding of how technology can aid your specific area within an organization can allow you to stand out among your peers. Since the alignment of business and information systems strategy has been a long lasting problem, your inputs could assist in bringing additional success to the organization. The approach described above guides communication between the technology group and the business functions. It provides a common language to allow answering questions that will allow added value to the organization. The company can see you as the catalyst that makes alignment happen, thus contributing to the success of the organization.

An advantage of communicating between unlike organizational units and determining where to add value is that the communication allows a more accurate cost and benefit analysis. By specifying both business objectives and system objectives, each group will have measureable targets to shoot at. They will know when they have met a milestone and can determine if project progress has occurred. You can help define when you are done rather than feeling as if you are in a never ending cycle of change.

Another advantage of clear communication is that you can help assure that the information systems in the organization are useful and used. If the performance of the business tactics can improve with information from meeting the system objectives, then business members will have an incentive to use it to make better decisions and to increase productivity. Both the business people and the information systems staff will know their roles in helping to achieve efficiency and effectiveness.

In summary, no matter what level you might be at in an organization, your contributions will be greater if you understand the role of information in the success of the organization.

Food for Thought/Aligning Systems and Business Strategy

- Why might technical persons feel most comfortable discussing system tactics? What would make a business person least interested in system tactics?

- What is the best way for a chief information officer to get fired?

- According to the Ross/Weill article, why is it dangerous to leave all IT decisions to your IT personnel?

- Could you as a new employee utilize the "Putting it All Together" diagram? Could you answer the questions on the diagram if your manager asked you to?

- How would you respond to a classmate who said that it was important to perform business objectives?

- Is it possible to achieve business objectives without performing business tactics? Why or why not?

- Can you think of instances where trying to answer all the questions in Figure 2.1 might be more trouble than it is worth?

A NEED TO WORK TOGETHER

T.E.A.M. Stands for
Together Everyone Accomplishes More

Often, business managers will avoid dealing with information systems problems and decisions. An article by Ross and Weill addresses this issue and makes a strong argument that it is dangerous to leave all IT decisions to the IT personnel, especially decisions that have an impact on business strategy. (Ross, Jeanne W. and Weill, Peter. "Six IT Decisions Your IT People Shouldn't Make," *Harvard Business Review*, November 2002, pp. 84–91.)

According to Ross and Weill, the six decisions that senior business managers cannot avoid include:

1. **How much to spend on IT?** This decision is highly dependent on the strategic impact of IT in the organization. IT managers need to know what the business managers would like to do. This can range from providing basic processing capability to excelling in segmented customer service based on customer loyalty.

2. **What is the priority of each business project?** The IT managers cannot decide value in terms of increased revenues and reduced costs without assistance from the business managers.

3. **What is the mix of companywide versus localized IT capabilities?** Economies of scale as well as commonly shared data from data warehouses are only possible with centralized capabilities and standardized system architectures. But standardization can limit flexibility.

4. **How dependent is the organization on the IT function?** Some organizations, such as financial instrument trading systems or air traffic control cannot be out of operation for more than a few seconds. Other systems such as auto insurance billing systems, could tolerate being down for a few hours without dire consequences.

5. **What are acceptable security and privacy risks?** IT managers cannot determine the sensitivity of data they are storing. This tolerance level must come from the business manager. Reducing risks is possible but comes at a cost. Business managers know best what cost is reasonable.

6. **What are the true business benefits in terms of increased revenues and reduced costs?** The business managers must generate the changed business tactics that can lead to achieving business objectives.

Business managers must "sponsor" and provide resources for the information systems group. If there is a need for people from the business organization to help define the systems project, then the company must free the best business people to work on the project. Someone whom the business organization would not miss is unlikely to add value to the systems project. Commitment, not just involvement, by the business managers is essential to success. Business managers can delegate authority to the information systems group, but on business projects they still are responsible. The above six decisions will aid responsible business managers in teaming up with information systems to improve the entire organization.

Exercise

Developing Your Analytical Skills: Using Information Systems to Add Organizational Value

Your task is to use the business/systems objectives/tactics model from this chapter to clearly present a report on the following situation. Waste Management Corporation is a garbage collection and disposal company. The company has a problem that it would like to turn into an opportunity. The situation is that garbage truck drivers encounter overflowing garbage containers such as dumpsters that are difficult to pick up. Once the containers fill over capacity, the automated pick-up cranes do not operate properly, the garbage falls onto the ground near the container, and the truck drivers must get out and manually load the garbage into the trucks.

A suggestion has occurred to use technology to help. The company would provide digital cameras to the drivers to take pictures of overflowing containers. The company sales staff would receive the pictures along with a short form detailing the time, place, customer and any other pertinent information. The sales staff would analyze the information from the drivers and combine the information with other data from the customer database. They then would develop a proposal for larger or additional containers at an additional cost to the customer. They would email the proposal to the customer.

The Waste Management team felt that drivers would spend less time on each pick-up if they did not have to get out of the truck. This would allow more pick-ups per day for each driver with less cost per pick-up.

The Readers' Task

Use the questions shown on the diagram in Figure 2.1 to help align the business and systems strategy. Questions you must answer include: What revenues would increase? From whom? Be specific about the type of customer. What would be a reasonable approximation of a percentage growth? What costs could be reduced? By how much? What would the business people have to do to make this work that they don't do now? Whose job will change? Is there a way to reward the people involved in the effort? Would this motivate them? What information would be necessary to do the new tasks? How often would it be required? What technology is necessary to support this effort? Could both the business need and the technology push directions on Figure 2.1 be useful to explain this new venture? Explain.

chapter 3

The Information Cycle

Data Is Everywhere

The Data Warehouse or Repository

Measurements and Dimensions

Transforming Data into Information

Moving from Information to Knowledge/Business Intelligence

Making Smarter and Faster Decisions

Smart Decisions Lead to Power in the Marketplace

Is Information Really Power?

Completing the Information Cycle—The Feedback Loop

The Foundation of the Information Cycle—Trust and Risk

Practicing the Information Cycle

Chapter Summary

Information is the lifeblood of an organization. The information flows through the veins or communication channels of the organization, informing persons in the organization and allowing them to manage better and to make smarter decisions. This chapter will examine the cycle of information as it moves through the organization and its members utilize it. Figure 3.1 represents the information cycle. The major components of the information cycle are data, information, knowledge/business intelligence, decision-making and power in the marketplace.

Data Is Everywhere

Data exists all around us. Data includes the raw numbers and text that describe activities that take place both in the organization and in its environment. A phone book contains data. Data does not inform. It does not provide such specifics as all persons who live in the 8000 block of 43rd Street. Another example of data is a list of all orders placed with Amazon.com on a certain date. Data is the raw unanalyzed numbers and text that are ubiquitous in our current world.

The predominant data types are internal data, generated by the organization's day-to-day activities or business tactics, and external data, generated by activities in the environment surrounding the organization.

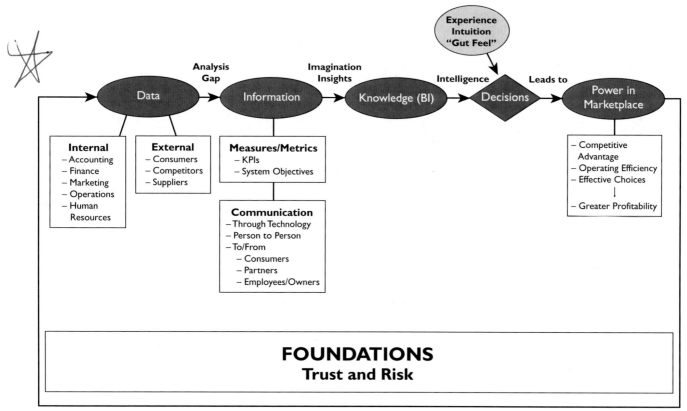

FIGURE 3.1—*The Information Cycle*

Internal data results from events performed in the organization. As described in Chapter 2, these events are the business tactics. There is a long list of activities needed to keep the organization operating. Customers place orders to obtain goods and services from the organization; suppliers send raw materials and finished goods to the organization; and customers receive the goods and services and pay bills. Suppliers receive payment for the goods and services; taxes get collected from customers and sent to the appropriate government units; people apply to the organization to become employees, applicants get hired; and employees receive pay from the organization. Employees also pay taxes and other deductions, such as for retirement plans or health care, and many more events occur during the daily activities of the organization. All events are recorded in great detail including who, what, when, where and how much.

The events generating internal data involve all organizational functions. Systems must process such events as customer orders, sending them to warehouses to fill from inventory and notifying shipping, so that the right department can send the completed and assembled orders. The company must notify customers that it has filled the orders and then bill the customers. We refer to these systems as online transaction processing systems (OLTP). Accounting gathers and records a great deal of data. There is data about money owed to suppliers called account payables, accounts receivables or money owed to the organization by customers. There are payroll data with details about money paid to employees, cost allocations to each business function and summaries of the accounting functions recorded in general ledger accounts. Finance gathers and records data about loans made to the organization and investments the company might make with the cash flowing into the organization. Marketing/Sales keeps track of customer orders, including who is buying what, available products or services for sale, and promotions and advertising, along with their effectiveness. Human Resources collects data on job applicants, the skills and knowledge of employees and benefit plans. Strategic management records business plans and actual results against a plan. Operations management tracks both raw material and finished goods inventories. It also tracks production plans that include the scheduling of machines and people, and logistics, which include how to transport products to retailers, wholesalers and customers. Information management keeps records on all the transactions and maintains data storage and communication to facilitate online transaction processing.

Besides general organizational data, individuals within an organization also record a large amount of data based on events or transactions. Each sales person in an organization keeps data about customers that may not be shared with the entire organization. For example, to establish good relationships with customers a sales person may keep records of each customer's family members, including such items as a spouse's name, children's names, birth dates and other personal information.

Within a university, a professor records data about each student in a grade book. The grade book might include collected data items, such as student name, student number, attendance for each class day, an exam grade for each exam, an assignment grade for each assignment, peer evaluations for team assignments and other data depending on the class design. The grade book also would contain calculated data items such as exam sub-totals and total points accumulated.

The holder of the data, in this case the professor, wants to assure that the data is complete and clean. This means that he or she records all scores, there is no missing data, grades are within an acceptable range so no student receives a fifty-five on a five-point exercise, and all calculations are accurate. "Dirty data" must get scrubbed, which could include assuring reasonableness and collecting missing data. For example, assuring the data is complete could include obtaining a makeup exam score for an excused student to fill in a missing score.

Besides the internal data generated by the events in the organization, personnel must obtain other data from events happening in the environment. The professor must utilize university-wide data, such as overall class grade point average guidelines. A business organization must collect data about industry trends such as product or service prices, salaries paid to different classes of employees and government tax rates or tax filing data that allows the organization to abide by any rules and regulations.

In a business organization, external data comes from many sources. Data about competitors, customers and the marketplace, and suppliers is necessary to survive as a business. Competitor data could include product pricing, advertising and promotions that the company may need to respond to, and news stories about new products or services.

There are huge amounts of data that companies must gather, check for completeness and cleanse to keep the organization functioning and to allow further manipulation and analysis.

The Data Warehouse or Repository

After accumulating and cleansing the needed internal and external data, the organization must then store it to allow examination and manipulation by many members. At one time, data was scattered throughout the organization. Many employees kept their own files of data. A current trend is to aggregate all the data in a central repository or data warehouse so that collection takes place once and its storage allows consistency and the avoidance of conflicts. Multiple versions of the same data often result in confusion when it is unclear which data is the most current or, if differences occur, which data is correct.

For example, "dirty data" could exist if personnel found the following data occurrences in a data warehouse:

Name	Phone Number
Ken Kozar	303-492-8437
Kenneth Kozar	303-492-5962
Kozar, Ken	303-492-8347
Kozar, Kenneth	303-492-8337

The data could indicate that all of these records represent the same person or that there could be as many as four different people. Verification should take place, often manually. If all four represent one person, then the organization should "cleanse" the data to verify which of the names is most representative and which phone number is correct.

There are hardware/software companies that specialize in creating systems that allow data management, including data storage and retrieval. These companies specialize in assuring that all the data is stored in a manner that makes it available for processing into information.

In many cases, organizations break down the data warehouse into data marts or segments of the data warehouse. The data marts are subject specific and address entities such as products, customers or suppliers. The data marts are directly linked to, or are a part of, the data warehouse, but they allow for easier understanding and manipulation to produce the needed information. In many cases, the data marts are simply a "virtual view" of the data warehouse that allow for needed data analysis. This means that the data still is stored only once, but there is a certain segment or view of the data that would satisfy a specific organizational member's needs.

Measurements and Dimensions

One can segment and examine data in several ways. Some of the data include a measurement of a particular type. A measure is a count of something, such as the number of customers, the number of customer sales, the number of numeric exam scores and the number of exercise scores. Although interesting, measurements do not provide much opportunity for analysis. The real power of analysis comes from examining measures by certain dimensions or categories. The key word is "by." We may want to know the number of customers by geographic factors and conduct an analysis by state, by city or by country. We could examine customer sales by time of day, by online versus telephone order or by product type. Dimensions give real power to analysis since we can "slice and dice" the data to provide real information. The next chapter will cover how this occurs.

Transforming Data into Information

Data provides the raw material that organizations extract, transform and load into data marts that can provide information to the organizational members. But, the information does not magically appear. Online analytical processing systems (OLAP) are necessary to bridge the analytic gap between data and information. We must condense, sort, summarize and further analyze the data to provide information.

Some of the information comes through standardized reports or screens defined in advance that allow the monitoring of both the organizational environment and the external marketplace. Information should provide an element of surprise, telling organizational members something they do not know. For example, managers may want to know if a product is costing more to produce than customers are willing to pay. Or, management may want to know if sales of a particular product are falling in a certain geographic area. Or, a sales manager may want to know who the top salespeople are and the salespeople who are not meeting sales expectations. Once this becomes known by meeting the system objectives and providing information to the manager, he or she can perform business tactics to address the situation and to take any action needed to meet business objectives.

Key performance indicators for each functional area provide the basis for information. Each business function must specify some measurements that indicate how well it is doing. Operations managers may want to know the number of units produced per employee. Sales managers may want to know the percentage of sales to both existing and new customers. Human resources managers may want to know about employee turnover or the percentage of hires based on the number of offers made. All areas within an organization have some measure of how well it is performing. As we mentioned in Chapter 2, key performance indicators are based on business objectives or desired achievements and how efficiently business tactics are performed. Chapter 4 will discuss key performance indicators for different organizational units.

Much of the information comes directly from people as well as from data warehouses and data marts. Customers, suppliers and vendors, owners and employees can provide information directly to organizational managers. Customers may ask for different products or services, or suppliers may provide product availability information. To receive this information, it is essential to have open communication with other individuals within organizational units.

Moving from Information to Knowledge/Business Intelligence

Along with communication with others, there is a need for managers to be part of the process of examining information and determining what the information is telling them. Two persons can look at the same report or screen and take away different interpretations. There is a great need for organizations to use human skills to gain insight into what they are seeing. A manager may invoke curiosity based on seeing a relationship between different pieces of information or by examining results or measures by different dimensions. For example, a manager might see falling sales in a certain region and, upon investigating further, find a competitor has invoked a price reduction for a set of products.

This type of analysis includes looking at results from different perspectives or dimensions. We call this multidimensional analysis. Again, the important word is "by." Many dimensions may exist depending on what one is examining. Dimensions could include such items as geographic region, customer gender, customer age, customer zip code, product color, product size, time of day, day of the week, and so forth. The list could go on and on. Often the manager must request specific multidimensional analysis because of his or her ability to detect differences based on some factor or dimension.

Knowledge and the ability to gain insights distinguish one manager from another. A good manager has curiosity and the ability to detect patterns in the information, to generate questions and to seek answers and intelligence by using analysis to gain insight. The knowledge or business intelligence allows the manager to become smarter about what is really happening both inside the organization and in the competitive marketplace. The opposite of knowing is ignorance and hoping for the best. Knowing is the preferable state.

The manager also should attempt to think about what could happen in the future. He or she should ask the question: "What are the consequences of any decision I make and actions I take?" We often refer to this as future state thinking. Although the manager may not have a crystal ball with which to gaze into the future, he or she might try to imagine different scenarios that could take place. This allows the manager to become prepared and to think in advance about how to react if the situation does take place.

Making Smarter and Faster Decisions

The intent of all of the data gathering and storing, transforming it into information with true meaning, and using insights and imagination to gain knowledge and business intelligence is to allow better decision making. Decisions on who, what, when, where, why and how distinguish one organization from another. Smart decisions allow the selection of the right people to do the right things at the right time in the right place; they are able to understand why they are doing what they are doing and how to do it. This reduces uncertainty, and each organization member can have a clear direction for action.

Some decisions are strategic, involving overall and long-term plans. The most general question for a business organization is: "What business are we in and what business are we NOT in?" This sets the general direction for a company and helps define its customers and products or services.

Some decisions are day-to-day and involve specifying what the organization members will do today or what business tactics they will need to perform. When people show up for work at any level of the organization, they must have a purpose of accomplishing something for the day. All the day-to-day activities should add up to aid in accomplishing the more strategic business objectives.

Besides the knowledge or business intelligence used by a decision maker, there also is a need for another component of decision making. Business intelligence provides the rational aspect of making decisions, but there is also an emotional component. The emotional component of decision making is based on attributes of the decision maker and includes experience, intuition and "gut feel."

Even though the knowledge may point to a certain choice, a hidden or disguised component also may exist. Although the information may lead in a certain direction, something might be missing. This is where the experience of the decision maker comes into play. The decision based on purely rational data just may not feel right. There may be more to the decision than meets the eye.

A historical example of using intuition or gut feel involved the Chrysler Corporation. The organization used survey data and focus groups to examine customer preferences in order to gather data on proposed new car and truck models. It processed and analyzed the data and provided information on supposed customer desires. This was formal information intended to provide knowledge that the marketplace would accept a car or truck. However, some of the managers, specifically the CEO Lee Iacocca, believed

mimnan=gut feel

that there was something missing in the data model. His experience, intuition and gut feel led him to make the decision to move ahead with the Chrysler Corporation mini-van. The rational data had shown that it was not really a car, not really a station wagon and not really a truck. It was something the public had not conceived, but Mr. Iacocca's gut feel indicated it would be a unique vehicle and have an audience. He was correct. This situation resembled a decision made at Chrysler Corporation a number of years later when formal business intelligence without emotional intuition would have led to a decision to abandon the Dodge Ram pickup truck.

A balance is necessary to include both rational business intelligence and emotional intuition. A manager operating solely on intuition should not ignore information. And, if a decision does not feel right based just on business intelligence, the decision makers should explore further to see if some component is missing from the decision making process or in the information generating activity.

Smart Decisions Lead to Power in the Marketplace

Making the right decisions can lead to corporate success. Although there are other factors such as economic conditions that can lead to the inability to survive, smarter decisions can lead to a competitive advantage over other firms in the industry.

Smart decisions can improve operating efficiency. The best description of efficiency is doing things right. The smallest amount of inputs results in the largest amount of output. An efficient operation does not waste resources. It reduces the amount of scrap in production processes, reduces the cost of returns of defective products and has advertising campaigns that reach the right people for the least amount of expenditure. Efficiency requires an examination of processes to ensure that the system has the best output for a specified input.

Smart decisions also result in effective choices. Effectiveness means that the right things are done. If organizations perform unnecessary business tactics and do not contribute to the bottom line by reducing costs or increasing revenues, then it wastes resources. Notice that effectiveness should come first since something that does not need doing does not need doing efficiently.

Smarter decisions lead to improved profitability since it increases revenues and reduces costs. Smart decisions not only retain existing customers, they can result in increased revenues because the customers buy products or services that they currently do not buy. An organization can find new customers since improved business intelligence can focus advertising campaigns on persons most likely to buy. It does not waste money on mediums that do not reach potential customers or on messages that do not impact the desire to buy.

Is Information Really Power?

Often, you will hear the phrase "information is power." As we have explored in this chapter, the phrase may be too narrow. Merely having information does not mean a gain in power. There is much more behind the statement. Our belief is that, in its simplest form, an organization can process and transform data into information; information can provide a decision maker with intelligence and knowledge; and making decisions with knowledge can lead to power in the marketplace. There is much more complexity involved in the entire information cycle than appears by just stating, "information is power."

We can relate this concept to meeting system objectives. As we learned in Chapter 2, achieving system objectives and providing information has no direct value. An organization must use the information when performing business tactics in a way that ultimately leads to increased revenues or reduced costs—true power in the marketplace.

Completing the Information Cycle— The Feedback Loop

Once an organization operates in the business environment, answers to questions will lead to more questions. Managers will find that they may need to collect more data to process into information that will lead to knowledge and power in the marketplace. Once a manager obtains intelligence about a customer or a supplier, he or she will start to ask additional questions to further increase intelligence. The company may have to collect data differently to allow a new dimensional analysis. This cycle will continue as long as the manager remains in a discovery mode. Learning never seems to end.

The professor in our example above will examine student data to assist in planning the next time he or she teaches the class. He or she may need more or fewer assignments to assess learning the material and meeting the course objective. The professor desires to be effective by doing the right things and to save students time and her time by being efficient.

The Foundation of the Information Cycle— Trust and Risk

The basis of the information cycle is trust. Managers must trust that both the internal and the external data are sound and trustworthy. The online transaction processing systems that generate the internal data must generate correct records and results, and they must calculate the results correctly. The external data must come from sources that assure accuracy and completeness.

The online analytic processing also must be trustworthy. Correct formulas, including the correct variables, measurements and dimensions, are essential to gaining trust.

Communication between persons or organizations as well as between persons and machines also must be trustworthy. Some persons have a fear of accessing information and gaining business intelligence through technology. But, that is changing in the world today with computing and communication so common. Managers must trust analysts to correctly conduct the analyses.

Along with trust comes a risk. If you trust someone or something, you are risking that whatever provided is accurate and reliable. Some risk is necessary in the business world to reap the rewards of working together.

Practicing the Information Cycle

An example of the use of a data warehouse to allow better information management for decision making and running the business is the case of Continental Airlines (Continental Enterprise Case Study by Teradata Corporation © 2004–2007, EB-4349). Although the airline industry is constantly battling in the marketplace because of challenging economic factors, such as increasing fuel prices, better information and business intelligence have aided Continental in its quest to excel in the industry.

In the mid-1990s, Continental was struggling as an airline. It had filed for bankruptcy twice and was not doing well compared to its competitors. Its ability to use business intelligence resulted in persons stating that Continental went from "worst to first." They were an airline once known for poor service and inefficiencies that became an organization that won many "best of class" awards.

Greater concern for good management led to many changes in priorities within the airline. Marketing management wished to understand what flights and services customers wanted and what they were willing to pay for them. Finance management wanted to know details about what each business tactic was costing and the needed cash flow to best finance the airline's operation. Operations management wanted to minimize costs but to get customers to their destinations safely, on time, with their luggage arriving with them. Human resources management wanted to hire the best people, to keep them happy and to retain the employees as part of the Continental team. All of these management desires dictated that Continental improve its information cycle and engage in a data warehousing project that provided the right information to the right people at the right time.

Continental's data warehousing effort assisted the airline in many of its management activities. The $25 million dollar investment in cleaning up data, storing it in an accessible form and changing the corporate culture to operate on information rather than "flying by the seat of its pants" led to a large payback. Some major sources of increased profitability came from clearly identifying its best customers and treating them in a special manner. This meant assuring that its routes, fares and schedules led to a more efficient operation, which Continental management created from its business intelligence.

A quick view of the data warehouse exhibits the immensity of the effort. Twenty-five internal operational systems all provided inputs to the data warehouse. These included scheduling, seat inventory, reservations, ticketing, operations coordination, frequent flyer programs, customer profiles, maintenance, employee payroll, crew payroll and customer care. The airline used two external data sources, competitor activity and alliance/partner data. Continental used all this data to focus on several specific areas where knowledge was necessary to perform business tactics.

One significant business intelligence activity is known in the industry as customer relationship management (CRM). CRM allowed Continental to know which customers were contributing the largest amount to the bottom line of the company, thus assuring that these customers would continue to fly Continental. Continental found that the top one percent of flyers paid high fares because they often had to take frequent and spontaneous flights. This top one percent was responsible for almost 12 percent of Continental's total revenue. Continental made the decision to know who these people were and to ensure that any dealings with the airline made them feel special. The airline aligned the business and information system objectives and tactics.

Good customers will often just go away and use competitors if they are not happy. Continental wanted to assure that this did not happen. In a small retail business, success often comes from recognizing when a good customer enters the store and then treating him with special care. A company should treat all customers well, but when it can do something exceptional, such as expediting a rush order or making a quick delivery, it should be able to recognize the valued customer and do something to please him. Better business intelligence, often gained through loyalty programs, can provide information for a quick response.

Continental also closely examined its operations to ensure that it was gaining the maximum revenue from each flight. By managing fare structures to sell the most seats based on demand models, Continental was able to use the right size aircraft for different routes and to assure that it filled the seats in planes on those routes.

Airline operations also were a challenge without a data warehouse. The appropriate data allowed for the production of information, which led to business intelligence that assisted managers in keeping both employees and customers informed about delays and schedule changes. Quick responses were possible if the company provided information to someone who could use it to perform business tactics. For example, if a flight was late, valued customers could have a personalized message with connecting flight directions directly sent to them, giving them a better opportunity to get to a connecting flight. If rebooking needed to take place, a Continental employee could handle this situation electronically without having the valued customer stand in line.

Managers also were able to manage flight crews better and to make changes to equipment allocations, meals and staffing. They could assign flights more efficiently, leaving fewer employees left in some remote location without the ability to work their way home.

Better information also led to improved business intelligence about potential fraud and security threats. Analysis of data patterns assisted in generating information used with managerial insights to detect fraudulent behavior, especially in the area of overbooking, ticket refunds and inappropriate fare reductions.

Labor relations improved with better information since managers conducted contract negotiations with information and not by just assuming something was set at a certain rate at other airlines. They used external data sources to assure that Continental employees got fair treatment, along with competitive wages and benefits.

Since the operating managers knew the key performance indicators and the information necessary for measurement and analysis by desired dimensions, they took an active role in creating and maintaining the systems. Having this knowledge about the information processes gave employees an added responsibility, made them feel more important and valued and improved their skill sets. This assisted in employability and made either new hires or experienced employees more attractive in the marketplace.

As shown in the information cycle, Continental employees had to trust management, each other, technical persons, outside data sources and suppliers. Without trust, employees would doubt the provided analysis and carry on without using the provided information. The area of potential fraud is the only place where a challenge of trust should occur and where employees must be suspicious.

Continental Airlines used the information cycle to its fullest, which aided its business success. The same would be true at both small and large companies throughout the world.

Chapter Summary

Data exists both in the organization and in the environment of the organization. Managers must use data as raw material to produce information that has some value for managing their organizations. They can use the information to utilize key performance indicators in order to determine how well the company is doing. By combining the information with the insights and the imagination of management to gain business intelligence, they can solve problems and locate opportunities. They can make better decisions using business intelligence along with managerial experience and intuition. Smarter decisions can lead to increased profitability through effectiveness and efficiency. All of the information cycle depends upon improved communication throughout the organization based on a foundation of trust. Managers learn from their decisions and improve the information cycle through feedback and continuous improvement of the business intelligence activities. The use of information, business intelligence and smarter decisions gains power in the marketplace.

Food for Thought/Information Cycle

- What is the role of business intelligence in an organization? How does it link to decision making?

- Firms desire competitive advantage. What could give an organization competitive advantage in today's world?

- Does all the data for effective decision making come from inside the organization?

- Note that the chapter mentions that BI impacts common business problems in sales, marketing, operations, human resources, finance and other functional areas. Is your area of concentration included?

- What must an organization do with data before it can analyze it?

☞ Why is there a belief that technology alone cannot solve a business problem? What else must one consider?

☞ Relate the mention of corporate objectives and the plan for achieving them to the earlier chapter on aligning systems and the business strategy.

☞ Are KPIs an end or a means to an end?

☞ What besides information is an important basis for making decisions?

☞ How can well-organized business intelligence lead to selling insights that may challenge conventional wisdom?

☞ What is the role of people in business intelligence? Do machines or software have insights and imagination?

☞ What is multidimensional analysis? Can you explain it by using the word "by" multiple times?

☞ Explain why we sometimes refer to dimensions of data as categorizations. What are some dimensions that often occur with business data?

☞ Why is it necessary to have operational processing and databases prior to having analytical processing and databases?

☞ We may define data warehouses differently. But they all have the purpose of creating data marts that are subject-specific. Why is being subject-specific important? What are some subjects that we can be specific about?

Food for Thought/Continental Airlines

☞ How is Continental Airlines doing today? Check out *finance.Yahoo.com* and get some background.

☞ What were the sources of data for the Continental data warehouse? Was all the data internal?

☞ Why was it so important to build employee trust when the real focus was on the customer experience?

☞ Why might matching aircraft with customer demand be easy for a small company where the owner would be aware of this situation but very difficult for an airline the size of Continental?

☞ Based on the discussion of fraud, how did Continental use the system to catch those who try to "beat the system"?

☞ What were the sources of system payback?

☞ Do the support people all have technical backgrounds? Where did they originally work in the organization?

Exercise

Find an organization that you are familiar with. This could include a business you work for, a family related business, a club, a church group, etc. Trace the information cycle for the organization. You may want to start at the decision-making part of the cycle or with the internal or external data that the organization generates or collects. Specify each of the components of the information cycle, including determining business intelligence, communication needed, trust/risk, etc.

chapter 4

Crossing the Information Chasm with Business Intelligence

Beyond Intuition

Baseball Turns into Moneyball

Crossing the Analysis Gap

Key Performance Indicators

Multidimensional Analysis

Rolling Up versus Drilling Down versus Going Across

Measuring Against Benchmarks

There Is Gold in Them Hills—Data Mining

Chapter Summary

As Chapter 3 mentioned, huge amounts of internal and external data exist in a business environment. The challenge is to process all this data and to reduce it into information that provides knowledge and business intelligence in an organization. People working in business organizations need to discover what knowledge is necessary to be effective and to do the right things, along with being efficient doing those things in the most expeditious manner. Once they make this discovery, work begins to create the knowledge.

We commonly call manipulating and analyzing data to create information business analytics. The information allows managers and decision makers to gain knowledge, to operate using intelligence and not to remain ignorant when making decisions. The topic of business intelligence is important in helping business people use analytics to measure key performance indicators that lead to management action and to tactics that have the most impact on the business objectives or the bottom line.

Beyond Intuition

The objective of this chapter is to take a closer look at the activities and structure needed to achieve better management through improved intelligence. When a manager accepts the responsibility for making business decisions, he or she should make those decisions not just by using intuition and gut feel, but with good sound information as well. Using analytics can change an entire industry. Many people view the industry we will investigate—baseball—as an important industry and one of America's greatest pastimes. (This is also true for other countries, such as Japan.)

At one time, people managed and ran baseball without much use of analytic information. History represented by collected statistics was important, but its use was often only to recall past players and their great achievements. The record book was a list of past greats. It presented a challenge to current players who wanted to break the records and be recorded for posterity. Managers did not use recordkeeping to attempt to make decisions that would affect the future but to wax nostalgic about the past.

Determining future player performance was more of an art than a science. One of the most critical business decisions made in baseball is who should be on the team and how much to pay each player. We call this human resource management. Business analytics suggest that a team could manage a limited payroll better when using revealing information. At one time, the team with the biggest payroll had the best players and won the most games. Then a major change in player personnel decision-making took place. Business analytics entered the scene and changed baseball forever.

Baseball Turns into Moneyball

Michael Lewis wrote his 2004 book *Moneyball: The Art of Winning an Unfair Game* (see References) with the objective of answering a simple question: How did the Oakland Athletics, one of the lowest budget teams in baseball, win so many games? The Athletics' 2002 budget was about $40 million while the New York Yankees' 2002 budget was $126 million. In fact, the bottom of the team standings included many teams with big budgets who spent too much money on the wrong things, such as keeping big names on the team roster. As an exception, the Oakland Athletics were near the top of the league standings and won more regular season games than any other team. *Moneyball* is the story of how they accomplished this.

There is a short list of major characters in the Moneyball story. Oakland's general manager Billy Beane was a former baseball player that many people thought had great potential, yet he had never succeeded as a player. Billy had an inquisitive mind and looked hard to find inefficiencies in the game and its management. He used himself as an example of someone who SHOULD have been successful based on attributes used at the time, but who never achieved star player status. Bill James was a legend in analyzing baseball success in a scientific way. Bill established many of the measurements and dimensions needed to analyze baseball from a different perspective. Paul DePodesta understood baseball and pursued a new way of looking at statistics that he believed could assist in gaining baseball intelligence. These three persons were up against the classic stereotype of cigar smoking "scouts" that believed that gut feel and keen eyes were the key to baseball personnel success. The scouts were members of the "Club," the media and other baseball "insiders" who wanted to preserve its traditions and existing ways of doing things, and to avoid any new-fangled technology.

Billy Beane and Paul DePodesta of the Oakland Athletics embarked on an experiment to rethink baseball: how to manage and measure it, how to play it, who is best suited to play it and why. They wanted to move from a field of ignorance to a field of intelligence. One reason for a needed change was that the athletic competition was turning into a financial one. Many believed that huge payrolls and prima donna stars were necessary to win. Science was starting to enter the scene, and it disturbed the scouts and the "club."

Much of the science revolved around using new measures to determine whether a player had potential or not. For example, the scouts sought out high school pitchers with a high speed fastball. Why was this factor a major consideration? Simply, it was easy to measure and only a few pitchers had a blazing fastball, limiting the evaluation set. Yet, many of these young players were immature and unable to handle the stress of the game, its tiring schedule and the constant travel during the active season. Thus, Bill James and Paul DePodesta believed a blazing fastball was not a good predictor of future major league success.

Billy Beane considered firing all the scouts and using information gathered and displayed on Paul's computer for all personnel decisions. Others had seen drafting young players as an art, and Billy wanted to make it into a science. His goal was to buy undervalued players who had great potential, let them play, develop and gain value, and then trade them for new value. In a finance investing sense, Billy was a value investor, looking for undervalued investments, selling them when their price increased and then buying new undervalued assets. At the same time, Billy's and Paul's statistics were great predictors of contribution to a team and led to a great won-loss record.

The head of scouts for the Oakland Athletics did not believe that computers could add any value when finding and drafting new players. Paul had collected a great deal of data about existing players. He statistically analyzed the data and presented it in a form that suggested that they take certain actions in the future. Although batting average was a measure that scouts held sacred, Paul was more concerned about on-base percentage, including the number of walks and getting on base from a pitcher throwing four pitches outside the strike zone.

A player with great potential and great value in Paul's eyes was cognizant of the strike zone and did not swing at bad pitches. The player got on base more often. Paul believed that it was important to get on base, no matter how it happened. He was introducing new measures and then examining them using new dimensions, such as on-base by inning, by home versus away games or even by certain ball parks. Suddenly, new measures examined by new dimensions were leading to a more scientific view of finding players and putting together a winning team. But this was happening with resistance. The scouts and "the club" called what Billy Beane and Paul were doing "performance scouting" and looked at it with disdain. They believed that the new guys were using numbers that could take away the charm of the game. But they could not deny success in winning through better information. Winning and getting into the playoffs—and ultimately the World Series—was an important business benefit and a great revenue enhancer.

To use the new scientific approach to baseball, Paul and Billy met many challenges. The data that existed was incomplete and "dirty." After all, the important things considered by many data collectors were batting average, earned run average for pitchers and wins/losses. No one really checked the other data for accuracy since seldom did anyone use it. Billy and Paul wanted data on pitch types, pitch locations, direction and distance of batted balls, pitch counts and other measures and dimensions that might reveal a pattern that could lead to better win/loss records. Billy and Paul wanted to assign values (measures) to the minute components of a player's performance and analyze them by slicing and dicing them into as many dimensions or views as they could to see if the data revealed some new insight. These guys were using baseball intelligence much as many organizations were using business intelligence. This answered Michael Lewis's question of why the Oakland Athletics had such great success with such a meager payroll.

But, as in many cases of change, the "Club" and the scouts who felt they were the real "baseball men" believed this kind of analysis was tarnishing the game and its traditions. As we will discover in Chapter 11, change can be like "dying a little death," and in this case the death was the processes and tactics currently used and the "art" of player evaluation. The tactics were tradition, in use for many years. But it is hard to argue with success. Often the external forces, such as the fans, could easily see the change in the win/loss column. They got behind the change and supported the move to baseball analytics.

Since the writing of *Moneyball,* a movement has existed in professional and even college sports to using analytics. The basis of decision-making now is the use of information and not just intuition and guesswork. Even football decisions such as play section, whether to kick or to try for a first down when confronted with a short yardage situation on fourth down or player selection for any given play takes place with information, not just gut feel. Baseball has gone beyond just player selection to team manager decision making. For example, Davenport and Harris relate an example of Boston Red Sox pitching ace Pedro Martinez pitching in a 2003 American League Championship Series game. (See References, page 18 of "Competing on Analytics.") The Red Sox manager, Grady Little, had the information that Martinez was easier to get a hit from late in the game, after 7 innings or 105 pitches. Statistics showed that opposing hitters batted .231 for pitches 91–105 and .370 for pitches 106–110. In the fifth and deciding championship game, Little left Martinez in the game after 105 pitches. Martinez faltered, the team lost, and Little ultimately got fired. Believing the analytics could have saved the game and manager Little's job.

Baseball has changed. Other baseball teams have followed what has taken place with the Oakland Athletics. The Boston Red Sox joined the movement by hiring Bill James, considered by many the father of baseball analytics. Other teams have had to respond but many are too steeped in tradition. New data sources containing much of the raw data have become available, and subscriptions for access are being sold. Fields even get broken down into quadrants, and teams keep records of where batted balls are landing with different pitches and pitchers. And, they consider each batted ball by many factors or dimensions, such as place in the batting order, pitch count when hit, etc. New dimensions used to analyze data are pitch type in different situations, such as by inning and by current batter. New analytic software has become available to examine all of this never before collected data.

The story of *Moneyball* and the Oakland Athletics has a direct relationship to business. Teams are collecting, "cleansing" and analyzing additional business data in new ways. They are making new measurements and combining them into new databases. These measurements have led to new key performance indicators. The new approaches are adding new dimensions to the databases to enable viewing the measurements from different perspectives and "by" different "slices and dices" of the data. It is a gain in competitive advantage.

The following *Moneyball* quote best summarizes the big question related to business organizations that we must ask:

> *. . . if gross miscalculations of a person's value could occur on a baseball field, before a live audience of thirty thousand, and television audience of millions more, what did that say about the measurement of performance in other lines of work? If professional baseball players could be over- or under-valued, who couldn't? (p. 72)*

We need to learn from the *Moneyball* example in order to excel by applying business analytics, which can help create the same kinds of changes in your career as occurred in baseball.

Examining the *Moneyball* case should open our eyes to new possibilities. Some of the major things that we learned include the fact that innovations are necessary to change how an industry operates, but that the needed data often is not available and not "clean." Furthermore, it is difficult to get people to change. Managers must be concerned with organizational culture and whether decision makers will really use business intelligence. Change is unlikely unless there is great support and even pressure from the top of the organization and a clear understanding of how the persons involved can benefit from the change. Top managers can use better intelligence and set an example for the rest of the organization. Learning from the *Moneyball* example, we next will explore some basics of business intelligence.

Crossing the Analysis Gap

Most organizations are drowning in data but gasping to gain valuable and useful information. If managers do not know how to gather, organize, sort, summarize and present data in a format that compels decisions, they often will avoid or even rebel against others who want them to become more analytic and less intuitive. As discussed in Chapters 2 and 3, managers must combine meeting systems objectives and providing better information with using the information to perform business tactics better. The *Moneyball* example exhibited how using information can change the nature of an industry. Once one organization in an industry makes use of new forms of business intelligence to make better business decisions and to gain competitive advantage, others must follow to stay competitive.

Information is not only critical in business organizations but in other endeavors as well. Government today must respond to citizens by answering concerns and demands. They must recognize and understand those concerns and how to respond to them. Messages from politicians are based on gathering data and massaging the data into information and finally presenting the information to the public to assure them that government is responsive. Voters should respond to facts and figures that present a compelling argument. This is especially true during political campaigns where politicians need to address issues to build confidence and trust. They must quantify statements going beyond just using the words "more" or "better" to be convincing.

Politicians who are campaigning must make decisions based on information to know where to visit and what to say to reach the greatest number of people. They analyze geographic and demographic data to target the right audience and present the right information. Businesses can do the same thing when approaching customers. Thus, we must examine how business intelligence can be used to excel, much like the Oakland Athletics who forced the entire industry to change.

You need to realize that this is more than a technical problem. Using information for better management requires putting together the right people with desire and motivation with the right processes, and then using the right technology to leverage all the needed activities. What is necessary is a coordinated system of inter-related parts that produces the right outputs based on the right inputs and processes. Much like the *Moneyball* example, the organization needs to utilize a systems approach to move to a culture of information usage.

Key Performance Indicators

Whatever career you intend to pursue, your superiors will measure you by the results they assign you to achieve. The results are critical since our belief is that if you can't measure it, you can't manage it. Thus, measures are critically important.

Key performance indicators are measures that differ based on their functional area within the business. Some examples of measures include the following:

- ☞ Measure marketing by whether it retains key customers and finds new customers. Measures could include the percentage of customers that bought our products every year for a stated number of years or the number of customers that bought products for the first time during the past year.

- ☞ Measure the sales group by the amount of purchases by each customer and the total customer purchasing that takes place. Also, measure how much money and time the company spends to take care of each customer.

- ☞ Measure accounting by the speed and thoroughness of providing transaction reporting to managers, as well as the timeliness of completing the processing and reporting of accounting information after an accounting period ends.

- ☞ Measure finance by the cost of capital to run the business and whether capital is available when needed.

- ☞ Measure the human resources group by the ability to fill needed positions and to provide agreed on benefits to employees at the lowest cost.

- ☞ Measure the entrepreneurship group by the funding found for new ventures.

Every organizational unit has some key performance indicator measurements that are critical to the success of the entire organization. These measurements may differ from organization to organization, even within the same industry. Witness the differences in the measurement of individual players in the baseball leagues from the *Moneyball* example.

Multidimensional Analysis

As discussed in Chapter 3, measurements take on more meaning when the analyst examines the measure by different dimensions or categories. Dimensions or categories could include different products, different cities or regions or different time periods. This type of analysis allows us to view a measure such as sales by product, by city and by quarter. When we combine these dimensions, we can view them as a data cube. A data cube is a multidimensional view of data that allows a manager to visualize the data as layers that intersect each other, thus creating a cell that reveals a measurement. You should think of a cube as a three dimensional spreadsheet with rows, columns and layers. It can represent even more dimensions, but it is difficult to visualize such a "cube."

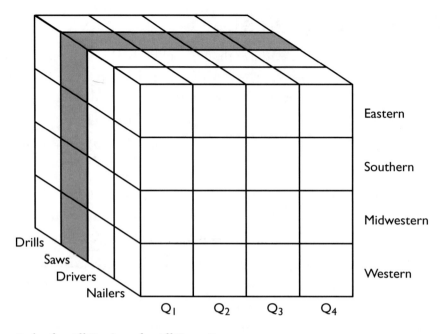

FIGURE 4.1—*Saw Sales for All Regions for All Four Quarters*

As mentioned in Chapter 3, managers need to break down and compare using differ-ent dimensions of the data. This is called *slicing and dicing.* A slice contains all the cells in a specific dimension. The figure below shows a slice of the sale of saws by region for each of the four quarters of time. The focus is on saws.

Dicing the data cube goes beyond a slice. Dicing is examining a slice of the data cube by the intersection of another dimension. In Figure 4.2, we could examine saw sales (a slice) by region, which means we will take the saw sales slice and cut it again by region.

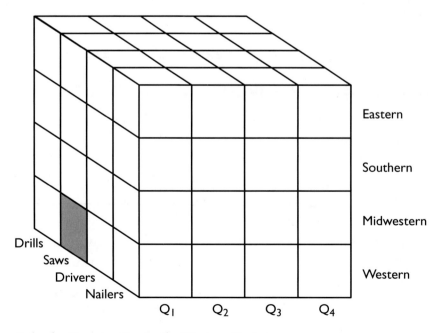

FIGURE 4.2—*Saw Sales for Quarter One in the Western Region*

You may want to think about slicing and dicing as a way of looking at tables of data and places where one table intersects another table.

We can use many different dimensions to give different views of measurements. For example, we could analyze sales by geographic region, by time or by organizational unit. For more detailed dimensional analysis, we could break down the geographic region to include continent, country, region, state or province, municipality, zip code or some other spatial breakdown. We could break time down by decade, year, month, week, day, hour or minute. Decision makers might even use some other measure.

For example, a dimension such as "by day of the week" or "by days prior to a holiday" could reveal interesting patterns such as very low sales on certain days of the week. Such information would lead the manager to action and suggest a business tactic of holding some kind of promotion on those days. We could break down organizational units by the organizational structure or by some other meaningful unit, such as the profit center or even an individual salesperson. The determination of the dimension is dependent on the needs of the manager or decision maker. This is similar to what the Oakland Athletics did when they used dimensions such as an analysis of scoring by inning, by pitch count, by batting position or by some other revealing dimension.

Dimensions allow the break down of measurements to analyze each significant and meaningful unit of analysis. The key word used when analyzing using dimensions is "by." For example, a sales manager might need to know sales by salesperson by zip code, by product or by product category. As you can see, these breakdowns can be endless, but they must add knowledge to the manager. This type of reporting to a manager really is achieving system objectives by providing information described in Chapter 2. The business tactics specify what the receiver of the information does with the information. The ideal as described in Chapter 2 is to use the information to perform better, which results in increased revenues or reduced costs, thus achieving business objectives.

Rolling Up versus Drilling Down versus Going Across

As we can determine from the above description, dimensions often can have different levels of detail, frequently referred to as a hierarchy.

For example, decades can consist of years, months, weeks, days, hours and minutes. In some types of analysis, summary data is more important than extremely detailed data. This especially is true when the manager wants to look for trends. Sales by minute by salesperson may not have much meaning. However, sales by week for each salesperson may be valuable in order to see if a salesperson's contribution is increasing or decreasing over time. If the company collected the data by the minute, it can roll it up or summarize it to a more gross measure, such as by hour to by day to by week. The manager can even roll it up further if there is further need. Often different trends will show up depending on the time interval chosen. A pattern on a graph or chart may appear erratic when shown over a short period, such as viewing sales by day over a two month period, but show an up or down trend when examined by month for a five year period. Each graph or chart would cover sixty measurements (for each of 30 days over 2 months; for each of 12 months over 5 years) but may reveal different patterns or trends.

Often a manager will examine data or information and be curious about one measurement and what makes it up. For example, examining monthly data over five years could show some peaks or low points. The curious manager can then look deeper into the data by drilling down. For example, he or she could examine data for one month by week, day, hour or even minute to see if some further pattern may occur. Of course, you only can drill down to the lowest level for which data exists. If the company collects sales data by the day, then that is the lowest level the manager can drill down to.

The manager also can examine the data by other dimensions by going across a dimension. For example, a restaurant manager may be curious about sales by day of the week. He or she may suspect that sales are low on Tuesdays. Then he or she could make an examination of Tuesdays versus other days of the week to see if it confirms this hunch. If so, the manager can pursue a business tactic such as running a special promotion, for instance a complementary appetizer on Tuesdays. The manager then can confirm whether there is a difference and even inquire of customers to determine whether they came to the restaurant on Tuesday due to the promotion. The manager can set objectives for increasing sales and see what business tactics works best to achieve those business objectives.

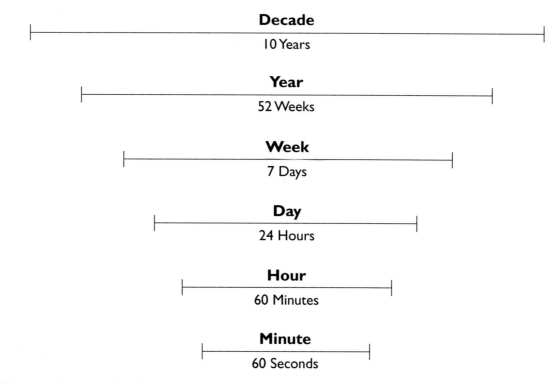

Decade
10 Years

Year
52 Weeks

Week
7 Days

Day
24 Hours

Hour
60 Minutes

Minute
60 Seconds

FIGURE 4.3—*An Example of a Hierarchy*

Measuring Against Benchmarks

Measurements need a comparison point to be meaningful. In baseball, a number giving an on base percentage for a player viewed in isolation would generate the questions "Is that good or bad?" and "In comparison to what?" To give some comparison, a benchmark or standard is necessary. Often we can examine a universe of data and create some aggregated measures to use as a benchmark. If your player had an on base percentage of 55 percent, and the average for all players was 43 percent, you could determine that the player is above average. Further statistics, such as the range of percentages, the categories of percentages and the variances could reveal whether your one measurement is good or bad and give you a basis for comparison.

We can refine benchmarks even further by examining dimensions. You might do this as a student if you compare your scores to other students based on the year of the other students, the major of the other students or some other meaningful measure. You may believe that your score on a math exam is only average when compared with math majors, but above average when compared against all majors. In essence, you must put the measurement in perspective.

There Is Gold in Them Hills—Data Mining

In some cases, managers will ask data analysts to search through large amounts of data without a specific search target or question in mind. The manager and analyst hope to find nuggets of truth among all the piles of data. Rather than seeking specific answers, the analysts are looking for potential problems and opportunities. This process is called *data mining*. Data mining is an attempt to find unexpected patterns in the huge accumulations of data often contained in a data warehouse.

There are two distinct types of data mining, descriptive and predictive. Descriptive data mining attempts to determine what patterns exist and what those patterns mean. One specific technique of descriptive data mining is affinity grouping. Affinity grouping looks for data that often occurs together. When one event takes place or a product appears, another event or product has a high probability of occurring as well. For example, if a customer buys one product, there is a strong possibility that he or she will buy some other product. The two products have a high affinity for one another.

Although there is some question whether the story is fact or urban legend, the tale goes that a convenience store chain discovered that two products with a high affinity were diapers and imported beer. The reasoning given behind this affinity is that a parent on the way home needing diapers for a youngster would not be likely to have an evening out but would want to reward himself with a special item. Thus, the diaper shopper bought imported beer as a reward for diaper shopping. This type of discovery could lead to product placement where the store might place diapers and beer in proximity to each other.

In some cases, the merchant may not be so subtle. Amazon.com comes right out and tells a person contemplating buying a book or other product that other people who bought that book or product also bought some other books or products that they display vividly on their Website. This is called *cross selling* and can increase revenues by increased sales and reduced costs, due to the low cost of advertising and promotion to a targeted audience.

Another type of descriptive data mining is clustering. Clustering is looking for smaller accumulations of data that have some similarity. The organization sorts and sifts the data to find a cluster with some common characteristics. For example, all customers that have a similar income, live in a similar price house, attend a certain kind of musical concert and have a similar number of children could form a cluster. If the members of this cluster turned in coupons at a certain kind of promotion or sale, the store could target the persons within the cluster when planning such a sale. Segmenting a larger potential sales audience could again focus promotions by contacting only those who the business should contact and reducing its costs. As described in Chapter 3, Continental Airlines used clustering to identify high value customers and to give them special treatment.

In some ways, we could view descriptive data mining as profiling. But the advantage to the customers is that they are targeted and not bothered with mass promotion campaigns. This is one of the major premises of database marketing, which contacts only those customers who welcome the promotion. For example, a frequent purchaser of a type of shoes might welcome receiving a promotion for a sale on that brand.

In contrast to descriptive data mining, predictive data mining attempts to create a model that will predict the probability of some event happening in the future. Businesses create, test and refine mathematical models until they feel comfortable that the model represents reality and can assist in decision making. For example, insurance companies may use past data to create a predictive model that indicates accident likelihood in the future. This would assist in setting rates or even in accepting or rejecting insurance applicants. It is interesting to note that they predicted that persons with a high credit rating score would be good insurance risks.

Companies could use the same kind of model for predicting the viability of applicants for home loans or for accepting credit applications. In essence, the models can classify risk categories or make estimates of viabilities. Often, techniques such as decision trees are part of these models. This method is similar to using a series of questions and answers to classify or categorize people with regard to some future behavior. Then the company can treat each of the classes as a special focus of organizational attention.

Chapter Summary

Businesses must organize data for it to be useful. Both measures and dimensions of those measures are necessary to give the data the most meaning. Even an industry like baseball needed to collect new data, to clean it up and to use it in new ways to increase organizational performance. Besides organizing the data into multi-dimensional data cubes and slicing and dicing those cubes, managers must think provocatively in order to ask the right questions. Then they must use data mining to go beyond asking questions to looking for patterns in the masses of data to find problems and opportunities that could stimulate new business tactics and ways of doing business. Business intelligence will change the way organizations conduct business.

In the end of their book, *Competing on Analytics,* Thomas H. Davenport and Jeanne G. Harris state on page 186:

> *"... analytical competitors will continue to find ways to outperform their competitors. They'll get the best customers and charge them exactly the price that the customer is willing to pay for their product and service. They'll have the most efficient and effective marketing campaigns and promotions. Their customer service will excel, and their customers will be loyal in return. Their supply chains will be ultra efficient, and they'll have neither excess inventory nor stock-outs. They'll have the best people or the best players in the industry, and the employees will be evaluated and compensated based on their specific contributions. They'll understand what nonfinancial processes and factors drive their financial performance, and they'll be able to predict and diagnose problems before they become too problematic. They will make a lot of money, win a lot of games, or help solve the world's most pressing problems. They will lead us into the future."*

The above summary of management using business intelligence should be a challenge for the way you will manage in your future. Competing on analytics could make you a winner in your career.

Food for Thought/Crossing the Information Chasm

- What is the gap between data and information called? Why?

- Why did other baseball teams have to respond to the Oakland Athletics?

- Do you think that other sports could use analytics now used in major league baseball?

- How would you respond to the baseball scouts or to the "club" as defined in the *Moneyball* story?

- Why might the *Moneyball* story be relevant to businesses?

- Explain what is meant by the phrase "reporting measures by dimensions."

- Are there any common dimensions that might appear on most data cubes? Think time, place, products/services . . .

- What is the purpose of data mining?

- Explain how Amazon.Com uses affinity grouping and clustering. Give some examples of your experiences.

- How could classification help in screening new credit applicants?

- What is the difference between descriptive and predictive data mining?

- How could an organization use segmentation and clustering to help with promotional or advertising campaigns?

References

Davenport, Thomas H., and Jeanne G. Harris. 2007. *Competing on analytics: The new science of winning.* Boston, MA: Harvard Business School Press.

Lewis, Michael. 2004. *Moneyball: The Art of Winning an Unfair Game.* New York, NY: W. W. Norton & Company.

Scheps, Swain. 2008. *Business Intelligence for Dummies.* Indianapolis, IN: Wiley Publishing, Inc.

Vitt, Elizabeth, Michael Luckevich, and Stacia Misner. 2002. *Business intelligence: Making better decisions faster.* Redmond, WA: Microsoft Press.

Williams, Steve, and Nancy Williams. 2007. *The profit impact of business intelligence.* San Francisco, CA: Morgan Kaufmann Publishers/Elsevier Inc.

Exercise

Developing Your Analysis Skills: Information to Make Better Decisions

Your task is to use the material in Chapter 4 to create and describe a possible business problem that suffers from the lack of business intelligence. Every business or organization needs to make decisions. Even student clubs need to make decisions, such as where they should place promotions to find new members, who they should encourage to join the group, how they should allocate the existing budget, etc. Your task is to describe an organization and to specify its key performance indicators, the measures used to evaluate performance and the dimensions that could aid decision makers in the organizations. You should focus on activities and tactics that would improve the organization's bottom line. For example, can the organization do something to increase revenues, even if this means obtaining money from dues or contributions or sponsorships?

Exercise

Interview a coach or a manager of a sports organization to determine what decisions the person needs to make and what intelligence he or she uses to make the decisions. Base your investigation on a situation similar to what you learned from reading the *Moneyball* story told in this chapter.

Exercise

Use a stock charting program such as the program found in Yahoo Finance to find different trends by changing the time dimension. Look at different stocks by month, by week, by day or by hour and see if different patterns occur. What can you conclude by changing the time dimension? Did different patterns occur? What principles from this chapter did this exercise exhibit? Summarize your results and what you learned from this exercise.

chapter 5

Finding Business Intelligence Opportunities

WHO SHOULD DO IT, WHAT SHOULD BE DONE AND HOW SHOULD BI BE PRESENTED?

This chapter explores who is involved in the processes of decision making and business intelligence, how to find business intelligence opportunities and how to present information to decision makers. More business intelligence opportunities will exist in an organization than people and other resources to address the opportunities. This chapter first examines the different roles of people in the organization who recognize and take advantage of business intelligence opportunities. Then it presents a process for finding and prioritizing these opportunities. Once an organization has created information and intelligence, it must present it to many different business managers and workers to make decisions and perform business tactics. Without presentation in a compelling format, managers cannot perform at a high level of efficiency and effectiveness.

Who Is Involved in Decision Making and Business Intelligence Activities?

Many organizations have a hierarchy with numerous levels of managers. There are senior managers, middle managers and lower level managers. Senior (or "top") managers typically provide strategic direction for the organization while lower level managers may be more concerned with the actual production of goods and services. Every organization has to produce something to receive revenue from customers. There also are other workers in the organization that may not be in a supervisory position but that still need information to make decisions. For example, customer service workers may need to decide what approach to take when dealing with a customer problem such as handling a warranty request.

Besides levels of managers, there are different specialties or functions in an organization, which Chapter 1 discussed. For example, you may remember that marketing is the eyes, ears and mouth of the organization that listens to and speaks to customers. Other functions include accounting, finance, human resources and operations, each of which acts to perform an important function in the organization.

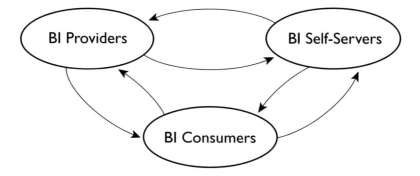

FIGURE 5.1—*Different BI Roles Played by Organization Members*

Business Intelligence Providers

We can take another view of business intelligence users based on their skill and knowledge. For example, the most skilled persons working with business intelligence applications will be the BI Providers. These persons are very technically knowledgeable and have a high technical skill level. Providers often exist in an information technology/systems business unit. They can specify the storage and retrieval structures and set up applications for other less skilled users. They can set up special commands or front-end tools with graphical interfaces that lead other less skilled persons through steps to get needed information. Some persons describe the BI Providers as the "button" developers who allow others to just "push the button" or click on an icon to get specific reports or the answer to a question. In most cases, this is a small number of people in any organization.

Often the BI Providers will be the chauffeurs who drive the front end tools to conduct ad hoc analysis. Ad hoc analysis is the interactive asking of questions of a data warehouse/data mart. The answers often lead to more questions. This type of analysis can involve drilling down or rolling up to change the level of the data being analyzed. The BI Providers also might need to seek other data sources to answer questions that a manager proposes. They might need to find external data to provide the business intelligence the decision maker seeks.

One other task that the BI Provider pursues is to perform both descriptive and prescriptive data mining. Teaming up with the business managers, the BI Providers will look for patterns in the data that may lead to seeking new opportunities or predicting problems prior to their occurrence. The BI Provider must have a keen understanding of the available internal and external data, the structure of the data and the retrieval and reporting tools that the organization will use to provide business intelligence.

Business Intelligence Consumers

At the other end of the spectrum from the BI Providers are the persons who want and need the added intelligence but who have a very limited technical skill set. Often, these are higher-level managers who are very busy and have limited time to do analysis, but who appreciate the need to operate beyond gut feel and intuition by utilizing information. The business intelligence consumer may detect a problem or opportunity and then ask others for assistance. The information consumer does not want to "drive the car" when others who specialize in chauffeuring can provide assistance. The information consumers may have other important tasks that need attention and don't believe that accessing information is a valuable use of their time.

Business Intelligence Self-Servers

Between the BI provider and the information consumer are the BI Self-Servers. This class of user believes in the information culture and in utilizing the power of business intelligence. Rather than being totally dependant on others, these are persons who can do some of the analysis for themselves. They do not need a chauffeur since they can "drive their own cars" and do some self service much as some car drivers who can fuel their own vehicles. They "pump their own" gas and can help themselves rather than waiting for or dealing with finding and interacting with a BI Provider. Often this class of business intelligence user will work with peers or others with similar skills and share solutions to information needs.

Hopefully in your career, you will aspire to the level of either a business intelligence provider or an information self-server. This will allow you the greatest opportunity to advance in your career and to survive in a knowledge-based business. To reach this level of skill and knowledge, you need to know how to find applications in your organization with the greatest impact that will provide the best opportunity for success using business intelligence.

Finding Business Intelligence Opportunities

Organizations must direct business intelligence initiatives toward specific areas that are "broken" in terms of lacking the appropriate business intelligence to perform business tactics and to make effective decisions. However, some BI initiatives are very costly and time consuming to develop, and some have greater business impacts than others. By following a step-by-step approach (See Figure 5.2), we will explore how to identify BI opportunities that will have the most significant business impacts. We must examine every opportunity to determine both its difficulty and its contribution and impact, and then rank these opportunities to obtain a mix of hard/easy and high/lower impact projects.

1. Who, What, When, Where, Why and How

The first task in finding business intelligence opportunities is to examine who may have some unfulfilled information needs. In some cases, managers will make requests for better business intelligence. In other cases, an analysis of different organizational

> ① Conduct 5W/1H Analysis to Generate Alternatives
>
> ② Specify Measures and Dimensions for Each Alternative
>
> ③ Categorize and Combine Similar Alternatives
>
> ④ Determine Contribution for Each Alternative
>
> ⑤ Determine Difficulty for Each Alternative
>
> ⑥ Score and Present Each Alternative to Create Project Portfolio
>
> ⑦ Implement and Share Discoveries

FIGURE 5.2—*A Process for Establishing a BI Plan*

levels, functions and locations is necessary. Once we gain an understanding of who has needs in the business intelligence arena, it is necessary to provide more detail and to specify what is needed, where, when and why. Some call this means of analysis the journalistic approach, similar to the method used by news story writers that addresses the 5 Ws and 1 H: Who, What, When, Where, Why and How.

In essence, the most basic question that we must answer is "What do we want to achieve by whom?" We accomplish this by gathering and brainstorming ideas to generate a number of possible alternatives and then by evaluating the alternatives to determine the business value and impact of each. Since we cannot implement all of the alternatives, we must prioritize them to achieve the greatest benefits for the most reasonable costs.

When examining questions for which managers have no answers, discussions may travel from "Why" questions, such as why some measurement is high or low, to "What" questions, such as what impacts the desired measure. Essentially, it is necessary to examine any causal chains or links. This could lead to new and different measures and calculations that address the unanswered questions. Curiosity should drive these business intelligence specification sessions. Managers should take the attitude of "I wonder why something is happening" and attempt to define applications where better intelligence can answer these questions.

Since there can exist a large number of business intelligence consumers and self-servers, we must identify them by organizational unit, functional area and management level. We also must take a process view that crosses functions, such as processing a customer order or building a product. Each functional area from the top to the lower levels must consider proposing potential BI projects. This includes such areas as accounting/finance, human resources, operations and marketing. It is part of the "Where" portion of the journalist model. One should be careful not to take a limited "silo" approach but to examine the processes of serving customers and acquiring from suppliers. This examination by the value or supply chain approach may require looking beyond the classic organizational hierarchy.

2. Measures and Dimensions

Next, one must specify what intelligence needs exist in terms of measures and dimensions and why this information is necessary. We can view the provision of this information to a person in an organization as meeting the system objectives that will aid in performing his or her business tactics. It is important to keep the business objectives of increased revenue opportunities and the problems of cost reduction in mind while conducting this analysis.

When examining managerial decision making in the organization, we need to understand that different managers can have different kinds and forms of information needs. Higher level managers may need more summarized information while lower level line managers may need more detail. Individual differences also can impact desires for information. For example, some managers will prefer tables of numbers and text and some will desire graphs and charts. Each can use the same information but displayed in a different manner.

We must package all of these needs together to create a bundle of unsatisfied needs in terms of information items that we can address. The question of "what information" must address both base and calculated measures, as well as the different dimensions that would allow examining the information. Many of the calculated measures consist of ratios where we view one number relative to another. Some areas that we must examine include product contributions and costs such as cost per product or cost per customer. For example, examine different groups of customers based on each group's contribution to profits. Many businesses have critical success factors or business performance indicators that address performance measures for each of the functional areas.

Dimensions usually include the examination of measures by time, by products, by customers, by demographics, by location, by employee, by work shift and by business unit or by other dimensions that an organization deems important. Recall the *Moneyball* story from Chapter 4 that tells how the development of new measures and dimensions changed the management of baseball. These developments impacted every level, all the way from the top of the organization in recruiting and hiring players to the lower operational levels of determining when a player should attempt to steal a base. All of these decisions should be made with better business intelligence and analytics.

An Example of Finding a BI Alternative

Who? Unique Bicycles Marketing Director

What? Advertising budget

When? Each month

Where? Newspaper, Internet, bike magazine, radio ads

Why? Impact of money spent is unknown

How? Analysis of sales to customers in each country based on Euros spent on advertising . . .

Following are statements that stimulated the alternative:

"I wonder why our advertising costs have been going up but our sales have not increased at the same rate" leads to

"I wonder where we should focus our advertising efforts?" leads to

"I wonder which countries in the European Union have persons who may buy a unique bicycle?" leads to

"What kind of customers bought a bicycle based on a response to one of our ads?" leads to

"Why were they impressed?"

This analysis of inquiries and questions led to a need for data on sales (measures) that required analysis by location/country by type of advertising seen; this stimulated buying a bicycle from Unique (dimensions). This type of demand analysis could lead to a change in advertising to high impact customers that could result in reduced advertising costs and increased revenues from customers in specified countries.

3. Summarizing and Categorizing the Alternatives

A record of discoveries found in such brainstorming sessions is essential. In some cases, the use of "sticky notes" or flip charts to post ideas is a good idea so all participants can see the recorded thoughts. An initial idea can stimulate other ideas to assist the creative process. Companies can also facilitate the process with groupware or software that assists in electronic brainstorming. Each participant can enter ideas anonymously through a networked keyboard that displays the ideas for all other participants. This process also can allow persons to participate in an idea generation session remotely.

- **Alternative 1**—Product Profit Contribution; Marketing; Are there any products that we should stop selling?

- **Alternative 2**—Geographic Region Sale; Sales; Are there areas where sales are unexplainably high or low?

- **Alternative 3**—Machine Age and Replacement; Operations; How much will we need to spend per year for the next three years to keep our factory running?

- **Alternative 4**—Product Pairing; Sales/Marketing; When customers buy our work boots, what else do they also buy?

- Etc.

What is shown above is a list of business intelligence opportunities or alternatives. Once established, there is a need to gather more detail such as measures and dimensions.

Once an organization has generated and recorded all the ideas for better intelligence, the next step is to look for commonalities and categories of ideas. Similar information needs may be grouped together, especially if they require collecting the same data. Some persons have called this activity "putting similar thoughts in one bucket." The result of this effort is a summarization of information requirements broken down by similarities. The categorizations may take place by similar measures or dimensions. Clusters of similar questions may exist that require similar data collection and analysis by similar dimensions. Some of these categories and clusters may not be immediately obvious and may take time to determine.

4. Contribution Determination

Organizations need to document each of the identified areas of opportunity along with the data needs, required analyses and bottom line impact. Once a list of alternatives is generated, it is important to examine each opportunity by level of contribution to the organization. The first consideration is the value based on the impact on the business objectives. The question that the business must address is whether increased revenues and reduced costs leading to profitability increase if the upgraded business intelligence exists. Another consideration is whether the business will actually use the improved BI. We must remember that an outstanding but unused BI application adds little value. The organization must carefully examine whether there is a need to evaluate the business tactics that allow taking advantage of the improved BI. Finally, it must examine where in the organization the BI applies. This examination will consider that a high organizational level may be more strategic and long term but harder to implement and achieve acceptance in the organization.

5. Difficulty Determination

The next step is to examine each alternative to determine its level of difficulty. An alternative that is cross functional would be more difficult to implement. It would involve several functions and thus impact managers in each of these functions. This would require cooperation and communication between the different functional managers. Assurance of use can be more difficult in strategic and cross-functional opportunities.

Another difficulty factor is whether complex calculations are necessary since this would add to the cost of building the application. Difficulty also could increase if data collection is complex and involves working with organizations outside the organization. The difficulty will also increase if the process requires new measures and collection by different dimensions, such as different locations or unusual time periods. Often the existing data does not have adequate detail, such as the new data required on where balls got hit in the *Moneyball* example in Chapter 4. It involved drawing quadrants on the baseball field and mapping each ball hit to the field.

One can always summarize data collected at a low level of detail, but this can become an expensive proposition. For example, collecting and storing each transaction from a point-of-sale terminal such as a grocery checkout may require too much storage and detail for many decision-making activities. Some organizations have found that collecting and storing the data summarized to an hourly basis was adequate for decision-making purposes. We can say the same about collecting data for geographic regions. The right level of detail must be discussed and determined.

Once we have examined all of the difficulty criteria we score each BI alternative on its degree of difficulty. This could be a five point scale from easy/low difficulty to hard/high difficulty. Of course, this is a somewhat subjective activity, but making some estimate of difficulty is better than ignoring this important factor.

The determination of difficulty and contribution cannot be left to the information providers and requires inputs from the actual decision makers, the self-servers and consumers. When you take a job in a business organization and gain experience in what it does, it may call upon you to participate in these kinds of sessions that determine information needs. Often different levels of employees take part in the brainstorming sessions that throw out ideas to assist in creative thinking about business intelligence needs. Inexperienced persons can lend great value since they don't have set ways of doing something and won't be locked into the thought that "we always did it that way."

6. Examining and Presenting the Scored Alternatives/Opportunities

Once the organization has scored each business intelligence alternative on contribution and difficulty, it creates a matrix of opportunities. Often, it creates a two by two matrix with a high/low for contribution and a high/low for difficulty with each alternative plotted on the matrix. Typical actions for each quadrant on the matrix would include:

☞ **High Contribution/Easy**—Go for it!

☞ **Low Contribution/Easy**—Consider as a confidence builder.

☞ **High Contribution/Hard**—Consider a pilot/proof of concept project

☞ **Other Alternatives**—Evaluate on a case-by-case basis considering resources

Again, this is a subjective activity based on organizational needs. Discussion needs to take place among the organization's members to create a portfolio of projects. A mix of both high risk/high potential reward and low risk/lower reward projects may make sense. Often, a business does early BI work to gain confidence and to exhibit the value of business intelligence efforts.

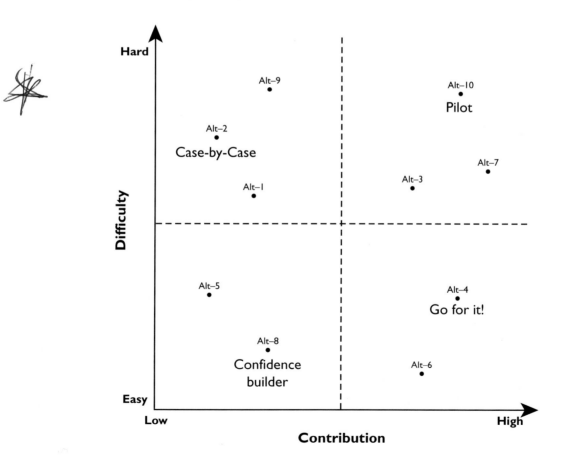

FIGURE 5.3—*Scoring Matrix of BI Opportunities*

7. Implement Projects, Learn and Share

There is a cycle of learning dealing with business intelligence opportunities. Managers and the organization should learn from both successes and failures. This only occurs when there is a conscious follow-up of business intelligence applications and the determination of what people learned from conducting the project and using the business intelligence. Some issues that a business must address include whether the business intelligence made a difference in terms of increased revenues and reduced costs, whether the original estimates and budgets for conducting the project were realistic and whether there are suggestions for further enhancements. Someone, usually within the information systems/information management function, should have a formal charge to conduct this post-project analysis.

The organization should publicize successes within the organization so other managers can see the potential and potentially apply it to their own areas. Success can breed other success in the organization and can lead to enthusiasm and an upward spiral of growing the business intelligence culture. Recall the *Moneyball* example where the number and impact of applications grew along with enthusiasm as the payoff from managing using information and analytics became obvious.

Usually the best utilization of successful business intelligence opportunities occur through a solid team effort with upper management executive support. The team must consist of the business users of the intelligence along with the technical persons who can make things happen. The company can leave the system tactics to the information system group, but it is essential to have business input and oversight.

The culture of the organization must move from one of making purely intuitive decisions to one where knowledge leads to power in the marketplace. Techniques that facilitate these kinds of efforts include doing some pilot projects and using them as examples. This is why some easily accomplished, lower impact projects make sense. The successes provide a "proof of concept" and serve as prototypes for further efforts. The "think big" and "start small" approach can help ease an organization into achieving benefits from the improved decision making.

Presenting Information to Managers

One essential component of utilizing business intelligence is to provide the information in a decision compelling format. Information presentation can make the difference between use and non-use and success and failure.

Two basic categories of information include pre-planned reports and ad hoc queries. Ad hoc queries are not planned and give the manager or an information provider the capability of asking questions that people may generate on the spot. These types of queries require the use of data marts that could include both internal and external data accessed with a special language included in a "front-end tool." Usually, the reports or queries may result in a numerical presentation of measures by dimensions in a table or textual results in the form of words. But, in some cases, there are analyses of textual data (see Analysis of Textual Data).

Analyses of Textual Data

Organizations can also analyze textual data to determine the frequency of words or ideas that indicate topics of interest. For an interesting view of the analysis of textual information on the Internet, conduct a search on Jonathan Harris and the "We Feel Fine" project. You will find some interesting videos about determining what is getting attention on the Internet. You can do this same type of analysis on corporate data, both internally and possibly from competitors. A manager seeking patterns in the data notes areas that may require further investigation. As mentioned in earlier chapters, each manager will monitor key performance indicators to determine the general health of the organization or some function within the organization.

Organizations need to report measures back to managers that are responsible for achieving the desired performance. One method of reporting an organization's performance is called a *balanced scorecard*. Robert Kaplan and David Norton (see References) propose four areas that comprise a balanced scorecard:

- ☞ Finances or information desired by shareholders that include cost per unit of production and market share

- ☞ Customers or information that could affect desirability by customers, including product/service quality and on-time delivery

- ☞ Processes or critical tactics that must be performed, including supplier performance, transportation costs, customer service response times and need to repeat, and inventory turnover/cost or backlogged orders

- ☞ Learning and growing or areas that need sustaining, which include quality management programs, technology usage such as order tracking or supplier communication through technology, and the ability to utilize employee suggestions or the percentage of new products yearly

Managers should measure and score each of the items mentioned above and put the results in both tables and graphs. They must observe and react much like an automobile driver reacts to gauges and lights on a dashboard. Each measure may have a gauge with a red/danger, yellow/caution or green/acceptable indicator.

Chart and graphs are essential in summarizing the huge amounts of data available when determining organizational performance and whether it is in an acceptable range. One method used is called a *control chart*. It exhibits an upper control limit (UCL) and a lower control limit (LCL) and then tracks performance to determine if it is "out

(© Mike McDonald. Used under license from Shutterstock, Inc.)

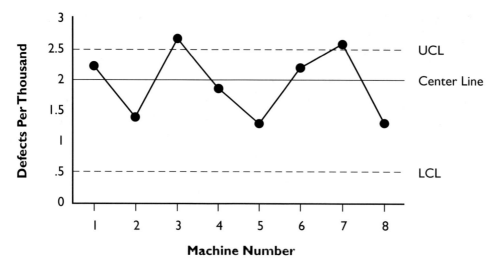

FIGURE 5.4—*Example of a Control Chart*

of control," which means it is outside the set limits. Often the organization sets the limits by using an average of some data and the number of standard deviations from the average.

A manager must examine the control chart and then take action if a process being sampled appears headed out of control. A student can do the same thing with his or her own life. For example, if the average on an exam is 80 and the standard deviation is calculated at 6 but the student scores a 60, he or she might determine that his class performance is out of control and more studying or outside help is in order.

Graphs and charts can take many forms, such as pie charts that show the composition of different items that make up the whole. For example, an individual could use a pie chart to show asset allocation between stocks, bonds or mutual funds. Then another pie chart could show the allocation between five funds of just mutual funds, such as small cap, large caps, indexed, health care and precious metals. This allows viewing the allocations that make up part of the whole and changing those allocations.

Line charts or bar charts can show trends over time. Usually, the horizontal axis shows time and the vertical axis shows some measure. Multiple lines on the graph or breakdowns of a single bar can show dimensions. For example, a single bar can consist of items that make up the height of the bar. Again, this is breaking down the bar, and you could consider it a view of the data using a dimension.

There are both good and bad graphs and charts. They should assist the manager in visualizing the data. Edward Tufte (see References) is an individual who has developed a cult-like following when it comes to graphically representing data. Tufte warns against clutter and extraneous "ink" used on a chart, which he calls "chart-junk." He suggests removing grid lines, unneeded headings and other decoration on the graph that can cause confusion. The best method of making sure that your presentation works is to test it with representative decision makers and see if your message comes through to them.

One thing that a chart or graph designer must be careful of is using graphics for deception. A simple example of deception is sloping the horizontal axis on a graph. This could make a line parallel to the axis that actually represents no change over time appear to be increasing. Another example is to start your vertical axis at some other number than zero when showing a trend. This will magnify any movement on a line graph. Tufte also cautions against using a two-dimensional representation to present a single dimension. For example, inflation over time really is a single dimensional measure. However, if you were to use the size of a dollar bill to show decreased spending power, you would be showing the measure as a two dimensional measure since the dollar bill would have both height and width. The real increase is the area shown, not the single measure. Keep in mind that the visual effect must be accurate and not present a "pretty picture" that misleads the viewer.

You can use color to advantage when presenting information but also misuse it. Color can show contrasts between different dimensions. For example, you can assign a color to each of five business units that a line graph can show. You can also use color alone as a measurement indicator. For example, you can show different categories of measurement on a chart or even a map. A map of the United States can show state boundaries with each state colored based on a performance measure. The simplest example of this is the voting result map that shows which political party dominated in an election. Thus, we have "red states" and "blue states." You can also use color as a signal. The color green often indicates "go ahead" while red indicates "stop." Keep in mind what you are communicating when presenting business intelligence.

Colors also can get a designer into trouble. Without adequate contrast, viewers cannot see colored fonts. We all have struggled with a purple font on a black background. It is very difficult to read. Another consideration is that estimates reveal that 5 to 10 percent of people have some degree of color blindness. One prevalent form of color blindness is the inability to distinguish between green and red. Keep this in mind when using color.

Chapter Summary

Different persons in the business organization play different roles and have different business intelligence needs. Each person has critical success factors in his job and measures of performance that relate to the success factors. Better business intelligence not only tells a person if he or she is doing well in his job but can provide clues to the impact of changes that could lead to better performance. Job performers must propose these business intelligence applications to assure as wise a use of organizational resources as possible. They should select among competing business alternatives with care and consideration of the impact on the bottom line of the organization. Once the application can provide the business intelligence through performance indicators, it is essential to design the presentation of the information to the manager for most effective use.

Food for Thought/Roles Played in Business Intelligence

☞ What skills are necessary for a person who would play the role of a BI Provider?

☞ Which of the three categories of BI players would you put yourself in? Explain why you feel this way.

☞ Which user role do you feel will likely advance most rapidly through management ranks?

Food for Thought/Identifying BI Opportunities

☞ Before starting a BI initiative, what are the "W" questions that need addressing?

☞ Do all workers need the same data/information? Do certain positions require more detailed data than others? Why?

☞ Should an organization define its information requirements before asking business questions? How can Post-It notes help organize and identify BI opportunities?

☞ What are some essential criteria for identifying the contribution of BI opportunities?

☞ What are some criteria that determine the difficulty of the BI opportunities?

☞ What is a "BI Opportunity Scorecard"? Are certain quadrants of BI opportunities more promising for BI efforts than others?

Food for Thought/Presenting Information to Management

☞ Tables of data can be overwhelming. What is a method of summarizing and visualizing data? Explain how even newspapers utilize this method. Finance majors, what is a key ingredient of technical stock analysis?

☞ What is a balanced scorecard? What is balanced?

References

Kaplan, Robert S., and David P. Norton. 2001. Transforming the balanced scorecard from performance measurement to strategic management. *Accounting Horizons* (March 2001), pp. 87–104.

Kaplan, Robert S. and David P. Norton. 2000. Having trouble with your strategy? Then map it. *Harvard Business Review* (September/October 2000), pp.167–176.

Scheps, Swain. 2008. *Business intelligence for dummies.* Indianapolis, IN: Wiley Publishing, Inc.

Tufte, Edward R. 1983. *The visual display of quantitative information.* Cheshire, Connecticut: Graphics Press.

Tufte, Edward R. 1990. *Envisioning information.* Cheshire, Connecticut: Graphics Press.

Tufte, Edward R. 1997. *Visual explanations.* Cheshire, Connecticut: Graphics Press.

Tufte, Edward R. 2006. *Beautiful evidence.* Cheshire, Connecticut: Graphics Press.

Vitt, Elizabeth, Michael Luckevich, and Stacia Misner. 2002. *Business intelligence: Making better decisions faster.* Redmond, WA: Microsoft Press.

Exercise

Developing Your Analysis Skills: Using Information Systems to Add Organizational Value

Your task is to search for successful business intelligence efforts and report back to the rest of your class. You may have personal contacts that have participated in such efforts or you may want to search using the Internet. Categorize any projects based on perceived contribution and difficulty. What level and functional areas in the organization did the projects impact?

Exercise

Search on the Internet for different methods of presenting information to managers. Try to find information on balanced scorecards and information dashboards. Report back what you found.

Exercise

Search for Edward Tufte on the Internet. How do persons who present information to others perceive him? Is his work only applicable to business applications? Explain.

Exercise

Look through business magazines and newspapers for graphs and charts. Try to find some graphs and charts that are misleading or deceptive. Explain why you believe this is true. Did the creator of the graph or chart further his or her argument by using an information presentation that could be misleading? Explain.

chapter 6

Making and Delivering Products and Services

In this chapter, we will explore how organizations manage their operations function to make and deliver products and services and how business intelligence makes a difference. We need to remember that Professor Lawrence described operations as the "muscle, sinew, and bone" of the organization that creates the outputs the organization sells. The production function is necessary in organizations since it provides the products and services sold to generate revenue to survive in a competitive environment.

The production function has many components. There must be forecasts of needed products and services that can satisfy predicted customer demand and raw materials must come from suppliers. The company must acquire people along with machines and other equipment and schedule them to produce its products and services. It must warehouse and prepare these products for distribution when demand occurs, and it must deliver them to customers or to those who buy the products to resell to their customers.

We often call the input/process/output system a *supply chain* because supplies of raw materials, labor and equipment are necessary. Supply chains determine how a particular business (or a group of businesses) acquires and converts raw materials in order to deliver a product or service that has more value than the inputs. A raw material inventory may require management to ensure having adequate supplies to do the production work, but not too much inventory since there is a cost to buy and carry it. We will look at the vital roles of supply chains and how Business Intelligence (BI) underlies efficient supply chain planning. Chapter 7 will focus in more detail on the transformation of the raw materials and concentrate on organizational processes. This chapter focuses on having the inputs needed to conduct the production of goods and services and getting those goods and services to the customers.

The Value Chain/Cycle

The production of a product or service takes place through performing processes, or the business tactics from our business/system objectives/tactics model in Chapter 2. We must add value by performing the processes. This is true for both goods and services. Combining all the inputs creates products to sell. Services must address a customer's needs to create something that the organization can sell in the marketplace at a price that offsets all costs and allows for a reasonable profit.

When considering the value cycle, it is important to realize the differences between goods and services. The production of goods requires raw materials and often production equipment; it produces scrap as a by-product and can be "stockpiled" or held in inventory for a period of time until a customer desires them. In contrast, the production of services often requires a higher percentage of labor costs; it needs fewer machines or equipment and usually requires a higher amount of customer interaction. Services are less tangible in the sense that you cannot hold them or touch them. In most cases, a product producer is in the "back room" and does not directly interact with the customers while service providers have a direct contact with the service consumer. A business cannot stockpile services, but the capability for providing services might be part of the human resources "inventory" that is ready to serve a customer.

Many organizations are both product and service providers. Restaurants, including fast food establishments, provide products such as the food and a service such as interacting with the customer if there is any problem with the product. The "back room" of a restaurant where the chef resides operates much like a production line, resulting in goods or products, while the "front" or the waiter deals directly with the customer and provides a service. Sometimes, the restaurant makes the product available to the customers who can then serve themselves. Most gas stations and salad bars operate in this fashion. Even fast food restaurants use self service when they provide you with a cup and ask you to serve yourself a drink. Services are critically important in the United States where almost 80 percent of the gross national product comes from providing services.

We often refer to the addition of value to goods and services as the "value chain." We could also see it as a "value cycle" since it is a continuous loop where a business uses feedback information on the outputs of products and services to alter the inputs and processes, which improves quality and customer satisfaction. Keep in mind that as goods move through a value cycle, each process is performed to make the product more valuable. The greatest value should occur when the goods are finished. Finished goods are ready to sell to customers in the environment.

As shown in Figure 6.1 below, once the organization determines the necessary goods and services, it can start the value cycle. The value cycle for both service- and product-oriented organizations consists of three basic system activities: procurement of raw material, labor, and equipment; production or transforming system inputs into outputs; and distributing the outputs in the form of products and services to the consumers or customers who exist in the organization's environment. Then the organization determines the need for any changes to the products and services as part of the feedback loop, and the cycle continues.

Procuring the System Inputs

Suppliers provide raw materials and equipment through the purchasing or procurement departments, and human resource experts acquire labor to work with the raw materials and equipment. Forecasts must occur of the amount of raw materials and labor needed to produce the desired outputs. The raw materials must arrive when needed, be inspected to assure quality and get sent to the locations within the organization that needs them.

If the raw material inputs take some time to arrive from the suppliers or if great uncertainty in delivery times exists, then it may be necessary to maintain a raw material inventory. If communication and coordination were finely tuned and lead times known precisely, then raw materials would arrive when needed, neither arriving too early so they have to be stored nor arriving too late and slowing down the production process. An inventory allows for being imprecise and provides "slack time."

Both raw material and finished goods inventories result in various costs. This includes the holding costs since capital is tied up in the inventory, the storage costs since the

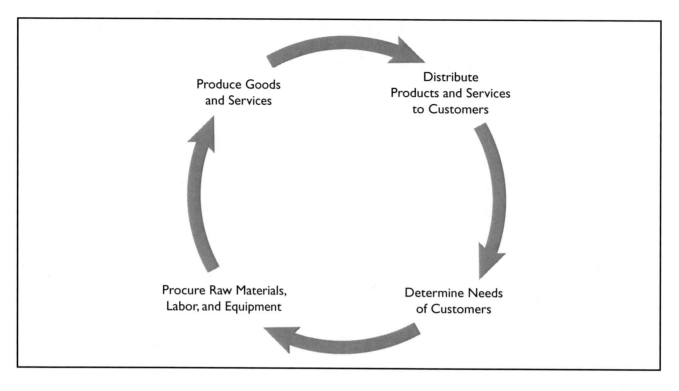

FIGURE 6.1—*The Value Chain/Cycle*

inventory takes space for storage and obsolescence costs since inventory could go out-of-date or a new style could replace it. If the product is not available, shortages of the product for sale could result in the costs of back orders or even cancelled orders. As you can tell, a balance is necessary, requiring close coordination. Open communication between the suppliers and the organization facilitates this type of coordination. Raw materials that arrive precisely at the time needed allow what is called *just-in-time inventory*. If there is a need to maintain and store inventory, we could refer to this as *just-in-case inventory* that serves as a buffer, allowing for less precision in arrival times. Information and communication allow for lower inventory costs.

To assist in providing information and communication, organizations often will utilize software systems during the procurement process called materials requirement planning (MRP) systems. These systems assist in estimating how much of any raw material is necessary based on past usage and what components are necessary to produce finished goods. They also provide help in placing orders for the materials, assist in paying the suppliers and aid in keeping track of the location of the raw materials. The MRP systems also provide coordination through the processing and distribution processes.

An organization must gather and store data to provide critical information when managing a supply chain. It may need a materials data mart to assure that the needed information to manage raw materials is accessible. Such a data mart would include a list of materials for each product. These would include sub-assemblies often called *work-in-process,* suppliers for each of the needed inputs, any alternative materials, costs for the raw materials, time needed from order to delivery, delivery options, etc. If the information is available, managers can quickly and easily evaluate alternatives to assure the lowest cost to the organization.

Procurement also includes acquisition of the right mix of employees to carry on the production of goods and services. The human resources function usually conducts this activity in conjunction with the business managers. Business managers must specify their needs in terms of the number of people and the various skill sets needed by each employee. They often use data marts to acquire the right labor mix. These data marts may include data on existing employees, as well as on potential employees who have applied to the organization or who may exist on external databases run by commercial human resource firms. These external databases may even include industry salary figures based on experience and geographic location. Since human labor is so critical to providing services, service organizations such as a consulting business may have very special needs for skills and knowledge and must work closely with both internal and external data.

Procurement also includes the acquisition of any needed equipment, tools or machinery needed to perform the processing of raw materials into finished goods. This equipment could include a wide assortment of machines and technology. For example, airlines may need airplanes, airport shuttle companies may need specially equipped vans, and construction companies could require everything from saws to paint brushes to electrical circuit testers.

Procuring quality people, raw materials and equipment requires a huge investment in information to assure having the right things in the right place at the right time. This often requires large databases and software to assist in the acquisition process. The simplest level is an inventory system that keeps track of raw materials needed to produce a product. At a higher level of complexity is a material requirements planning or MRP system that we referred to earlier. This type of system assists in keeping lists of needed components, often called a *bill of materials* (BOM), which show where to acquire the components.

More complex software that assists the operations function within an organization is called *supply chain software.* However, most manufacturing companies have replaced much of this supply chain management activity, or included it in an even more complex software system called *enterprise resource planning* or ERP software. This software is more complex and wider in scope than supply chain software. It includes the following three functions: the finance function that provides management of the capital to procure the needed labor, equipment and raw materials; the accounting function that handles all of the billing and payments to suppliers; and the marketing function that focuses on understanding and dealing with customers. We will cover this topic of how an ERP links the organization more fully in Chapter 8 where we will examine all the connections between the functional areas in a business and view the organization as one large interacting system.

Managing the Supply Chain

Within any organization that focuses on producing finished goods is a high need to plan an efficient set of processes to manage raw materials and partially finished products or product components. We often call this work-in-process. Less raw material inventory can reduce an organization's capital needs since inventories cost money for a company to acquire and store. An efficient supply chain results in accurate usage estimates, acquisition from a low cost supplier with high quality raw materials to reduce waste and scrap, backup suppliers and an accurate prediction of quantities based on careful analysis. The analysis could include the consideration of demand forecasts, production mix estimates, time cycle considerations and even seasonal variations.

Supply chain management requires business intelligence to assure management decisions are based on measurement, not guesswork. The past history along with an anticipation of future conditions can lead to more accurate estimates. If an estimate establishes that demand will increase in the future, a manager may decide that acquiring either the actual inventory or an option to buy it in the future at a currently determined price may be a prudent strategy. Airlines who anticipated high future fuel prices hedged against these increases by buying futures that guaranteed the fuel price in the future. This made planning easier. But, this type of hedge could be a liability if prices of fuel decreased. We do the same type of thing when our gas gauge on our car gets to half. If we anticipate prices will go up, we think it best to buy now. If we anticipate prices will decrease, we wait to fill our tank. But it would be great to make such a decision based on information and analysis rather than on intuition and guessing.

Supply chains are very intricate and include many interdependencies. Understanding all the connections can save a company from getting into trouble when one change ripples through the system and affects many other parts of the chain. A quote from a book by the Dalai Lama and Howard C. Cutler exhibits this dependency and interconnectedness (see References). On pages 74–75 Cutler related an instance that we could apply to a supply chain:

> "... Although I've always valued and enjoyed my friends and family, I've considered myself to be an independent person. Self-reliant. Prided myself on this quality in fact. Secretly, I've tended to regard overly dependent people with a kind of contempt—a sign of weakness.
>
> Yet that afternoon, as I listened to the Dalai Lama, something happened. As "Our Dependence on Others" was not my favorite topic, my mind started to wander again, and I found myself absently removing a loose thread from my shirt sleeve. Tuning in for a moment, I listened as he mentioned the many people who are involved in making our material possessions. As he said this, I began to think about how many people were involved in making my shirt. I started by imagining the farmer who grew the cotton. Next, the salesperson who sold the farmer the tractor to plow the field. Then, for that matter, the hundreds or even thousands of people involved in manufacturing that tractor. And all the designers of the tractor. Then, of course, the people who processed the cotton, the people who wove the cloth, and people who cut, dyed, and sewed that cloth. The cargo workers and truck drivers who delivered the shirt to the store and the

salesperson who sold the shirt to me. It occurred to me that virtually every aspect of my life came about as the results of others' efforts. My precious self-reliance was a complete illusion, a fantasy. As this realization dawned on me, I was overcome with a profound sense of the interconnectedness and interdependence of all beings. I felt a softening. Something. I don't know. It made me want to cry."

As Cutler states, there is an intricate supply chain with a great deal of interdependency and interconnectedness involved in creating a product that could continue all the way back from a thread in a shirt to a tractor, the fuel for the tractor, the seed for the cotton plants, the fertilizer and all of the other components needed for something as simple as a thread.

Production Facilities for Goods and Services

The next chapter will discuss how all the raw materials, labor and equipment come together in an efficiently designed production process. Process design and re-engineering can provide efficiencies that eliminate steps and reduce costs. However, part of the production activities includes having the right facilities in place to produce the products and services.

One essential component of getting things built is having the necessary capacity or an appropriate amount of people, raw materials and equipment in place. Capacity planning is highly dependent on forecasting demand for products and services. Both short-term and long-term forecasts are necessary. Short-term forecasts dictate how much labor and raw material the business must acquire and when it needs to arrive at the organization. In some cases, the company hires temporary workers or asks existing workers to work overtime to increase labor capacity. In other cases, it can outsource production needs to other organizations, especially to create partially assembled components, often called work-in-process inventory. For example, an automaker can have a supplier provide an engine, an axle or suspension components rather than starting from scratch by assembling the basic parts.

In essence, there is a need for *forecasting* demand to know what and how much raw material, equipment and facilities and people are necessary. *Capacity planning*, or having the appropriate amount of human labor and machine resources to deliver the needed system outputs, is necessary to assure efficiency and avoid over- or under-capacity. Then the actual production to meet demand includes *scheduling* humans and machines and assuring that trained and experienced people and fully maintained machines are ready to perform the production processes. The business must schedule processes so the right people with the right skills have the appropriate raw materials and any needed machines or equipment to do their jobs. They must do these processes in the most efficient manner. This requires careful analysis to assure that all the right components needed for production of goods and services are in place and that trained workers know what they need to do to produce a finished product or service.

The day-to-day production planning is part of the overall strategic production plan. For example, some manufacturers have learned that they can reduce high labor costs by utilizing sub-assembly in foreign locations and shipping to an assembly facility in another location. The lower labor costs offset the shipping costs. They could even send services such as individual income tax form completion to other countries where labor is cheaper. Chapter 12 will discuss some of these outsourcing or "off shoring" activities, along with the implications of a "flat world."

We must also consider growth potential, making sure that production capacity for now and the future is in place. An organization desires ample facilities and labor to allow flexibility to grow, but it does not need so much capacity that there are idle resources, either in labor or raw materials. Another part of capacity planning is plant location or determining where to locate geographically distributed production facilities. Considerations would include availability of labor, shipping costs, climate, incentives from government agencies such as tax breaks and any other factors where costs could increase or decrease based on the location of facilities.

An example of facility location is a large telemarketing facility that required persons to work short shifts at all hours of the day. The facility was a customer service operation that handled product questions. This took place by phone after the consumer dialed a toll free number. After much analysis, the company found skilled and personable labor by locating near a military base where spouses of the persons on the base desired to work at various times of the day, to get out of their homes and to earn some extra money.

Some service organizations such as hotels may consider proximity to other services part of their location strategy. For example, a restaurant may locate next to lodging or near an airport or other places where business-persons may be traveling. Some hotels may locate near other lodging facilities with a different price structure. For example, a mid-price hotel may locate near a high price facility in an attempt to increase occupancy through overflow from the other facility.

Once an organization locates a facility, it must make decisions on layout within the facility. For example, the placement of machines within a factory can greatly affect throughput. Personnel must move the raw material from a loading dock to production facilities and then to a location for finished goods. They can do this in many different ways. Even a self-service hotel breakfast area can have different types of layout to allow for the quick movement of customers without any bottlenecks. You also might think of a kitchen planning expert and how he or she would try to assure that the layout facilitates meal preparation with the least amount of movement. Organizations such as fast food restaurants are experts on using the available space to service a maximum number of customers with the highest quality and the fewest number of errors.

Producing Quality Finished Goods or Services

One critical aspect of the value cycle is assuring product or service quality. All processes can lead to defects or exceptions to the expected outputs. This can include the production of products, the entry of data into a data warehouse or even the recording of student grades into a grade book. Errors are costly since the company must detect, correct and notify anyone affected. For example, some large scale notification efforts include the need for product recalls if products do not meet a standard. Defects such as in a car braking system could lead to costly lawsuits and repair work. They even could result in death. The same is true of the medical products industry where contaminated drugs have led to costly recalls and even more costly advertising campaigns to regain consumer trust. The challenge to have zero defects and outstanding quality still confront companies. Thus, quality is of great concern to businesses today. The analysis of quality could include quality control, such as TQM or Total Quality Management, Six Sigma or qualifying for the Malcolm Baldrige Award.

Total Quality Management (TQM)

Poor quality can lead to lower revenues and increased costs. For example, scratched furniture or kitchen cabinets could result in product returns or repairs and would not lead to repeat sales. This also could lead to a consumer telling many others about the experience, which would lead others to avoid the business or brand. Cold meals at a restaurant, dirty airplanes or products that do not live up to advertised claims all result in unsatisfied and non-returning customers. This negative feedback has had a larger impact in recent years due to the ease of sharing bad experiences on the Internet.

Quality comes from taking a customer focus and understanding customer needs. It also comes from continuous improvement and attention to whether customers are satisfied, even if your organization produces work-in-process or subassemblies for others. Returns and rework are very expensive. You could consider your customers as others along the entire supply chain.

We can define poor quality by different things. If a customer expects something at a certain time, then lateness could be part of the quality definition. Not meeting expected specifications could be part of the quality definition. Higher cost than expected due to rework or warranty work could be part of the quality equation. Quality often is in the eye of the beholder so the company must understand the beholder. Great quality can save money and help increase revenues as customers expect quality, whether they are buying an electronic device, a car or a truck or taking a flight on an airline.

Workers—especially those who deal directly with customers—must be empowered and given the ability to use resources to solve customers' problems. Although there is a cost in solving a customer dilemma, it is more costly to try to find new customers, especially when unsatisfied customers are telling all their friends and acquaintances about their experience with your business.

There are many techniques that are part of quality control programs. *Control charts* mentioned in an earlier chapter provide a visualization or a chart of produced items that are within and outside of a certain standard. Scatter diagrams also indicate whether something measured falls within tolerable limits. Since not every item will be measured, especially if you need to destroy a product to measure it, *sampling* may need to take place to determine quality. For example, a manager may take a beverage from a production line and test it to assure that it meets all standards, such as sweetness or color saturation. *Inspection* may become part of the quality process. For example, a manager might examine bottled beverages as they pass through the bottling line to assure they are filled to the correct level.

Cause-effect diagrams can assist in improving processes that can assure higher quality. If quality does not meet a standard, what might be the cause? Poor quality materials, badly adjusted machines, inadequate worker skills or training all could be clues indicating where changes are necessary.

Six Sigma

Six Sigma is a quality control movement that started at Motorola Corporation in the 1980s. It is a statistically based quality control approach that works toward reducing product defects and approaching a zero defects objective. Much of the quality control effort evolved from early pioneers in the field, namely Edward Deming and Joseph Juran.

Six Sigma refers to the very small number of errors found out on the tails of the product defect probability distribution. Assuming a normal bell shaped curve, six standard deviations or six sigma from the mean would indicate 3.4 defects per million operations. The approach also allows finding the source of the defects in order to take corrective action.

Six Sigma not only applies to manufacturing but to any repeatable process where measureable results occur. For example, a driver's license renewal office can search for and detect errors in renewal transactions and assure that there are very few errors. They can find some errors immediately and check them through online editing with instant error correction. Matching a zip code against city and state tables can detect and point out potential errors. They can detect and correct other errors by having the customer proofread data before it officially enters the system for processing. They can find and correct simple errors such as the order of the first name and the last name for a person named Anthony. It is very costly to send a license to Robert Anthony and then have him go through a time-intensive error correction exercise.

If there are common sources of errors, it may require changes in processes. These process changes might not only include additional error checking processes, but they could include the order of the processes. It also could include who performs the processes. With the availability of online systems accessible from customer computers, a company can offload much of the responsibility and effort expended for the correct input of data to a system to the customer. Note that Amazon.com immediately sends a copy of your order to you via email so that you can verify if it is correct. This could also reduce time spent by the company, resulting in cost savings.

Six Sigma efforts have been popularized and have led to certification programs. The top certification is a "black belt" in quality management. As an employee, participation in these programs could lead to job opportunities and a better understanding of what is necessary in businesses today.

Malcolm Baldrige Quality Award

Many companies attempt to win the Malcolm Baldrige Quality Award. The President of the United States awards it to organizations that have achieved high levels of quality in their products and services. Motorola Corporation pursued the goal of zero defects and quantitative quality control and in 1998 won the Malcolm Baldrige National Quality Award for its quality work in its manufacturing operations. Other institutions have pursued quality in their operations, including the University of Northern Colorado Kenneth W. Monfort College of Business, which received the award in 2004 (*http://mcb.unco.edu/Newsroom/Baldrige/*).

Concern for quality outputs has led to improved business practices. The advantages of these practices include improved product and service quality, improved customer satisfaction, less waste in industry, fewer returned products or revisits for service and repeat purchases due to satisfaction with product and service quality. All of these advantages can lead to reduced costs and increased revenues, clearly affecting the organization's bottom line in the form of business objectives.

These activities have led to greater satisfaction with businesses that are paying attention to their customers. But, just having improved quality is only part of the puzzle. Quality is required, but not sufficient. There is more to success in business, including building the right products, offering the right services, ensuring customers are aware of your products and services, instilling customer trust in your organization and having the right mix of motivated workers, all of which contribute to the organization's bottom line. Outdated products and services that are perfect in quality, but undesired by customers, likely will lead to an organization's demise. To perform at a high level, an organization must measure what it is doing and then use these measurements to assure it is meeting customer needs at the lowest cost.

Distribution of Goods and Services

Once the company produces quality goods, or the services are available to perform, it must make them available to the customers. This is the all important "shipping and handling" that we pay for when we buy something from a distant company. Think of an organization such as Amazon.Com that must fill your book or merchandise order and then get it to your home.

To fill orders, companies often need to maintain a finished goods inventory. They can maintain and store inventory as part of a manufacturing facility or put it in a warehouse where they hold goods in preparation for customer orders. To minimize shipping costs, a manufacturer selling its own products even could maintain different distribution centers. Other businesses, such as large catalog stores, could save finished goods in their warehouses for aggregation to prepare for a customer order. A manufacturer could ship other parts of a catalog order directly, especially if it is a large and bulky item.

In some cases, organizations outsource the distribution processes to companies that specialize in this activity. For example, a company could provide a distribution center as a service to other organizations and perform their handling and shipping activities. There are parts inventories maintained in Memphis, Tennessee, as part of the Federal Express warehousing network. Federal Express provides services to other companies by accepting customer orders from the companies, filling them and putting them into the Federal Express shipping network for delivery.

Federal Express maintains a complex distribution network that uses a hub system. One of the major hubs is in Memphis, Tennessee, and other smaller hubs exist in Indiana and California. Federal Express gathers and assembles packages by ground transport dropped off throughout the United States at collection centers. It then flies them to a centralized location in Memphis every day. In Memphis, they re-sort and aggregate the packages according to the desired destinations, load them onto airplanes and then fly them out to destinations. There they put the packages on trucks for local or regional delivery. (For an interesting view of 24 hours of flights in and out of Federal Express hubs, see *http://www.youtube.com/watch?v=CzsXqawswPc,* which is a depiction of the "Federal Express Ant Hill.")

An organization often seen as a master of the supply chain and distribution of products is Wal-Mart. Wal-Mart has great business intelligence in that it knows the location of each product it sells, both in warehouses and in stores. If events take place that cause demand for a product to grow in one store while another store has less demand, Wal-Mart can move products from one location to another. For example, if Wal-Mart knows a hurricane is approaching a certain location, it can move both convenience foods such as breakfast bars and clean up supplies such as mops and pails from low demand to high demand store locations to maximize sales and satisfy customers.

A Unique View of a Supply Chain—eChoupal

We have described a supply chain as managing activities from resource acquisition from suppliers, to producing/manufacturing, to getting the goods to customers and receiving payments, and handling any other problems. An example can help us understand the importance of this concept. Supply chains occur in the smallest company that makes a single product up to a large conglomerate company that produces hundreds or even thousands of different products.

A unique story of a supply chain in India involving many dependencies is based on a Harvard Business School case entitled *eChoupal* (see References and a very informative overview video at: *http://www.youtube.com/watch?v=Fx4gukMYTGA*). This case study describes changing the supply chain by putting personal computer/network connections in Indian villages. The move eliminated middlemen and made price and other information available at common areas in small villages to enable farmers to become more efficient and effective. Let's review the eChoupal story.

Some of the key players in the case included a company called ITC, the farmers and some middle people called Commissioned Agents (CAs) who work in market yards called a *Mandi.* ITC is a large company that has a business unit that processed and sold soy beans. ITC was concerned with the very slow growth in the soybean commodity area. ITC needed the soybeans to process into high protein soy meal and into soy oil that it exported to other countries.

The soybean farmers who were the source of soybeans had small village farms in rural areas of India. The farmers had low crop yields due to many factors. These included the quality of sowing seeds, not using herbicides to control weeds, not using pesticides to control destructive insects and the lack of information such as weather forecasts. The farmers belonged to a social group that assembled and shared with each other at choupals or community gathering places. These choupals often were in the home of a leader of the farmers or in other local buildings. Finally, the Mandis or market yards had Commission Agents (CAs) that ITC hired as middle people who brokered for the larger company and acquired the soybeans from the farmers.

The diagram in the figure below represents the original supply chain for obtaining soybeans:

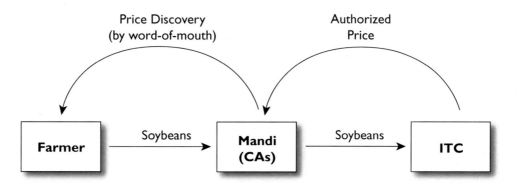

FIGURE 6.2—*Old Supply Chain*

The farmers were not happy with the supply chain. They did not know what the price would be when they headed off to market with their carts of soybeans. And they did not have access to weather forecasts, which could cause them to lose their harvested crops to torrential storms that they did not know were coming. Although the farmers were supposed to be paid once they turned over their crops, the CAs often delayed payment to them. Selling the soybeans was the farmers' livelihood and could mean how they and their families lived until the next crop was ready for sale. They often accused the CAs of corruption as they could misrepresent price and also could "nudge" the scales to give a weight favoring themselves. The entire supply chain was subject to manipulation and utilized only informal communication.

After some analysis and study, the company determined the needed changes in the supply chain. The new players and roles included the eChoupal, which changed the village meeting place to an electronic source where real knowledge seeking and sharing could take place. The eChoupals served as a source of information since each gathering place had a personal computer linked to the Internet and a special site created by ITC (*http://www.echoupal.com/*). The site contained a weather page with localized forecasts, a best practices page with items such as crop spacing suggestions, a crop information page with soil testing guidelines, a market information page with demand and price lists and a market outlook from the Chicago Board of Trade, a Question/Answer page where experts or other farmers could share information, a news page with agricultural happenings and a suggestions page where site users could make requests for more/different information.

The original Commissioned Agents (CAs) now played a new role called the *Samyojak*. They set up the new eChoupals, managed warehouses for soybean storage, sold some of ITC's products, such as seed, and selected another new role player called a *Sanchalak*. A Sanchalak was the lead farmer who would serve as the liaison between ITC and farmers and who managed the personal computers and their connection to information sources. The Sanchalak was an entrepreneur who could now make additional money by selling other ITC products such as tools and fertilizer. ITC also worked out a process where farmers could have the ability to sell directly to ITC and bypass the Mandi. The farmer could have a sample of crop tested by the Sanchalak for quality and get an estimated price without going to the market for an auction. The new supply chain now took a different form:

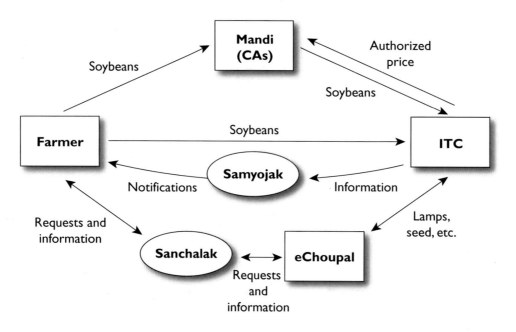

FIGURE 6.3—*New Supply Chain*

When ITC made a direct purchase, the farmers would take the crop to an ITC hub. The farmer would have the crop weighed on a computer scale and receive payment at an advertised price. The farmers also received reimbursement for transporting the crop to the hub since this saved ITC transportation and temporary storage costs. The hub also provided services such as soil testing and recommending fertilizers, and it sold other products such as soy oil at an attractive price since middle people were eliminated. It conducted these sales through the Sanchalak who received a commission since he or she aided ITC's buying process.

The new supply chain facilitated the development of better informed people and groups that were a part of the value chain. The interactions between the key players exhibited a number of factors related to information and business intelligence. ITC realized the importance of understanding the supply chain and its players and what motivated them. They needed to understand their rewards and what was in it for each of them so that they could address motivation. The eChoupals also exhibited the importance of business intelligence, especially for the farmers. Once their isolation kept the farmers "in the dark." This changed as they became aware of supply, demand, weather, prices, etc. Information had empowered the farmers to better understand the marketplace. Many informal processes now became formalized and enabled information for the supply chain members.

The eChoupal case exhibits the importance of utilizing systems thinking and why understanding inputs, processes, outputs and feedback allows for improvements in both effectiveness and efficiency. By increasing efficiency through information flows, the soybean supply chain became a situation where all of those involved could be winners rather than participating in a zero-sum game where a gain could only occur when someone else lost. By making the "pie bigger," all of the participants could be winners by growing the economy and increasing the standard of living to a degree where the poor could now become consumers and buy products they could not afford when their incomes were smaller. This type of economic growth could lead to a prosperous economy.

Chapter Summary

A company cannot have revenues unless it produces products or sells services to a customer who is willing to pay for them. We refer to the process of getting materials, humans and equipment, and producing products and services and selling them to customers as the *supply chain.* There must be careful planning and management of the supply chain for it to be effective and efficient. Information is essential to have a high quality supply chain as the eChoupal case illustrates. The case shows how the components of people, organizations, technology, communication and equipment combine to streamline the acquisition of inputs and finally deliver outputs.

Food for Thought/ITC eChoupal

- What information were the soybean farmers missing that caused the unproductive cycle?

- What problems did the "Mandi" introduce? Did the middlemen known as CAs serve the farmers' best interests?

- What was the original supply chain used to get the soybeans from the farmers to the market? What were the issues with this supply chain?

- What is a "choupal"? How did ITC utilize choupals to introduce the e-Choupal initiative?

    ☞ How did the e-Choupals change the supply chain? What role did "sanchalaks" have in this new supply chain?

    ☞ Did the new supply chain introduce new efficiencies? What benefits did the new supply chain have for the farmers? How about ITC?

References

HH Dalai Lama, and Howard C. Cutler. 1998. *The Art of Happiness: A Handbook for Living.* New York: Riverhead Books, pp. 74–75.

Worthen, B. "ABC: An introduction to supply chain management." *CIO Magazine.* *http://www.cio.com/article/40940/ ABC_An_Introduction_to_Supply_Chain_Management?contentId=40940&slug=&.*

Upton, David M., and Virginia A Fuller. "The ITC eChoupal Initiative." Harvard Business School case 9-604-016, January 15, 2006.

Exercise

Consider what you might need to acquire to create a simple product such as a pizza. What are the raw materials, equipment and labor needed to create a sausage and mushroom pizza? Explain why this might be similar to a list of pizza ingredients on a recipe. What would you need to conduct the procurement activities? Next, consider the creation of the pizza. Note how this is similar to the steps on the pizza recipe. What might be the necessary steps?

How is the pizza operations process more complex for a pizza delivery restaurant? Think about the procurement activities. What do you have to procure? Then, how do you conduct the actual production process? Finally, what would you need to do to get your pizzas to your customers? Are there alternatives?

Exercise

This chapter gives an example of Wal-Mart moving low demand products from one store to another store where high demand may occur. They might move convenience foods, mops and pails to an area where bad weather is predicted. Think of and record all occasions where such a strategy might work. Try to consider both weather-related and special events that could create high demand and a need to re-distribute products.

Exercise

Why might you consider your refrigerator a "warehouse" that holds an inventory? Why do you put things in the refrigerator or store non-perishable items in a pantry? How could we turn this into a just-in-time versus a just-in-case system?

chapter 7

Representing and Redesigning Business Processes

Processes Transform Inputs Into Outputs

Conducting Process Analysis

Understanding Business Processes

Mapping Business Processes: A Closer Look

Using Business Intelligence in Process Management

Reengineering Business Processes

Example of Process Reengineering

Job Design

Chapter Summary

Businesses must perform processes to produce goods and services and to sell them to customers in the environment. Generating revenue through sales and ultimately achieving a profit is necessary for organizational survival. Without sales of products and services, the organization only has expenses with no offsetting revenues. Using our more familiar language from earlier in the book, we can say that organizations must perform processes that they can consider business tactics that they must perform to achieve business objectives. Thus, it is critical to understand business processes to assure the production of the products and services in the most expeditious manner to generate revenues at the lowest cost.

Processes Transform Inputs Into Outputs

As discussed in an earlier chapter, we can view organizations as systems with inputs, processes and outputs. Once a business accumulates all the resources that are inputs and it is clear what product and service outputs to provide for customers, it must determine how to transform the inputs into outputs. A process receives inputs from other processes or the environment and produces outputs that go to another process or the environment. Within each process, there are sub-processes that also have inputs and that produce outputs. When we get to an elemental process level, we have a series of tasks or activities. We often call these *procedures*. As you can imagine, there are many steps between knowing a customer need and satisfying it. The transformation process requires a clear view of the steps or activities needed to produce the products and services to satisfy customers and generate sales. This clear view allows assurance that the processes operate with the greatest efficiency and produce high quality products and services.

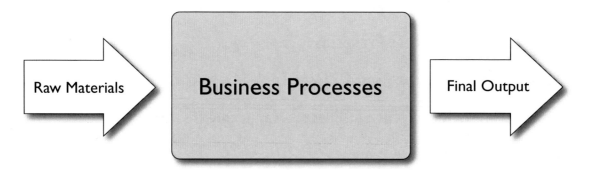

FIGURE 7.1—*What Is a Business Process?*

Conducting Process Analysis

All organizations need to perform processes. In fact, we could commonly define performing processes as "work." Something must happen to the inputs to make them more valuable by combining, finishing and packaging. Organizations have found that there is potential for cost reduction when processes are efficient. They must perform the business processes used to produce the goods and services to use the least amount of resources for each unit of production with the highest degree of quality. Less human resources are necessary to perform well-designed processes.

Revenue increases also are possible. If customers find that efficient processes provide quicker delivery and quicker response to customer service requests, the image of the company improves and repeat orders and sales are more likely. Some organizations have found that process improvement is so important that they have made it a company focus, creating jobs and possibly even hiring high level managers to assure effective and efficient processes.

Sometimes process designers make minor and incremental improvements to the existing processes. In other cases, they ignore the old processes, and the process designers start with a blank slate. We often call this process *reengineering*. We will look at how, why and when organizations should just incrementally improve or reengineer processes, and the principles involved. The first challenge of all process redesign is to understand the processes well enough to improve them through redesign.

Understanding Business Processes

Organizations can accomplish process understanding in many ways. Some of the process design work could include observation and recording or mapping of existing processes with an eye toward finding bottlenecks or slow down points. Some of the work could include data collection to determine arrival rates of orders and the people who desire products or services. Some process work to gain understanding could include creating complex mathematical models in order to build a model that is a virtual re-creation of the processes. A model allows simulation and changing inputs and processing capacity to determine the effect on the output of goods and services.

Some business processes involve manufacturing and some involve information and data handling. It is important to examine and understand manufacturing processes from the initial acquisition of raw material to the distribution of finished goods. In between are the production activities utilizing the materials, machines and human labor. Information processes involve accepting some data or documents and using them to instigate an action or to process it into information. For example, a customer order can be an input used to provide data to perform the processes of filling the order, billing the customer and adjusting the inventory. We must analyze and design both types of processes to be efficient.

Manufacturing Processes

In manufacturing processes, it is essential to take into consideration the product being produced. If there are more variations of the product, then there is more management needed since there are more possibilities and production paths that may need to change. The process may require different raw materials, machines and skilled people, depending on the product or service that needs delivery. Usually, the less variation, the lower the cost for each item produced. For example, Henry Ford tried to simplify car production when he stated that you can have any color car you want as long as it was black. This made the process easier to manage since only one color of paint was necessary; interiors did not have to match a variety of colors, and painting equipment could become minimized.

Manufacturing processes can vary quite a bit depending on the amount of demand for the product. Craftspeople perform some processes to produce customized one-of-a-kind products. For example, a skilled cabinetmaker might build a specialized cabinet that fits in a non-standard sized opening. Or, a skilled woodworker may build a breakfast booth in a unique space in a kitchen. You can't go out and buy the product at a local chain store. Someone has to design it, acquire the materials, construct it and finish it to fit in a specialized space.

Another kind of manufacturing is to create an assembly line to build many cabinets of a certain size and material. This type of mass production, such as building similar cars and trucks, will lower the cost of each item. Rather than building a customizable product, often the standard used in manufacturing today is to follow the principles of acquiring large amounts of raw materials, using interchangeable parts and having people perform a specialized task over and over again. Of course, there are different levels of customizing that we can achieve. Often, we can assemble interchangeable parts to make a product, but then differences will appear once we specify the outer color or aesthetic design. Thus, the product design and specification will dictate different kinds of processes.

Information Processes

Information processing differs in that the input is data and the output is information. The data can come from many different databases or warehouses and becomes combined and manipulated to produce information that gives intelligence and knowledge. This could be as simple as processing a customer order to producing a budget for a large organization. We have examined the information cycle in an earlier chapter and much of the processing is either transaction or analytic processing. We also need to produce information about the products, services and required processes to assist management. We will discuss this later in this chapter.

Whatever the product, service or information, it is necessary to clearly understand the processes needed to produce the desired result. Some specific activities performed in process analysis in order to understand the processes include:

- Process charting or diagramming—creating systems views of processes including the inputs/processes and sub-processes/outputs. This understanding of what occurs can lead to obvious places to improve. However, when we discuss reengineering later in the chapter, we also will discover that there is a disadvantage in knowing too much about current processes since the knowledge could blind us to making changes. We will go into detail about flow diagramming in the next section.

- Cycle time analysis or determining where time is spent performing processes or sub-processes. Time analysis can help focus attention on places where we can make the greatest improvements. Study of the differences in time distribution spent on each of the sub-processes can reveal variations between the fastest and the slowest times taken by different persons or groups performing the processes. Often we can study the fast processors to learn if we can record their techniques and share them with others. Then we can teach the slow performers new approaches or techniques to increase productivity.

- ☛ Bottleneck analysis or finding where the greatest delays take place. For example, if orders are held up by sitting in the inbox of one person, it could be beneficial to determine whether or not to add additional persons at the bottleneck or whether we can split up the tasks performed by the bottlenecked person or work station to bring more efficiency. Overall, this type of study will increase throughput and improve productivity.

- ☛ Simulation or building a computer-based model with a distribution of historic arrival rates at a process along with a distribution of times collected from past experience to perform the process. Through the use of random arrival rates and random service times, we can analyze performance to determine if changing the number of arrival "gates," as well as the number and speed of "service stations," can increase overall performance. This type of analysis can lead to different mixes of process performers between different types of people or machines.

The use of advanced software and technology has improved many of these approaches to process analysis. For example, drawing tools have aided the creation of system diagrams and recording processes for cycle time analysis. Computer simulation software with improved interfaces has assisted process analysts in creating process models and running them to examine performance.

Mapping Business Processes: A Closer Look

In examining business processes, it is extremely helpful to represent the system and its processes in a set of diagrams. We often call this process mapping or diagramming. There are many approaches to process mapping, but all approaches attempt to achieve the same objective: to provide a visual view of the processes to better understand them, to evaluate them and to change them. Manufacturing processes may have different methods and symbols than information processes. But all the methods attempt to represent a system with its inputs, processes, storage, outputs and movement of either data or physical objects in a visual representation. Because of this similarity, we will discuss all types of diagrams together.

Processing mapping gives a spatial, not a textual, view of a system. This allows a process mapper and reviewers a view that allows them to see problems, opportunities, bottlenecks and delays, and it allows for training others since it is like a map that shows "you are here now." Maps allow sharing and putting the processes in perspective. They also allow further mark-up to indicate where one might take measurements and include quality control checkpoints. Once we have developed a process map, we can examine the pictures to try to visualize what changes to make to gain efficiencies.

The purpose of flow diagrams is to provide a semantic bridge between process modelers and those that must perform the processes. The diagrams are:

- graphical, eliminating thousands of words;

- hierarchical, showing systems at any level of detail; and

- jargonless, allowing user understanding and reviewing.

The goal of flow diagramming is to have a commonly understood model of a system. Other techniques support flow diagrams, such as data structure diagrams that show the relationships of data in a data warehouse, data dictionaries and procedure-representing techniques such as decision tables or decision trees.

In most cases, system diagramming starts at the highest level and then goes into more detail, creating a hierarchy of diagrams with different levels of detail. The highest level diagram attempts to put the system in context, thus the term *context diagram.* A context diagram is the highest level graphic representation of a system. It shows inputs to the system and destinations from the system. We call these sources and destinations *external entities,* since they are external to the system boundary. In some cases, the diagram also may show flows of data and resources between external entities, especially if a system boundary is unclear to the analyst.

In the context diagram below, the squares are external entities. The diagonal lines in the external entity corners indicate that there is a duplicate of the external entity somewhere on the page. Note that the circle in the middle of how the professor does her evaluation of a student is still considered a "black box" since no detail is provided on what actually takes place in the circle, but the diagram identifies the sources/destinations and the flows into/out of the system. The system accepts the inputs from four different sources, processes them and sends them off to three different destinations.

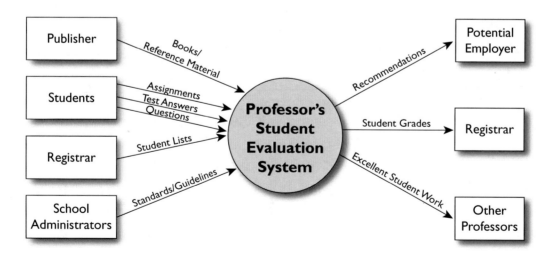

FIGURE 7.2—*An Example of a Context Diagram*

Once we identify the context of the system, we need more detail about the processes inside the circle in the center of the context diagram. Flow diagrams are a network representation of a system. The diagrams use four symbols to represent any system at any level of detail. The four entities that must be represented are:

- **Flows**—movement of data or resources to or in the system

- **Stores**—repositories for data or resources (inventory) that is not moving

- **Processes**—transforms incoming flow(s) to outgoing flow(s). The processes often add value. A label at the bottom of the process can indicate the group or job position that performs the process.

- **External entities**—sources or destinations outside the specified system boundary.

Flow diagrams do not show decisions or the timing of events. Their function is to illustrate sources, destinations, flows, stores and transformations. The capabilities of flow diagramming align directly with general definitions of systems and implement a method for representing systems concepts, including boundaries, input/outputs, processes/sub-processes, etc.

The flow diagram is analogous to a roadmap. It is a network model of all possible paths with different detail shown on different hierarchical levels. Some flow diagram advocates call the process of representing different detail levels "leveling" or "partitioning." Like a roadmap, there is no starting or stopping point, no time or timing or steps to get somewhere. We just know that the data or material path must exist because at some point we will need it. A roadmap shows all existing or planned roads because the roads are necessary. If we were to add usage patterns or great detail to the road network on a state roadmap, it would become unusable to plan routes. When we look at the roadmap of Illinois, we know we could find more detail of the main roads in the Chicago vicinity, and then find even more detail of the street network within the Chicago vicinity.

Consider the flow diagram of a professor's grading system in Figure 7.3. Note that the diagram shows the details within the large circle on the context diagram shown earlier. The flows to and from the external entities shown on the context diagram all appear on the flow diagram. Note that only four symbols are used.

The flow diagram does not include repetition, or how many times a procedure is performed or when it is performed. Remember that the flow diagram only presents a network of paths. It presents the network at a degree of detail that is understandable and usable for a select set of users. Different views at different levels of the same system are necessary for users at different levels of authority and responsibility to understand and review their relevant system portion. Detail not shown on the different levels of the flow diagram, such as volumes, timing, frequency, etc., appears on supplementary diagrams or in a glossary or what we call a *data dictionary*. For example, store contents may appear in the data dictionary that would include things like a bill or materials.

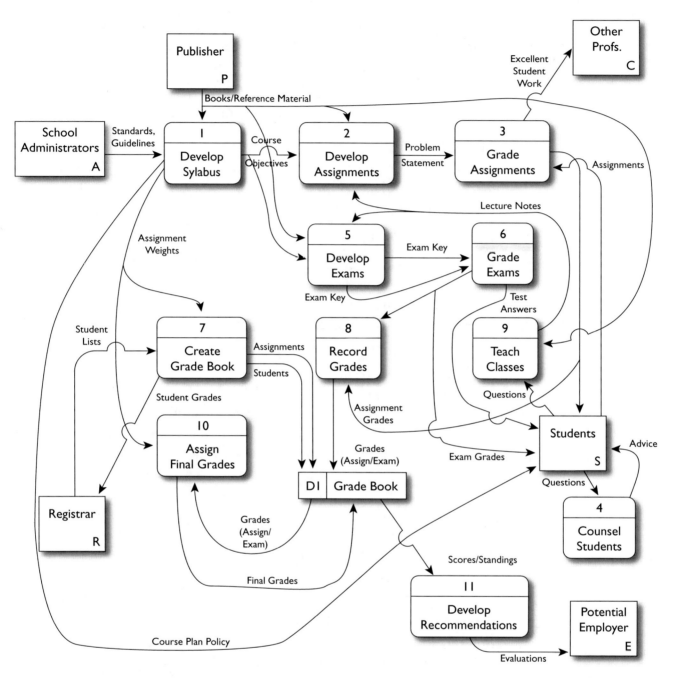

FIGURE 7.3—*Flow Diagram of a Professor's Grading System*

Knowing how to produce a flow diagram can be a valuable skill. We will review a procedure for creating a flow diagram. Keep in mind that flow diagrams are composed of the four basic symbols shown below.

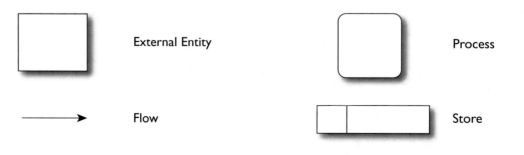

The ***External Entity*** symbol represents sources of data or material to the system or destinations of data or material from the system.

The ***Flow*** symbol represents movement of data or material.

The ***Process*** symbol represents an activity that transforms or manipulates the data, raw material or work-in-process (combines, reorders, converts, etc.).

The ***Store*** symbol represents data or material that is not moving (delayed data or inventory not being used at the moment).

These four symbols can represent any system at any level of detail.

External Entities

- Have an appropriate name.

- Can be duplicated, one or more times, on the diagram to avoid line crossing.

- Determine the system boundary. They are external to the system being studied. They are often beyond the area of influence of the mapper.

- Can represent another system or subsystem.

- Go on margins/edges of flow diagram.

Flows

- Are represented with a line with an arrowhead on one end. A fork in a flow means that the same data or product goes to two separate destinations. You can also join the same data or product coming from several locations.

- Are ALWAYS named. Names should clearly identify what is moving.

Processes

- Show transformation or change. Data or materials coming into a process must be "worked on" or transformed in some way. Thus, all processes must have inputs and outputs. In some (rare) cases, data inputs or outputs will only appear at more detailed levels of the diagrams. Each process is always "running" and ready to accept data or materials.

- Are represented by a rounded corner rectangle.

- Are named with one carefully chosen verb and an object of the verb. There is no subject. The name should be descriptive beyond the word "process." Each process should represent one function or action. If there is an "and" in the name, you likely have more than one function (and process).

- Should generally move from top to bottom and left to right.

Stores

- Are generic for physical storage (parts, materials, computer or human memory, etc.)

☛ Have an appropriate name.

☛ Can be duplicated, one or more times, to avoid line crossing.

☛ Are detailed in the data dictionary, glossary or with data description diagrams.

Developing the Diagram

The procedure for producing a flow diagram is to:

1. Identify and list external entities specifying the providing inputs/receiving outputs from the system;

2. Identify and list inputs from/outputs to external entities;

3. Create a context diagram with the system at center and external entities sending and receiving flows;

4. Identify the business functions or processes included within the system boundary;

5. Identify the data or material connections between business processes;

6. Confirm through personal contact with process experts that they receive sent data or material and vice-versa;

7. Trace and record what happens to each of the flows entering the system (data/material movement, storage, transformation/processing);

8. Attempt to connect any diagram segments into a rough draft;

9. Verify that all flows have a source and destination;

10. Verify that data or material coming out of a data store or inventory goes in;

11. Redraw to simplify—ponder and question result;

12. Review with "informed"—those persons who know about the processes and flows;

13. Explode any process where more detail is necessary and repeat above steps as needed.

Diagraming Is Not Easy

There are a number of challenges that others have encountered when creating flow diagrams. We can learn from their experiences.

☛ System boundary establishment is an important judgment call. External entities aid in determining where to establish the boundary. An interfacing system can be shown as an external entity. It may become necessary to dictate the input of the external entity to assure quality in the supply chain. For example, customers may be required to submit orders or refund requests containing specific information. An interactive system linked to a data warehouse may assist the data provider by retrieving data needed in completion of a form. Use of output such as reports by management may require some agreement on tactics to perform, which may mean the entity becomes part of the system, not external to it. When in doubt, include the external entity as processes within the system and then evaluate with those concerned.

☞ Label your processes carefully and vividly. A process labeled "Produce Report" and that has the output of "Report" tells a reviewer and designer very little. If you have trouble labeling anything on the diagram, it often is because you do not have adequate understanding. Choose names carefully.

☞ Flows are pathways for data or materials. Think about what data or materials are necessary to perform a process or to update a data or inventory store. Think about the flows, processes and storage needed to move data or materials through a system.

☞ Concentrate first on what happens to a "good" transaction. Systems people have a tendency to lose sight of the forest because they are so busy concentrating on the branches of the trees and handling exceptions.

☞ Confusion will not convince reviewers. A quality flow diagram will be so simple and straightforward that people will wonder what took you so long.

☞ Do not try to put everything you know on the flow diagram. The diagram should serve as an index and outline. The index/outline will be "fleshed out" in the data dictionary, in other diagrams such as organization charts, and in procedure specification techniques.

The way to really learn about process mapping is to do it and to have persons review it who perform the processes or who supervise other performers. Experience is the best teacher.

Using Business Intelligence in Process Management

When determining how well processes are working and what you should change, you must make decisions based on business intelligence. As discussed in earlier chapters, there is a need to determine what measurements you must make and how to interpret them. There may be a need for standards or benchmarks to compare to actual performance. Tolerances specifying the acceptable level of performance are necessary. Once you have specified measurements, multidimensional analysis can be revealing.

Dimensions are comparable to specifications. Any specification would mean that there are differences within the dimension. For example, you could examine a car by model, by engine type, by drive train, by body style, by color, etc. You could analyze a piece of clothing by size, by design, by material, by color, etc. to determine if there are differences in processing needed to produce a product. Even if there is a service produced and sold, you could analyze it by different dimensions, such as by server, by time of day, by type of service, by shift, etc. to reveal needs for changes in processes. Information leading to business intelligence is essential for efficient and effective business processes so managers will know what is going right and what is going wrong.

When process design takes place, a need may exist to include special processes. This may include a lack of needed material, an inability to contact a customer to suggest substitution or upgrades or a need to involve external constituents, such as suppliers, transporters or labor unions. Better business intelligence could provide contact information that could keep a process operating.

The following example details what can happen if needed materials are not available. An auto maker had to shut down its assembly line:

> *Chrysler Corp. DETROIT, Oct 2, 2009; Soyoung Kim writing for Reuters reported that Chrysler Group LLC said on Friday it will idle production of its Jeep Wrangler SUV for a week starting Monday due to part shortages from an unidentified supplier. Chrysler said its Toledo, Ohio plant, which produces the Jeep Wrangler and has 525 hourly factory workers, will be shut down due to the "continued stress in the automotive supply chain." Chrysler spokesman Max Gates did not identify the auto parts maker or the parts supplied by the company. Chrysler sold 65,045 Wrangler SUVs in the first nine months of the year, flat from 2008, making it one of the few vehicles to avoid a steep decline in sales. U.S. auto parts suppliers have been hit hard by a steep downturn in North American auto production, the lack of financing and the bankruptcies of General Motors Corporation [GM.UL] and Chrysler earlier this year. Even the failure to provide a single component by a supplier has the potential to disrupt production quickly at automakers due to the manufacturing practices of having parts delivered just before assembly of the vehicles. (Source: 10/3/09, Denver Post)*

Shutting down an assembly line is very costly. Not only are there no finished goods to sell, but a need may exist to pay for work not being done due to contractual obligations. People get paid to be idle rather than to be productive. Better business intelligence could have alleviated the above situation by providing indicators about a problem in parts delivery.

Assembly lines are very intricate and can easily get out of sync with arriving parts and needed labor. Management of these processes often requires asking a large number of "what if . . ." questions. An automaker may ask: What if we don't have enough crème colored paint? What if there is a delay in a suspension part for a certain model? Or what if there will be a delay in a certain sound system? Each of these situations will require decisions and process changes. We can aid answering "what if" questions through the use of simulation that can provide needed business intelligence. Based on past data and probabilities, we can evaluate different scenarios to determine which approach will give the most throughput. The car maker Audi used a simulation of their assembly line to better manage their operation. (See Vick book in References)

Audi learned from its simulations that it could be beneficial to change production patterns in certain circumstances. Essentially, if there was a wait for parts for a certain car model, they could move different car models if all their parts were available. They could pull other cars from the line. Different sequences could be more beneficial to allow cars of a certain color or engine type to get priority or belong to a batch allowing greater efficiencies. They could take corrective action based on better business intelligence and clear communication lines. If there was a delay, they could keep customers up to date or even ask whether substitution of a different accessory (a higher priced sound system) was acceptable. The customer might get a more expensive component, but it might be worth it if the assembly line could have greater overall optimization.

To accomplish this better business intelligence at Audi, there was an operations data mart with over fifty dimensions and hundreds of measurements, a database "engine" to manage all the data, front-end analysis software to help convert the data into information and business intelligence and an extraction/transform/link (ETL) data transformation service. This approach to process management served both operational/day-to-day and long-term analysis needs. Audi managed by using information, not by using best estimates, guesses and intuition.

Reengineering Business Processes

Reengineering business processes was popularized in the early 1990s. The book entitled *Reengineering the Corporation: A Manifesto for Business Revolution* by Michael Hammer and James Champy was published in 1993. The theme of the reengineering gurus was not to make incremental changes when examining processes, but to start from scratch with a blank sheet. "Don't Automate, Obliterate" was the cry. It encouraged radical rethinking of what is. When reengineering, the words "we've always done it that way" are discouraged. A new perspective on the organization and its information processing is necessary.

One belief about organizational processes is that they have evolved over time. Processes are added but few get deleted. Few process examiners ask the tough question: "Is this process or sub-process really necessary?" Often processes remain because they always have been there. This is the reason to start with a blank sheet, to determine what really needs doing and to specify the necessary business tactics or processes. This may require some difficult management decisions.

For example, many accounting control processes exist due to a lack of trust. If it requires many signatures to purchase a low-cost, twenty dollar item, then process engineering may be needed. We must ask the question: "What should the limit be before we really need multiple approvals?" and "Do we truly trust our employees?" At other times, rather than seeking specific approval through a signature, the organization managers just want awareness of a purchase or decision. For example, a finance person may require management action to *disapprove* a travel expense while he or she can review accepted expenses and after a short time period move them forward. This can lead to efficiency where fewer tactics are performed.

Just as with making incremental improvements, before we can reengineer processes it is essential to understand the desired end result and why the current processes are performed. However, knowing too much detail about what is done and how it is done may stifle creative and new thinking. Redesigners can become locked into what already is there. Knowing the desired output and why it is necessary is a good starting point. Then the designer can ask herself questions and determine if there is a "better way." Changing WHAT is done, HOW it is done—including the use of technology—and WHO does it can lead to improved processes.

One example is a company that is receiving and fulfilling orders. Customers send in orders as an input. The company examines the orders to assure that they are complete, including customer identification and address, items ordered and means of payment. The customer receives a notification either that the order is complete and the products are available or that the company needs more information. The company fills the order, charges the customer and notifies him or her when to expect the order. It also provides a tracking number.

The company may examine these processes and find that some of the customer contact is unnecessary. It can check the order for completeness, and, if it can fill the order, charge the customer and then send only one notification. The revised processes are simpler and less costly to perform. There may not be a huge savings on each order, but there could be great savings on a large number of orders.

When conducting reengineering process analyses, a basic change in mindset is necessary to view the organization. In the past, analyses viewed many organizations using a functional or silo view. Each function operated somewhat independently, and each department only did one type of work. The task-based approach focused on what was done within a functional unit, not on the output to the customer. The biggest difference was that information flowed vertically so a message or concern from operations would go up the hierarchical chain of command to a higher level manager who then would pass the information across and then down the silo to another function, such as marketing or accounting. To do something different required a radical change in information flow.

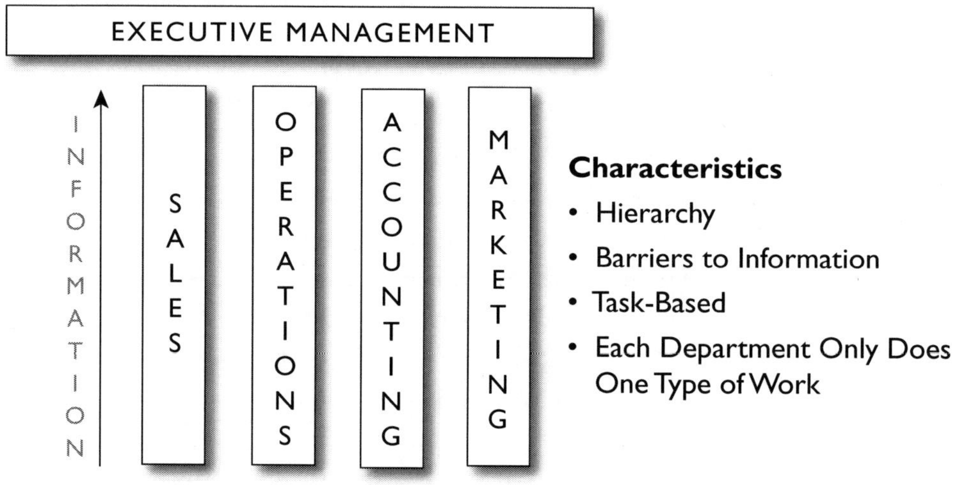

EXECUTIVE MANAGEMENT

INFORMATION

SALES   OPERATIONS   ACCOUNTING   MARKETING

Characteristics

- Hierarchy
- Barriers to Information
- Task-Based
- Each Department Only Does One Type of Work

FIGURE 7.4—*Silo (Functional) View*

More organizations today are taking an outcome-based process view of the organization. The process view is beneficial for information flows since the information does not have a long path up and down the hierarchy but goes horizontally to other functional managers or workers. This requires less management involvement and results in better communication and information flows, and ultimately, better business intelligence. The customer also benefits since the different functions act more as a team and provide better service to the customers.

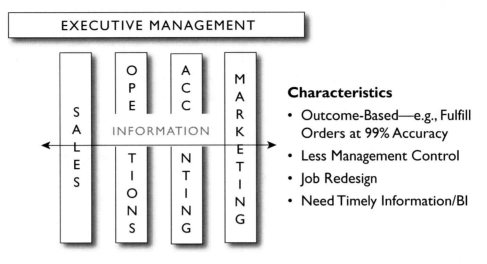

FIGURE 7.5—*Process View*

Taking a horizontal or process view rather than a functional silo or vertical view of an organization can lead to some major changes in the performance of processes. This radical change often can lead to a reengineering of the processes.

Example of Process Reengineering

An example from Michael Hammer's article (see References) shows us a vivid reengineering example and allows us to apply the process mapping tools described earlier in the chapter. The example describes the accounts payable process for acquiring new goods (e.g., tires, engine components) at Ford. A flow diagram of this process appears below. The present process required Ford to send a variety of documents between its departments and the vendor who was providing the goods (e.g., Goodyear tires). The accounts payable department had to match three documents (purchase order, an invoice and a receiving document) before submitting payment to the vendor. When accounts payable was unable to match one of the documents with the others, it had to investigate where the disparity arose. A bottleneck formed that required extra work. The vendors became frustrated by the length of time it took for them to receive the payment for their goods.

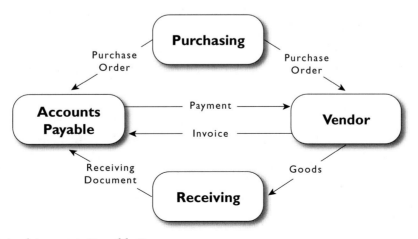

FIGURE 7.6—*Original Accounts Payable Process*

Ford decided to improve this goods acquisition process. Instead of making incremental improvements, it reengineered the process. This required Ford to change the underlying assumptions of how accounts payable works. Instead of paying for the goods when an invoice arrives, they would now pay for goods when they arrive at the receiving dock. In fact, Ford determined that invoices were not necessary at all. As the flow diagram of the reengineered process below shows, Ford added a centralized database so that the accounts payable, receiving and purchasing departments could update the status of the order directly. For example, when the goods arrive at the receiving dock, an individual from the dock will indicate this, and accounts payable can submit a payment to the vendor. This eliminated unnecessary paperwork, and matching errors no longer occurred. The reengineered process vastly improved the efficiency of acquiring goods at Ford.

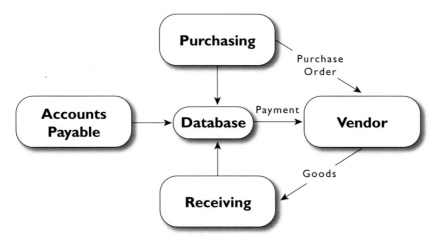

FIGURE 7.7—*Reengineered Accounts Payable Process*

According to the Hammer article, Ford reduced its headcount for these processes by 75 percent rather than the original incremental process enhancements that had projected a 20 percent cut. The radical change saved time and costs, but it did require a new way of thinking and required some jobs to change.

Job Design

When any processes change through incremental improvement or more radical changes in reengineering, an employee's job will change. This requires the operations, information systems and human resources units to work together to redesign jobs in the organization.

We might consider job design the most detailed part of the redesign effort. What employees do when they arrive at their jobs can change as the processes change. The company must compartmentalize and combine the tasks so it can train persons to perform the tasks with their necessary knowledge and skill sets. Remember an earlier chapter when we asked "Will someone's job change?" when referring to changing business tactics.

Analysts, including persons from operations and human resources, must work together to decide what is done by whom and whether it is done by machine, by a human, done as a group of subcomponents or outsourced as a finished product or as a component or subassembly. This is part of the supply chain analysis. But once analysts determine the human activities, they must specify what each person must do. In some cases, they state the activities in very general terms, such as "interview customer to determine problem," while in other cases, they determine a detailed checklist. For example, fast food restaurants may have a seventeen step procedure for making French fries down to the level of how many shakes of salt go on each batch.

Each person performing a process must have the appropriate qualifications. Job qualifications could include education, training, skills, licenses or strengths. The need to know how to operate certain machines or tools may exist. There may be a need for a certain amount of time or experience such as driving a truck or a forklift. Testing for certain knowledge or skills or a certification from a certifying body may be part of determining whether a person is qualified to perform a job.

Compensation also is part of the job specification and human resource process. A company may have to do wage surveys that take into consideration regions of the country and the amount of demand for similar workers. It also must consider unions when determining work processes and job designs. The unions may set requirements for work conditions and worker safety.

All in all, the human resources and job specification function is an interesting and challenging part of process and work design. It is beyond the scope of this book, but organizations need to carefully consider it when conducting process analysis.

Chapter Summary

We can view performing processes in an organization as the "work" done. The work is done so that the business can sell products and services in the marketplace to generate revenues. To do the work efficiently, careful analysis of the processes occurs and changes take place to ensure the business is competitive in the marketplace. This important role can consist of incremental improvements or radical changes through reengineering. Business intelligence is necessary to perform process redesign and to utilize resources in the most expeditious manner. Often, the situation requires job changes to assure that all employees are making the greatest contribution to the organization's mission.

References

Damelio, Robert. 1996. *The basics of process mapping.* Boca Raton, FL: CRC Press.

Hammer, M. 1990. Reengineering work: Don't automate, obliterate." *Harvard Business Review,* July/August 1990.

Vitt, Elizabeth, Michael Luckevich, and Stacia Misner. 2002. *Business intelligence: Making better decisions faster.* Redmond, WA: Microsoft Press. See Chapter 4, "Operations/Assembly Lines and Scheduling with BI, Audi Case Study."

Exercise

Developing Your Analysis Skills: Representing and Redesigning Business Processes

Diagram the process you use to register for classes every semester. Are all the steps in the process necessary? Are there steps that the school could eliminate or combine? Would information that you had filled out earlier reduce the time for your registration if it could be accessed from a data warehouse and used to fill in a form?

Exercise

Think back to a visit to either a doctor's or a dentist's office. These service providers must perform processes to assure that you receive quality service. Providing the service requires information. On your visit, what questions did they ask of you? Do you know the accurate answers to the questions? Does this information exist somewhere else? Could they store and access it whenever you have medical treatment, no matter where you are? How could they do this?

Exercise

Conduct a search on the Internet to find out what companies might use simulation to represent their processes and to test changes to the processes. What did you discover? Are there software packages that exist that make simulation easier?

Exercise

As part of a team, brainstorm examples of poor quality. The chapter gave several examples. Can you add to the list? How would you define quality in classes you take? What would you change within reason to improve the quality?

chapter 8

Enterprise Resource Planning

Now that we have explored how supply chains can assist in creating and delivering products and services and that we understand the importance of processes, we will move on to learn how to manage information and business activities for the whole organization. This often takes place by utilizing enterprise resource planning systems.

Enterprise Resource Planning (ERP) software systems support and connect supply chains and an organization's vital functions, such as marketing, finance and accounting. ERP helps to integrate all computing and information associated with business operations. The software systems link the once independent pieces of software into an integrated whole that expedites data exchanges. It is similar to a continent where all individual units speak the same language and don't need translators. Many organizations today utilize ERP systems to manage their operations systems since the ERP systems allow the storing, linking and managing of data usable by all functions and levels in a business organization. ERP facilitates the data warehouse concepts discussed earlier in this book.

Evolution and Definition of Enterprise Resource Planning (ERP) Systems

ERP systems consist of software modules and are part of an organization's information technology systems. The systems are offshoots of and enhancements to early materials requirement planning (MRP) systems. These systems have been around for over twenty-five years. ERP helps to link functions in the organization involved in creating products and services. Besides operations, the supporting functions are essential to building and delivering products and services. This is because accounting helps pay for resources used in operations; finance helps acquire capital to purchase materials, labor, machines and facilities used in the production of goods and services; and marketing needs to know the availability of goods and services for sale to customers. Often, the ERP systems consist of four major sub-systems: finance/accounting, sales/marketing, production/materials management and human resources.

The finance/accounting sub-system addresses the question: *What's our money doing?* Finance/accounting includes such modules as:

- Accounts receivables to pay bills, including invoicing and billing

- Accounts payable to collect money and to deal with vendors

- Activity-based cost accounting to understand fixed and variable costs associated with goods and services

- General ledger to integrate the financial functions

- Payroll to pay employees and allocate benefits

- Asset management to acquire and depreciate assets

- Capital management, including acquisition and allocation of money to build plants and facilities

- Expense handling to manage the cost of doing business

- Investment management to assure money is working
- Cost management, including assistance in estimating, job costing and proposal composition

The sales/marketing sub-system addresses the question: *What are our existing and potential customers doing?* Sales/marketing includes such modules as:

- Products and services available for sale
- Product and service availability and projected delivery
- Order processing from customers
- Sales analysis and planning
- Sales commission management
- Delivery options for purchases
- Pricing models evaluating sensitivity of different prices
- Promotion management, including costs, potential and effectiveness
- Discount and rebate management
- Customer profiles, including VIPs and slow pays
- Warranty management, including returns and complaint handling

The production/materials management sub-system addresses the question: *What are our "factories" or operations facilities doing?* Production/materials management includes such modules as:

- Product drawings, including computer assisted design (CAD) modules and component diagrams
- Engineering analysis
- Bill of material management, including materials comparison analysis
- Supplier management, including costs and ability to respond to orders as well as purchasing
- Production scheduling capability
- Quality assurance management
- Inventory management, including adjustments and replenishment
- Equipment/machinery management, including maintenance and replacement schedules

The human resources sub-system addresses the question of: *What are employees doing?* Human resources includes modules such as:

- Workforce planning
- Salary histories and comparisons
- Benefits planning tools

- Training capabilities and plans

- Job opening management and promotions

- Job applicant pool management

- Job descriptions

- Organizational structure management

All of these modules linked together in an ERP allow the systems a comprehensive ability to manage the data and information resources of an organization. At one time, many of these functions were independent modules with non-standard formats so little linking was possible. ERP aids in addressing this problem.

We can diagram and manage the data flows between the different functions and processes, as Chapter 7 described. The capability of building an accurate and comprehensive data warehouse and providing front-end analysis tools facilitates the use of data analytics. This fits with our theme of better management through measurement in many dimensions and the use of business intelligence.

A major advantage of ERP systems is the communication that can take place all along the supply chain. Passing on information about customer orders can help alleviate the bullwhip effect, where quick reaction to customer demand without adequate analysis causes over-ordering of raw materials and ramped up production not based on full information. ERP allows the sharing and coordination of production and distribution through the use of a centralized source of data. It also provides an accurate reading of measurements or pulse on the entire set of processes from customer demand back to supplier replenishment.

Figure 8.1 exhibits all of the components and linkages in an enterprise resource planning system.

What Can an ERP System Accomplish?

Note that Figure 8.1 shows an integration of all computing and information needed to manage the supply chain and operations as well as the financial and customer data. The central database/warehouse allows the usage of data by all functions and levels of management. It facilitates the process view rather than the silo view of an organization as described in Chapter 7.

A major advantage of Enterprise Resource Planning (ERP) systems is to offer an off-the-shelf solution to managing information flows in an organization. One of their key advantages is the ability to solve the dilemma of data fragmentation and multiple data storage locations. An organization could have hundreds of small systems, each addressing a problem. This results in different storage schemes and many different data definitions for the same data. This then creates inconsistent and redundant data and an inability to communicate and share. ERP was designed to alleviate this problem.

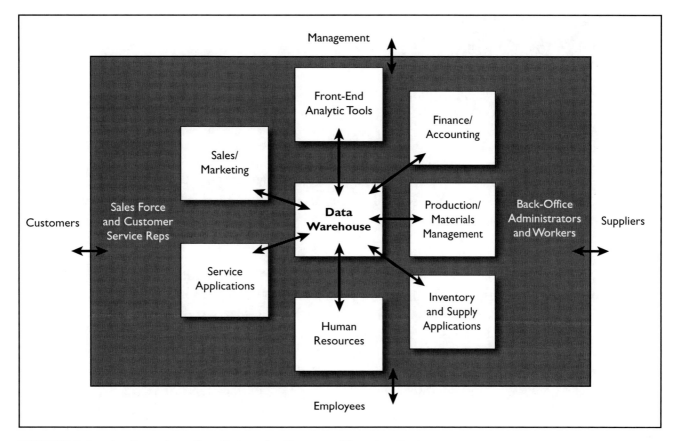

FIGURE 8.1—*An Overview of an Enterprise Resource Planning System*
   (Adapted from Thomas H. Davenport—See References)

ERP can assist in connecting customer demand with supplying products or services. This capability links sales with production and allows real supply chain automation since the ERP system takes an enterprise-wide view. For example, consider what happens to a customer order. The order ripples through the organization and adjusts the data warehouse to reflect changes in inventory, parts supplies, accounting entries such as accounts payables and receivables, production schedules, shipping schedules and even the balance sheet and income statement. The ERP allows a real systems view of the organization since the basis of its design is a "set of interrelated parts that exist for a purpose," our definition of a system from Chapter 1.

Another advantage of an ERP is that it can expand the boundary of an "enterprise." The system boundary can include customers and suppliers. Suppliers even can monitor raw material inventories and replenish them on the basis of some agreed-upon order quantities. For example, Wal-Mart has five thousand suppliers that access its data warehouse to check sales and replenish inventory. In order to automate from one end to the other, some versions of the systems can even use the Internet to link to the suppliers supply chain and to customers. As we learned in our information cycle diagram found in Chapter 3, all of this information sharing is based on the important principle of trust, in this case between a business and its suppliers.

ERP Characteristics

Although ERP systems are internally complex since they offer so many capabilities, they attempt to achieve simplicity in handling transactions and providing information to all organizational members. One obvious improvement from many old and non-integrated sets of systems is a single transaction source. This means a business enters an order once and only once and carefully error checks it. Once entered, the transaction moves through the linked processes automatically. One order can impact order filling, inventory adjustment, billing, communication to the customer, notification of a supplier, etc., and this all takes place automatically.

With all of these clear links, the audit trail for transactions becomes vivid and easy to recreate and examine. Conversions involving currency, language, rates and taxes, etc. all take place automatically. The ERP vendor assists in all necessary updates, such as changes in currency exchange rates and taxes down to the local level. This kind of mass change helps offset the cost of the ERP system.

The ERP system also has some built-in reporting capabilities. Organizations can access data through the reporting functions linked to the data warehousing function. Managers and stakeholders shown in Figure 8.1 can receive reports and make inquiries to keep track of the business's pulse.

The ERP system also provides other normal processing capabilities. The system has the ability to create backup facilities to reduce the chance of data loss. It also includes the ability to recover from any possible disasters such as floods or fires. It can also facilitate security through established processes and routines.

Is ERP Critical in a Business Organization?

SAP, the largest vendor of ERP systems and based in Waldorf, Germany, estimates that 80 percent of all business transactions in the world touch an ERP system. There are ERP systems of different sizes and capabilities to allow both larger and smaller organizations to utilize them. There are several major ERP vendors, including SAP (60 percent of ERP market), Oracle (30 percent) and PeopleSoft. This market has had several mergers and acquisitions.

As an organization takes a more global view and does business across company borders, the ERP system can assist in making this transition. Just think of the complexity of running a payroll in many countries with varying tax rates, retirement plans, benefits such as health care, etc. The ERP vendor will help replace hundreds of old traditional legacy systems that may have been in effect for many years. The ERP systems also can incorporate advanced technologies such as Radio Frequency Identification programs (RFID) that can assist in keeping track of things such as finished goods inventory.

We can expect that an ERP system will provide substantial benefits. These include reductions in inventory with fewer ordering and carrying costs, fewer staff resulting in reduced labor costs, better handling of orders so they are not lost and customers lost at the same time, reduced costs from closer examination of financial reporting and better cash flow management reducing capital costs. All can save an organization money. Assistance and cost reduction in transportation and logistics as a result of better management and control of shipments also can reduce costs. Better information about customers, suppliers and areas where cost reductions can take place may result from easier access to data and the ability to transform the data into information and business intelligence.

Cautions for an Organization Considering ERP

Undertaking an ERP implementation also can have some downsides. It can take a large amount of money, time and expertise to take full advantage of an ERP system. Eventual savings must offset the huge investment of from $50M to $500M or more. Essentially, the cost of the system tactics must be offset by the business objectives and the impact on the bottom line by increasing revenues or reducing costs. Many ERP attempts have failed, so careful management is essential for success.

Besides the actual cost of the ERP software, organizations may encounter other costs. Researchers have estimated that the cost of implementing an ERP system can be two to three times the cost of the software. Often, organizations hire consultants who are familiar with the different software packages to assist with the installation and training of internal persons. The organization might need new hardware to run the ERP software. If the company does not have an integrated approach to data management and data warehousing, there is the additional cost of creating an integrated database that links finance and accounting, marketing and sales, operations and production/materials management, and human resources. These efforts can require major expenditures within an organization as they involve getting the "house in order" prior to running the software. And the organization must maintain and run all of the other business activities while this effort is taking place.

ERP can level the playing field, but it can become a negative for those who already have achieved prominence. It could force your organization to "fit a mold" rather than to use your uniqueness that differentiates you in your customers' eyes. Another factor beyond the financial issue is the need to change organizational processes to conform to the ERP system. An organization might have to change the way it interacts with customers or suppliers that it currently may see as an existing company advantage. In some cases, not having an ERP system could give your business a competitive advantage since the costs and change needed with an ERP could destroy the benefits of what you currently do.

As mentioned earlier, some disasters have occurred in the ERP implementation arena. For example, Shane Companies, the Colorado-based and family-owned jewelry retailer that sought bankruptcy protection in 2009, told the bankruptcy judge that the company's decline was partly based upon delays and cost overruns for an ERP system. The system implementation took three years, and costs went from an estimated $10M to $36M. Shane Companies said they were "substantially overstocked with inventory, and with the wrong mix of inventory." They claimed that the software "adversely affected sales." (From the *Rocky Mountain News,* 1/14/2009, page B5.)

ERP Implementation Suggestions

Many of the challenges of installing and implementing ERP systems go beyond technical challenges. Although there are complexities in implementing the systems on the available hardware and software systems, many of the problems are of a business nature. The organization must be ready to make ERP part of its way of conducting business. The system must be part of the organizational culture. This starts with commitment and support by top management.

Implementation involves many decisions about the capabilities that the organization will add. It must choose modules to implement and create data and configuration tables. For example, the ERP may offer many choices of accounting methods or inventory approaches, and their implementation must carefully consider implications for the business. Often, this work takes place in phases where the organization implements and tests the most critical modules before moving on to the next implementation phase. There usually is a need to customize the ERP to fit the organization. There are many decisions about what to implement, including the countries or states that the organization operates in and the currencies that it will accept for payment. Some of these decisions may require the organization to just take an approach where it accepts the defaults set by the vendor on initial installations.

Along with the modules and configuration tables, ERP might also require organizational changes. Establishing ERP is not just a technical problem. Jobs and organizational structures and culture may change. Processes and structures must fit with the way the ERP operates. The designs of many ERPs incorporate best practices from industry leaders and include templates from the ERP vendor, but these may require significant changes in processes and organizational structure.

Organizations should be careful not to lose their exclusive differentiation and make the organization too generic. Implementers must keep the customers in mind and not lose any uniqueness that a customer may desire. Some ERP systems include a special class of software for dealing with customers called Customer Relationship Management (CRM). Often, these systems allow custom features for dealing with customers, such as one-on-one marketing campaigns, specialized customer service and custom ordering. An organization can utilize data mining or prospecting for customers based on the data in the data warehouse. The key word in many of the CRM applications is building a "relationship" with your customers with better intelligence.

An examination of assuring value from the ERP system must take place. It would be helpful to use the business/system objectives/tactics (BSOT) model to assure cost/benefit advantages that we mentioned earlier. It should be clear how better information (system objectives) will assist in performing business tactics, thus leading to increased revenues/reduced costs (business objectives).

Relating Business Functions to ERP Systems

To assist you in understanding the importance of ERP systems and their relationship with your own business major, we will view the major functional areas from the operations and information management perspective, in terms of information flows to and from the function.

Since Operations Management and Information Management is the focus of much ERP activity, we will examine how the other business functions relate. As Figure 8.2 shows, there are links:

- Between **Operations** and **Accounting**: Billing information, Accounts Payable, Accounts Receivables and Process Improvements go to Accounting, and Cost Accounting Details go to Operations.

- Between **Operations** and **Finance**: Capital Requirements and Planned Capital Investments go from Operations to Finance. Financial Measures, Budgets and Stockholder reporting needs must flow to Operations.

- Between **Operations** and **Engineering**: Production Capabilities and Design Needs Specifications go to Engineering, and Product Specifications go to Operations.

- Between **Operations** and **Human Resources**: Labor Requirements go to Human Resources, and Labor Skills Inventory and Labor Costs go to Operations.

- Between **Operations** and **Marketing**: Production Capacities, Finished Inventory Levels and Output Rates go to Marketing, and Customer Demands, Customer Feedback/Concerns and Need for New Products go to Operations.

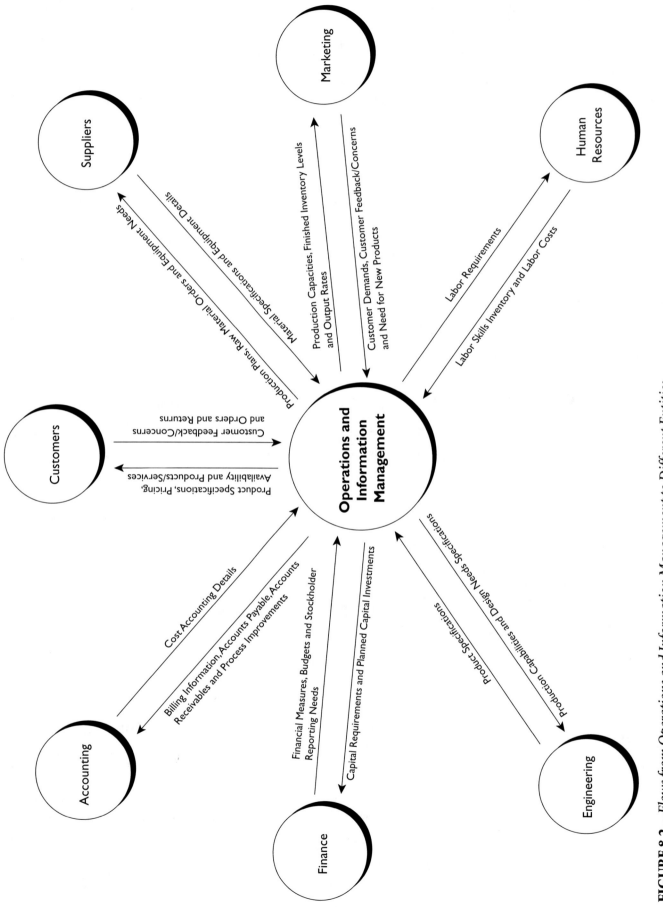

FIGURE 8.2—*Flows from Operations and Information Management to Different Entities*

☛ Between **Operations** and **Suppliers**: Production Plans, Raw Material Orders and Equipment Needs go to Suppliers and Invoices. Material Specifications, and Equipment Details go to Operations

☛ Between **Operations** and **Customers**: Product Specifications, Pricing, Availability and Products/Services go to Customers and Customer Demands. Customer Feedback/Concerns and Orders and Returns go to Operations.

All of these flows may currently exist in the business organization, but they will flow in a consistent and standard manner using enterprise resource planning systems.

Chapter Summary

Enterprise Resource Planning (ERP) systems allow a total systems view of the implementation of an organization. This view reduces fragmentation of the organization and enhances communication between the major organizational functions. No matter where you intend to work in an organization, an ERP could impact you. It can enhance your career opportunities to understand and appreciate the capabilities of an enterprise view of an organization.

Food for Thought/Enterprise Resource Planning

☛ What is an Enterprise Resource Planning system (ERP), and what problems do ERPs attempt to solve?

☛ Why do many ERPs fail to live up to companies' expectations? Are technical problems the sole source of blame? Explain.

☛ How do the failures of ERPs relate to the system/business objectives and system/business tactics model discussed at the beginning of the semester?

☛ What problems might an ERP introduce if you work at an organization that has a very distinct organizational structure and processes?

References

Brady, Joseph A., Ellen F. Monk, and Bret J. Wagner. 2001. *Concepts in enterprise planning.* Boston, MA: Course Technology.

Davenport, T. 1998. Putting the enterprise into the enterprise system. *Harvard Business Review,* July/August 1998

Retailer puts blame partly on software. 2009. *Rocky Mountain News,* January 14, 2009, p. B5.

Exercise

Developing Your Analytical Skills: Using Information Systems to Add Organizational Value

Different organizations can have different enterprise resource planning needs. Examine Figure 8.1 and fill in the detail for a university, especially in the area of student services. What are the accounting (billing and costing), finance (capital expenditures such as buildings), human resources (faculty and staff) and marketing (students and contributors) functions that require support? Are any of these functions linked? In what way?

Exercise

What is the student information that a data warehouse would include to fit in an ERP system? Is any of this data of interest to the various business functions?

Exercise

Visit the Website of an ERP vendor. What did you find out about the company? Report back and share with the rest of the class.

Exercise

How can an ERP help you do your job in your major in business? For example, if you plan on being an accountant, how would an ERP system affect you and your ability to do your job?

Exercise

Trace what happens to a book order that you place with Amazon.com. Look at the four basic sub-systems within an ERP and state how it could involve the modules listed in this chapter. Write a story about the order and all the modules triggered.

chapter 9

Projects and Project Management

Many of us conduct our lives around projects. We have projects at work, at home and at school. This chapter will explore what a project is and what information is necessary to manage a project. Whenever you have a student team project, you should keep the principles covered in this chapter in mind.

Managing Business Projects

Many activities that business organizations must perform take place in projects. Although much of the work in organizations follows the supply and value chain with processes performed in a repetitive and continuous fashion, special requests come up that require a unique and often one-time need for some work. These are projects. Projects are sets of activities combined to accomplish a specified objective, a final result. People can do projects in teams or individually. Projects come in various sizes and cover different topics.

We manage projects in school, including term papers and team activities/projects. We manage projects at home, such as painting the bedroom or repairing the sidewalk. Larger projects could include building a new warehouse or even an office building. We manage projects at work, such as putting together and delivering an advertising campaign or writing a computer program. Much of the work in information systems, such as creating a Website or a computer software program, takes place in projects. The same is true for consulting organizations where companies request a team of persons with special skills to solve a problem or to take advantage of an opportunity.

Projects have some distinct characteristics. They have a specific start and end time and are not regularly scheduled business tactics, such as processing customer orders or the company payroll. Projects are put together to get some task or tasks accomplished that the organization usually does not repeat. Thus, a project is temporary and assembles resources until achievement of its objective. Then the organization disbands the resources. Projects have clear objectives that allow us to determine when we are done. For example, we will know when we have put two coats of paint on the bedroom walls and ceiling. Estimates of when we will complete the project become clearer as we progress. This especially is true of large construction projects, such as building a bridge, since many factors can delay the work, including bad weather, labor disputes or problems.

Projects must be managed just like any other business activity. This includes planning, organizing, staffing, directing and controlling, the typical functions of management. Project planning includes determining what needs accomplishing (objectives) and what needs doing to reach those objectives (tactics). And, a plan must include a budget and an estimate of resources needed since an organization does not have unlimited resources. Organizing includes determining the specific activities that need accomplishing and in what order. It includes scheduling the human resources and needed equipment. Staffing includes determining who can perform the activities and assigning them to the project when it needs them. Directing means supervising the performance of the activities and assuring they have the resources when needed.

Controlling includes measuring actual results, comparing them with the planned results and taking action to assure the project is on plan. Controlling also includes comparing actual expenditures with budgeted allocations.

Once an organization has assigned a project to a manager, the project manager must attempt to answer some questions, including:

- What is the scope of the project, including what will it do and what will it not do? This is necessary to ensure that the project scope does not "creep" to become larger without additional resources, a source of budget overruns.
- What activities must the organization complete to reach the project objective?
- How long will each of these activities take?
- Do the activities have to be done in a certain order?
- Are there intermediate reviewable and definable results that help us determine if we are heading toward our target objectives?
- Are there people skills needed to perform the necessary activities?
- Are there any equipment or tools needed for the project?
- Are there deadlines for any of the activities?
- Are there any activities that, if delayed, will delay the entire project?

No matter whether the project is as small as painting a room or as large as constructing a large office building, we must answer the above questions.

Why Is Project Management Part of Operations and Information Management?

Although every person in an organization might have to play the role of project manager, project management in business organizations often falls within the domain of operations and information management. Projects consist of a set of interrelated parts that interact with each other to achieve a result. As you might notice, this definition is very close to our definition of a system. Project management is systems management. Successful project management is a human activity that allows for the orderly completion of required activities or tasks in a minimum amount of time with a minimum of resources. Project managers are concerned with effectiveness, efficiency and productivity. This is why project management often is within the domain of operations and information management.

Another reason that project management is closely related to operations and information management is that complex projects often require using specialized software running on information technology. Skills to use this type of software often exist in the operations and information management group. Good project management also requires the use of data from past projects that fit in the domain of database and information management.

Thus, since project management is a systems oriented and information based type of management, we consider it part of operations and information management and will discuss it in this chapter.

Project Planning

Project plans become established to inform people what they must do, by whom and with what resources. Plans cannot be cast in stone but must be flexible. A project manager is responsible for establishing a project plan with the assistance of others who might have additional information from being close to the situation where the project is taking place. The project manager must implement the plan by acquiring needed human and other resources. Then the manager must control against the plan to assure that reality aligns with the plan and, if not, by adjusting the plan. As mentioned above, the plan should become more accurate as the project progresses and receives better information.

A plan is necessary to perform management control activities. The organization compares expectations from the plan with actual results. Then it makes adjustments. Many people wonder if someone who says a plan is not necessary would argue that "don't plan it, just do it" is the correct management approach. We all know what happens if we do not plan what we write in our term papers. We don't know when we are done (many believe we are done when the time is up and they must hand the paper in). If you don't know what you are going to do, it is difficult to do it and even more difficult to know when you are done. Home builders certainly would not start construction without a plan!

So what are some discoveries that good project managers have made about plans and planning?

- Those affected by the plan must approve the plans, including performers of activities in the plan as well as those who must accept the final results.

- Plans must be revised and updated as new discoveries occur.

- Changes in plans take time and consume resources and should lead to revisions in needed time and resources.

- Plans should become more accurate and clearer in specifications for activities that need doing sooner.

- Resource assignments will change as the plan progresses due to unpredictable events such as illness or other changes in the environment.

- Some activities that seem finished will need redoing. (Just talk to any house or construction contractor about redos.)

- We must consider global and cultural differences since different countries have different holidays, work habits and accepted standards, such as overtime and a defined work week.

Plans are living objects that must be adapted and adaptable in the world in which they exist. They are not carved in stone, and all people dealing with the plan must be flexible.

You should monitor and approve intermediate results from activities in the plan. If you are writing a term paper, you will have an outline that you should review and approve. Then you will have a rough first draft that needs review and approval. We often refer to these intermediate results as *milestones,* and they result in a deliverable that should be subject to review. A deliverable is either ready or not. The intermediate result is not 90 percent done. Full completion is necessary. For example, there must be approval for a set of blueprints prior to the construction of the actual house. Then other intermediate results such as a cement foundation must receive approval prior to framing the house, and plumbing and wiring must have approval prior to covering the walls with drywall. Inspections and reviews must be part of the project management process. If the milestone or deliverable review results in revisions, there also must be revisions to the plan and resource allocations. Otherwise, the project is moving toward being out of control. A house contractor certainly would not allow changes in size of rooms or upgrades to the house without changing the project plan and a budget adjustment.

Each milestone must have a responsible person assigned. This person must use judgment to determine when the milestone is ready for review. As mentioned above, the responsible person should have been working with the project manager to jointly set the milestone deadline. If the milestone is not ready based on the project plan, the project manager must investigate, determine the reason for the delay and make necessary revisions. You likely have encountered delays in your school team projects when one of your team members has not accomplished his or her part.

One significant challenge to any project plan is staffing. Part of the challenge is that the staffing plan is not static, but it is constantly changing as people get removed from the project for other perceived "emergencies." This state of flux makes management difficult and something the project manager must constantly monitor.

As the project progresses, there must be updates and revisions to the project plan. New information on how long activities take and whether there must be an addition of new activities or tasks will alter the plan. Gaining this knowledge will make the plan more accurate as the project progresses and allow for more accurate estimates. Estimating is a skill that all project managers need.

Estimating

Estimating is establishing the amount of time needed to complete a task. Adding up all the time needed for all the tasks will give an estimate for total time for the project. Estimates are easier to make if using some history from past projects for similar tasks or a standard rate and time book. Often you will see these types of time estimates if you have auto repairs done. Some persons can finish the task more quickly than others. But, a rough estimate is better than no estimate at all.

Good estimates eliminate surprises for the customer or recipient of the work. For example, if a painter estimates that painting the trim on your house will take fifty hours at $35 an hour, you could budget somewhere around $1,750 for the project. If the estimate is too low and the project takes seventy-five hours, the customer will be surprised and likely unhappy. And, if another project such as some stone work depends on completion of the trim painting project, then the stone mason will not be able to start work and will be unhappy. Thus good estimates are desirable.

We often specify project time estimates for a task in "person-hours." As mentioned above, these task estimates are aggregated and, for a larger project, specified in "person-months." However, we should be cautious when using a measure such as person-months. Frederick Brooks, the author of a book entitled *The Mythical Man-Month,* declared the person-month a myth. The reason for this is that people and months are not interchangeable. A month of work by one person is not equivalent to a month of work by another person. You likely experienced this on your school team projects. Some of your teammates and you likely had great variability in the amount of time required to accomplish a task. Skill and experience as well as the amount of motivation will make a large difference.

We also must realize that some tasks will take a certain amount of time no matter how many persons are assigned. In fact, if there are too many persons working on a task in a confined space, they can get in each other's way. Brooks also reminded us that having a child will take around nine months, no matter how many women get assigned to the task.

Brooks also warned us about the project management tendencies that may get us in trouble. As a project falls behind schedule, the natural tendency is to add more people. This could slow the project down due to the geometric increase in the number of communication channels and interactions between people assigned. New persons assigned to a project may slow down the entire project since the team members may have to train the new person to "bring them up to speed," introduce them to the work and the other team members and maintain the communication channels necessary for the project. This will reduce the productive work done by the original team members.

Some factors that project managers must consider when estimating include:

- Size of the activity (number of rooms added to an existing house?)
- Complexity of the activity (run-of-the-mill versus custom work?)
- Management commitment and interest in the project
- Environment, including the number of locations that may require travel
- Experience of team members in doing similar work
- Skill level of task workers
- Interest and motivation of task workers in building team spirit
- Whether the team has worked together previously

The estimator cannot just use a rate book, but must take both individual and team camaraderie into consideration. You likely have experienced many of the same factors when working on your school team projects.

Project managers should heed the following:

- Base estimates on careful thought. WIGUs (Wild Guesses) will not result in accurate specifications.

- Be careful if the boss asks "how long will this two day project take you?" He or she already has made a determination.

- If after some careful analysis, you determine that a project will take you twenty hours and your boss guesses that it will take fourteen, you should not split the difference and say it will take seventeen. Estimating is not negotiating.

- Keep in mind that a delay in one part of a project that is critical to starting some other tasks will delay the entire project.

- A point estimate may not be as accurate as a range estimate. Saying something will take five hours will create an expectation that it will be done in five hours. However, it may be more accurate to say that if all went perfectly, it could take four and a half hours, and if you ran into some problems, it could take five and a half hours. We need to realize that some estimators are pessimists and some are optimists. We hope to be realists.

- Do not ignore obvious time consumers such as meetings, travel time, vacations and even the time to re-estimate and plan the project.

- Creative activities are difficult to estimate. For example, estimating how long it will take to write a novel or paint a painting requires an unknown factor of inspiration. It is much easier to estimate the time required to write a factual newspaper article since it involves less creativity and the task likely has been performed many times before.

Putting the Project Plan Together

As the project manager accumulates a list of all tasks needed to accomplish a project, he or she can put a project plan together. The tasks can include a time estimate for each task, the people assigned to each task and the precedence or order that they must accomplish the tasks. When considering task precedence, you need to remember that some tasks do not depend on previous task outputs and can start at any time. You can do some tasks in parallel or concurrently if people are available for assignment to them.

Project management can become very complex if it involves many tasks. Project management software can help a manager. After inputting all the above information into a table, the software can create a network diagram, such as the one shown in Figure 9.1. A popular type of network diagram is a CPM (Critical Path Method) diagram. The critical path method shows start and end times and the path of tasks, which, if delayed,

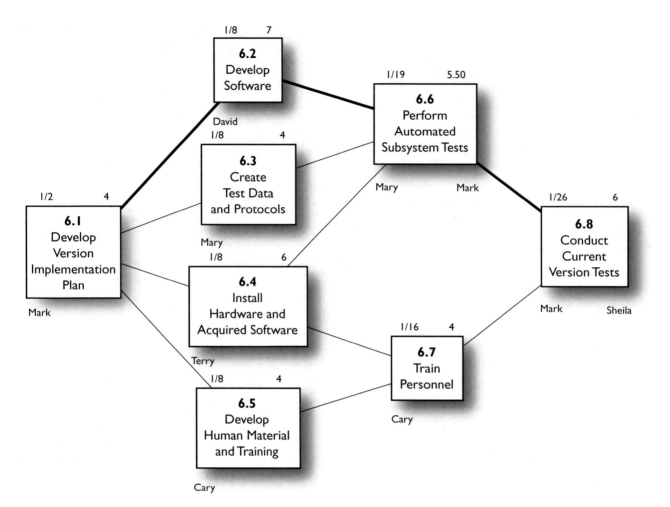

FIGURE 9.1—*Example Critical Path Method Diagram*

will hinder the entire project. This is the critical path. The critical path is shown on Figure 9.1 by the bold lines connecting processes 6.1, 6.2, 6.6, and 6.8. The other activities or tasks have "slack time" in that they would not delay the entire project if not completed on time.

You should read the diagram in Figure 9.1 from left to right. Each of the boxes is a task or an activity. The number in the upper left-hand corner is the earliest start time; the number in the upper right-hand corner is the number of days estimated to complete the task; and the names at the bottom are the people assigned to the task. The dark connector lines show the critical path. Note that task 6.1 must be complete prior to starting task 6.2. However, tasks 6.3, 6.4 and 6.5 can take place concurrently with task 6.2. The amount of slack time is the difference between the time to complete task 6.2 (7 days) and the time to complete task 6.3 (7 – 4 or 3 days slack), task 6.4 (7 – 6 or 1 day slack), and task 6.5 (7 – 4 or 3 days slack). The manager should keep her eyes on task 6.4 since delays could put this task on the critical path. Note that task 6.6 cannot be started until completion of tasks 6.2–6.4. This is called *logical precedence.*

Another diagram used by project managers is a Gantt chart or a task timeline as shown in Figure 9.2. Note that many of the same things appear in the CPM chart in Figure 9.1.

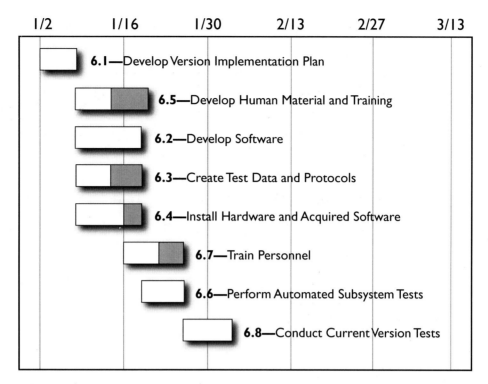

FIGURE 9.2—*A Gantt Chart*

One difference is that the slack time appears in the shaded part of the bar on the diagram. If the bar is not shaded, it is on the critical path.

The power of a computer software package such as Microsoft Project is that as we gather more information about the project, we can change the charts and tables easily. One change into the input table will show up in all the other tables and charts. This ability allows a project manager to monitor and control the projects and determine if any resource allocation changes are necessary. The manager also can test alternatives, such as increasing the hours a worker can work per day or allowing for vacations and their impact on the overall schedule. The manager can ask "what if . . ." questions to try to determine if changes could be made. As the project manager gains additional knowledge, it is easy to make changes and review the implications. Likewise, the software can assist in gathering data to use in estimating and planning future projects.

Being a Good Project Manager

Project management is more than just keeping track of things. A good project manager also helps build a team and motivates the team members to work together. All of the team members must share the project objectives and understand their purpose, as well as what is important to the persons who will receive the project's outputs. The project manager constantly thinks about what can go wrong and what will help reach the project objectives. He or she looks for deviations from the plan and ways to adjust both the plan and the workers in order to bring the project back on schedule. Interpersonal skills that can motivate project workers without angering them are important. The manager must exude confidence and act like a manager, not just like another worker.

The project manager must work with people and develop people skills. Conflicts may occur between team members, and the project manager should attempt to mediate these conflicts with open communication and trust. The manager must help build loyalty to the project and to the project team. You can develop all of these skills if you think like a manager when you work on your own individual and team projects in school.

The project manager plays an important role in completing the project. There are some projects with specific, hard deadlines. For example, a stadium needed for a professional football team that plays its first game in August must be complete well in advance of that date. October is not satisfactory. Completion delays can be very costly. For example, a non-functioning automated baggage-handling system that intended to use computers and conveyor belts delayed the opening of the Denver International Airport. They finally scrapped the cutting edge systems and replaced them with a standard cart system that we often see at airports today.

Chapter Summary

Keane, Keane and Teagan (see References) provide some good guidelines for project management. The principles include:

- Know what you have to do and what you need to do it. Define the job or project in as much detail as you can. Know the project scope, the objectives and the activities that require doing. Specify the deliverables and milestones and measure against them.

- Be sure to get the right people involved. Know who can do what and match them with what needs doing. Get all people involved committed to the project and keep them informed. Jointly develop goals and objectives and keep communication lines open.

- Carefully develop estimates based on information, not guesswork. Estimate each component of the project separately. Avoid planning back from a deadline and squeezing a project into the time allowed if this is not realistic.

- Use an eighty-hour rule where you attempt to manage small "chunks." Break the project down as much as possible and work hard to fit the chunks together.

- Establish a change procedure to assure that changes get managed and do not sneak in. Changes mean adjustments in time, required resources and in money needed for the project.

- Establish acceptance criteria so you know when you are done. This may mean clear review activities by the appropriate people. Again, communication is needed so the results are clear to all involved parties. Don't try to hide out without sharing results with others. Surprises are not welcome.

Project management is both a science and an art. Good structure can assist in accomplishing complex projects. Good people skills can assist in motivating people to be active participants, making work fun.

Food for Thought/Project Management

- Why is processing customer orders not considered a project?

- Why is estimating so difficult? Have you had difficulty estimating how long a school project might take, such as writing a term paper? Why?

- Is there more to project management than plugging activities and times into a software package?

References

Brooks. F. P. Jr. 1975. *The mythical man-month: Essays on software engineering.* Reading, MA: Addison-Wesley.

Keane, John F., Marilyn Keane, and Mark Teagan. 1984. *Productivity management in the development of computer applications.* Englewood Cliffs, NJ: Prentice-Hall, Inc.

Exercise

Developing Your Analytical Skills:
Becoming a Project Manager

Use Google or another search engine to find some information on project management and project manager skills.

Make a list of skills you feel would be necessary for a project manager.

How many of these skills are behavioral and how many are technical skills?

Explain why a project manager may not have all of the skills that people assigned to the project might have.

Exercise

Developing Your Analytical Skills: Discovering More about Project Management

Check out the Website at *www.pmi.com* and pay special attention to the project management section.

Examine the project management certifications and see if there are common themes that are part of product management certification. What are some of these themes?

What kinds of courses are available for you to learn more about project management? How much do these courses cost?

Why would people pay for project management certification? You may find some of the answers to this question in the marketing of the courses.

Exercise

Developing Your Analytical Skills: Discovering More about Project Management Software

There are a number of computer software packages that assist project managers. They are available from Intuit, IBM, Microsoft and others. For examples, see the table at:

http://en.wikipedia.org/wiki/Comparison_of_project_management_software

Take a closer look at one of the packages.

What is the name of the package?

Who is the vendor of the package?

Does the package support the principles mentioned in this chapter?

What kind of diagramming and networks can the software produce?

Why would someone pay to acquire such software?

Exercise

Developing Your Analytical Skills: Using Project Management in Your Final Class Project

You will be completing final class projects in some of your courses. Apply some of the concepts from this chapter to your projects.

What activities will you need to perform to complete the projects? List as many of these activities as you can.

You will need to assign different activities to different people. How will you choose who will do which activities?

Are there some activities that will need doing before other activities can proceed? What are they?

Draw a rough sketch or diagram of the project plan and share it with your teammates. Did they suggest any changes? What were they?

Optional

Create a project plan using project management software and share it with the class.

chapter 10

Electronic Commerce / Building Your Online Store

Building an Online Store
The Internet and the World Wide Web ("The Web")
Key Characteristics of the Internet
Intranets and Extranets
The What, Why, Where, How, Who and When of E-Commerce
E-Commerce versus E-Business
Prerequisites to Performing E-Commerce
Designing Your Store
Hosting Your E-Commerce Store
Creating and Maintaining an Online Store
Getting Known
Building Trust
Making a Sale
Getting Paid
Delivering Your Product or Service
Responding to Questions and Issues
Protecting Your Property and Consumers
Chapter Summary

The material on electronic commerce and the Unique Bicycles example was developed as part of the Eurasia Project at the University of Colorado/Boulder Leeds School of Business.

One specific system has dramatically influenced our society and business environment: the World Wide Web (WWW) or simply "the Web." The Web has revolutionized our everyday lives. It has provided us with instantaneous information about nearly anything that we can think of. Some key characteristics of the Internet and the WWW have made this possible, and we will elaborate on them in this chapter first. The growth of the Web has also facilitated drastic changes in how businesses and organizations function. The potential consumer base has expanded from a certain geographic location to the over 1.5 billion (and growing) users. The growth of the Web has also opened the doors for small businesses to open their doors (onto the World Wide Web) at a very low cost.

Building an Online Store

This chapter's first objective is to provide a basic understanding of the Internet and the differences between the WWW, the Internet, intranets and extranets. Once you have an understanding of the underlying characteristics of each of these terms, we will turn our attention to e-commerce.

You will also learn how to successfully start an e-commerce business. Anyone can start an online business, but creating a successful online business is a challenge. This chapter introduces how to make potential customers aware of your store, how to get them to trust you, how to make a sale and the various methods of getting paid. You must keep your online store up-to-date with careful maintenance. Once you have sold a product or service and received payment, you must deliver it. We will discuss delivery methods so you can make a wise choice about getting your products to your customers. Customer relations are important for repeat sales. We will introduce methods of responding to questions and issues. You also must protect yourself and your customer as you will be handling and storing sensitive data. This chapter gives you some hints about how you can keep a safe environment. It will help you understand the questions that you need to ask yourself and the steps required in creating your online store that you need to consider before opening the virtual doors of your e-commerce storefront.

The Internet and the World Wide Web ("The Web")

Alaska's former senator, Ted Stevens, claimed that the Internet is a series of tubes. However, the Internet is a massive network of computer networks linked together using copper wires and fiber-optic cables, not tubes. In other words, the Internet is a network of networks that provides the infrastructure for computers (and other devices) to communicate with each other. The World Wide Web is one of these networks on the Internet—the Internet is the network on which the WWW was built. Specifically, the Web utilizes Web browsers such as Mozilla Firefox and Internet Explorer to allow individuals to easily access Web pages that interconnect with each other through the use of hyperlinks.

Key Characteristics of the Internet

First of all, the Internet is based on open standards. Everyday standards such as measurement systems and electricity voltage standards give us a common "language." When we buy appliances that rely upon electricity in North America, we do not need to worry whether they are compatible with the electricity outlets in our homes. Similarly, standards relevant to the Internet, such as HTML (Hyper Text Markup Language) and TCP/IP (Transmission Control Protocol / Internet Protocol), give the Internet a common language. As a consequence, a wide variety of devices can easily connect to it and communicate with each other. When you create a Web page or an online store, you do not need to worry whether your potential consumers will be able to view it via their Web browser.

The Internet is also asynchronous. Communication via the Internet is broken down into parts called packets. For example, to send an email message or a video clip to your professor, the message first becomes disassembled into a series of packets, and then your computer sends these packets through the Internet to your professor's computer (or other device such as a smart phone). When all the packets arrive (each can take a different amount of time to arrive, called "inherent latency"), they become reassembled into your email message. Unlike making a phone call, you do not need any prior coordination or direct connection when communicating via the Internet. The packets travel without having a bi-directional connection, and your message will go even if your professor's computer is off.

Finally, we can attribute the Internet's explosive growth and spread across the world to the distributed and scalable nature of the Internet. No single organization or company manages the Internet or controls access to it. As a consequence, organizations can add (or remove) additional links when the need exists. The additional links also provide more paths through which to route packets, so that when a particular part of the Internet is interrupted, packets can travel via an alternate link. We can characterize the Internet as an organic mechanism that can adapt and react as needed.

Intranets and Extranets

By default, communication via the Internet is open and accessible to all. If you post content on the Web, anyone in the world is able to access it. For many uses open access might be desirable, but for others access needs restriction. Intranets and extranets both restrict access to a specific group of individuals, but they have different purposes.

Intranets restrict access to the boundaries of a specific organization. At your university, you might have several intranets that only members of your university community can access such as course registration, university announcements, benefits enrollment and so forth. Your classes may have a Website restricted to your class members. Intranets can also facilitate the quick distribution of internal resources, such as meeting minutes, announcements, bylaws and calendars that should not be visible to the broader community of users. On the other hand, extranets provide a link between an organization and its partners, clients and consumers. For example, a company like

Amazon might need to receive confidential information from various suppliers in its supply chain concerning inventory levels and delivery estimates. An extranet provides this gateway and allows for more effective, real-time communication.

Now that you have a basic understanding of terminology and the underlying characteristics of the Internet, we will turn our attention to the main focus of this chapter: how to conduct business on the Web through an e-commerce Website.

The What, Why, Where, How, Who and When of E-Commerce

What Is It?

E-commerce is the buying and selling of goods and services through the use of the Internet.

Why Do It?

E-commerce is an alternative marketplace that allows a business to reduce costs and increase revenues without having a physical "brick and mortar" storefront. It is low cost, has relatively low risk, has few barriers to entry (it can also be a disadvantage since others can enter easily), can build customer loyalty, can be open around the clock, can allow for cross-selling (the selling of related products); and, most importantly, it increases the potential market size for a product or service. E-commerce allows us to quickly establish a store and to sell to a wide audience.

Where Is It Done?

E-commerce takes place on the Internet through the use of an online/non-physical store. A Website contains your online store and gives you a presence as an available outlet. Your Website also provides other essential information, such as customer service information, contact information and the company's policies.

How Is It Done?

You build a Website that allows visitors to browse, search, shop and buy products and services.

Who Is Involved?

Roles played in e-commerce include that of the merchant, the Web designer, the Website builder/Webmaster and the visitor/buyer. Sometimes the same individual can play multiple roles. For example, an individual could be the merchant, the Web designer, and the Website builder/Webmaster.

When Is It Done?

E-commerce takes place on a twenty-four-hour basis, seven days a week, when the merchant believes that the benefits offset the costs.

E-Commerce versus E-Business

E-commerce refers to the buying and selling of products and services online. On the other hand, e-business is a much broader term. E-business encompasses not only the activities relevant to buying and selling on the Internet, but also to providing services to customers and collaborating with business partners, suppliers and distributors. E-commerce is a form of e-business. This chapter will focus specifically on e-commerce.

Prerequisites to Performing E-Commerce

Many e-commerce stores fail. To increase your chances of succeeding, you should make sure to have the following before you attempt to build an e-commerce store:

- A *business model* for your business that includes how you will make more money than you spend. Your revenues must offset your expenses. You need to know that you are price competitive and attractive to potential buyers because comparison shopping is easy on the Internet.

- A *financial plan* for obtaining any necessary financing you need for your business

- An *operations plan* for obtaining your goods and services and paying for them (a supply chain)

- A *marketing plan* to reach your potential customers

- An *internationalization plan* for dealing with items such as currency, customs and other related issues. You must decide where you are going to sell your products, since your Website will be accessible worldwide.

Once you have a concrete business model and have devised the necessary plans, you should undertake a systematic process to design and develop the e-commerce Website. The following sections describe each of these steps.

Designing Your Store

The first step in creating your e-commerce Website is to think about its design. You must design your online store in a compelling manner to attract and retain customers. Why? Because the customer is in control. The customer can easily leave an online store with one click and feel very little guilt about leaving. You do not have a chance to hold the customer captive. The customer has a free will.

To retain customers and not drive them away to another online store, your store must be effectively designed—in other words, it must be usable. Usability means that your customers can efficiently, effectively and with satisfaction (and not with frustration!)

find the information about the products and services they are looking for and be able to perform the essential tasks on your Website easily, such as purchasing your products.

If usability is vital to an online store's success, how does one achieve it? You achieve usable design by making sure that your online store and Website accomplish the following:

Simplicity

Simplicity is a key to getting people to visit your online store and keeping them there. Complexity will confuse potential consumers and drive them to other locations. Simplicity allows customers to find the information they are looking for easily. This means that you should not include anything on your Web page that the customer does not need. Do not introduce unnecessary complexity or include images or content that have nothing to do with your products. Often, being "cool" or "fancy" will hinder the shopping experience. These factors keep the customer away from effectively performing the task that is vital to the success of your store—purchasing your products.

Navigability

A good Website has an accommodating architecture, much like a house or a building has a good organization. We must design the overall structure (or "architecture") of a Website from the perspective of the customer or visitor. Your Website must have easy-to-find navigation (usually on the top of each Web page) structured in a way that allows the customer or visitor get to the information with ease. The name of each hyperlink in the navigation must be clear, so that the person who clicks the link understands where it will go. After the individual clicks the link and moves to the appropriate Web page, it should be clear to him where he is within the overall structure of the Website, and how he can return to where he started if needed.

Consistency

Each page of your Website should have a consistent "look and feel." You should keep colors, fonts and the overall structure of each page as consistent as possible. The navigation should always be in the same location, so that the customer always knows where to look for it. The text should have a consistent size, color and font. Your company logo should be on each page in the same location (usually in the top left corner of each Web page).

Readability and Content Relevance

People are not going to read long strings of text on the Internet. As a result, you must attempt to make your writing scan-able and succinct. Also, you must make sure that you are including the information that your potential customers want and need. You should state policies for returns, shipping and billing clearly and address any questions from your customers. You also need to make sure that the content is up-to-date. For example, when an item goes out of stock within your online store, you must update its availability quickly to keep your customers from becoming frustrated.

To ensure that your store design exhibits simplicity, navigability, consistency and relevance, you must validate its usability before implementing your online store. Before you release your Website to your customers, you should test a prototype with representative users. A simple means of testing includes assigning a person representative of a user a task such as ordering; then watch the person go through the process. You should ask the person to "think out loud" and to keep a record of her thoughts. This will help you find trouble spots and places that need changes. Places where a person gets frustrated and confused are where the potential customer will abandon your site. This is especially critical for the purchasing process. People may put things in a shopping cart and then abandon the cart if they get confused.

Hosting Your E-Commerce Store

Once you have created and evaluated your design, the next step is to find a place to host the online store. You want to pick the hosting solution that makes your store reliable and fast and that can handle your customers' Web traffic. If your Website is not reliable or is too slow, most customers will not return. However, very reliable and fast hosting solutions are also extremely expensive, so you must make a trade-off to find a solution that is right for your particular store.

There are two broad hosting options that you should consider: standard Website hosting and merchant accounts. We consider the advantages and disadvantages of each below.

Standard Website Hosting

There are thousands of companies that offer hosting for your online store. These Website hosting companies provide a place for your online store for a monthly fee that can vary greatly (from a few dollars to thousands of dollars). When choosing a hosting plan at any of these companies, some of the important factors that you need to consider include:

- **Advertising:** Some hosting companies place unwanted advertisements automatically on your Website, which can be frustrating and distracting for your customers. This could reduce your sales.

- **Amount of disk space:** You want to make sure to have enough space to include your product pictures and other essential documents and files. Most businesses will find 200–500 MBs (megabytes) sufficient.

- **Reliability:** You want to make sure that your online store is fast and reliable during both peak and off peak hours. You should avoid a hosting company that cannot promise that your Website will be available at least 99 percent of the time.

☞ **Bandwidth:** You want to make sure that your hosting plan can handle the Web traffic that you expect. Usually, about 3 GBs (gigabytes) per month of bandwidth is enough for most stores. As you gain more customers, you can purchase an additional bandwidth allocation from the hosting company.

☞ **Technical support:** When you have a question or a problem, make sure that someone knowledgeable is there to help you. You should not pick a host that does not guarantee response within twenty-four hours to your inquiries.

☞ **Security:** If you are going to be storing and processing credit cards without the help of a third-party company, you should make sure that the Web hosting company offers SSL (Secure Sockets Layer). We will discuss SSL later in the chapter.

Most of the standard Website hosting companies simply provide you a place to put your store; they do not help you build your online store. Therefore, you will need to learn to use additional software, such as Macromedia, Dreamweaver or Microsoft Expression Web to create your store. Further discussion is beyond the scope of this book.

Storefronts/Merchant Accounts

Storefront (or "merchant") accounts combine Web hosting with online tools that allow you not only to create your online store, but that often provide credit card processing, inventory management and other important services. Therefore, merchant accounts are popular with individuals who are starting their first online store and do not have a lot of technical experience. Merchant account providers such as Yahoo! (*www.yahoo.com*), Google (*www.google.com*) and PayPal (*www.paypal.com*) provide a variety of plans that charge different monthly fees depending on their features (e.g., credit card processing) and factors that we discussed above (e.g., reliability and bandwidth).

After you find a place to host your store, you should register a domain name. A domain name (or "URL") gives your store a unique identity on the Internet. In addition to choosing the name, you must also choose a specific extension. The most popular is ".com" for companies, but other extensions such as ".net" and ".bz" are potential alternatives.

Creating and Maintaining an Online Store

Once you have made a decision about where to host your online store, you need to turn your attention to gathering information about your products and creating your product catalog. On the Internet, your potential customers do not have a chance to physically interact with your products, so you have to carefully describe each product with great precision and detail. For each of your products within your online catalog, you should include at least the following information:

☞ The name of the product

☞ A short description of the product

- The price of the product
- A picture of the product

Depending on the type of product that you are selling, you should also consider adding information about such product attributes as:

- The weight of the product
- The color of the product
- A unique item number of the product
- The physical dimensions of the product
- The manufacturer and country that make the product
- A video showing how to use the product

The single most important piece of information used to describe any product on the Internet is its picture. Therefore, your product pictures should get extra attention. First, you will either need to purchase or gain access to a digital camera or a scanner to create digital product images. You can purchase these products online and connect them easily to most personal computers.

You will need to make sure that the pictures are in the correct file format for viewing online. Acceptable file formats (or "extensions") are: JPG, JPEG, GIF, TIFF and PNG. It is preferable to use the JPG or JPEG file formats for all of your pictures. If your digital pictures are in a different format, you will need to convert each one to an accepted format. Most computers have free software programs such as Microsoft Paint that allow you to accomplish this.

Most importantly, you must not only build your online store, you must maintain it. You must keep your catalog of goods and services current. You need to keep prices and the availability of any items up-to-date. If you have any announcements specifying a date, you must remove them as you pass the date.

Getting Known

There are thousands of other Websites that will compete with your online store. Thus, you must allow potential customers to find you easily and offer something unique for them to purchase. Competing on price and wide variety is a difficult business proposition. There are too many well established, large and well-funded competitors. Selling unique crafts or items from your region of the world may result in a successful strategy. But, potential customers still must be able to find your Website/store. In the following sections we offer some strategies for improving your chances that customers worldwide will be able to find your online store.

One area of particular concern is how to allow your potential customers to find your business easily when they use a search engine. Search engines have become the dominant mechanism for finding new online stores such as your own. When a potential customer enters a relevant word in a popular search engine such as Google and Yahoo!, you want your Website to appear high on a ranked list (and preferably at the top). Potential customers often will only scan the first ten or twenty links, so having your link on the first page of the results is vital.

One way to optimize your online store for search engines is to include specific keywords within your Website that are relevant to your online business. For example, when selling pottery online, an online store should include such keywords as pottery, pots and clay. Also, you can improve your placement on search engines by having other Websites link to your Website. For example, if there are any informational or community Websites that discuss your product category, you should make sure that they link to your online store.

You also can improve the chances of potential customers finding your online store by paying for placement on search engines. The most widely used search engines such as Yahoo!, Google and Microsoft Live Search allow businesses to bid on specific keywords relevant to their product offerings. Then, when a search engine user searches for one of these keywords, your business will appear in the list of "sponsored ads" of the search engine results. Your business pays a small fee only when the user clicks on the link to your Website.

In addition to getting known through search engines, you should also consider doing the following to get the word out about your online business:

- Contribute to blogs or message boards that are relevant to your products
- Buy banner advertisements on other Websites
- Write an online newsletter and email it to potential customers
- Advertise on popular social networking Websites such as Facebook and Myspace.

Building Trust

Your customers must trust you and your company to buy your products. The key to trust is open and honest communication and a satisfying interaction. This is true whether you deal with someone in person or through your online store.

Trust is even more vital when selling products online (as opposed to a physical storefront) due to the lack of direct contact and the large physical distances between the buyer and seller. Most likely, your online customers have never met you and have never actually seen any of your products. If trust is lost, the customer is only one click away from leaving your online store and moving to another location on the Internet.

Your customers must have their FUDs (fears, uncertainties and doubts) reduced or even eliminated if you intend to earn and retain their trust.

Fears include losing their money, not getting the product that they paid for and getting taken advantage of. A very high fear is identity theft where someone poses as you and performs activities in your name. To reduce fears you will need to include the following on your Website:

- A privacy policy (how you will keep personal data safe) and a security policy (precautions that you have taken to keeping the customer information safe)

- A shipping and return policy (how you will deliver the product(s) and how customers can return items that do not satisfy them

Uncertainties come from unclear feedback and information. You can reduce anxiety for those dealing with you by providing confident and satisfying experiences. Include the following on your Website to reduce uncertainties:

- Contact information (including an email address, phone number and mailing address)

- Customer service information

- Complete and detailed information about each of your products (including pictures, dimensions and other necessary information)

Doubts come from customers' inability to conduct business over the Internet and at unexpected surprises when dealing with you. Initial Web customers must have their doubts removed and believe that shopping and buying on the Internet can be more efficient and effective than actually going to a physical storefront. To reduce doubts you can:

- Include feedback and testimonials about your business from previously satisfied customers

- Allow customers to present reviews of your products on your Website

- Have third-party businesses review certain aspects of your online store, such as its security

Making a Sale

Once you have gained the trust of customers and visitors, you need to encourage them to make a purchase on your Website. It is vital that the sale process be intuitive, i.e., customers should not feel forced to think extensively about how to purchase the products. That will drive them away to other sites that will allow them to get the product they want with less frustration.

There already are certain conventions with which online customers are familiar that you need to follow. The three steps typically involved in making a successful sale through an online storefront are:

Step #1: Find the Desired Products in Your Catalog

The customer must first find the product that he or she is looking for in your product catalog. Typically, customers utilize two different approaches to find the products they desire—searching and browsing. Your product catalog must support both approaches because some customers prefer to search for products, while browsing draws many others.

When searching for desired products, the customer enters a series of keywords to find the most closely related products. In order for a successful search to take place, your product catalog must describe each of the products in sufficient detail, so that they can be matched via the search. Alternatively, customers can browse for a specific product. To support browsing, you should divide your product catalog into categories that will make sense to the customer. The customer then clicks on a certain category of products and a list of products within that category appears. If your catalog contains a large number of products, you might also need subcategories to keep your product catalog organized.

Step #2: Use a Shopping Cart to Keep Track of Products

Once a customer finds a product that she is looking for, she needs the ability to save it for later while continuing to shop on your Website. We typically call this process "adding an item to a shopping cart." This is a common convention used by most online businesses. You have not yet paid for the items or services in the cart, but you still possess them. A shopper should also be able to examine her shopping cart contents. She will want to know what she has selected, along with the total cost. The cost should include any shipping costs or taxes. The shopper also should have the ability to add more items to the cart, to delete items in the cart or to change the quantity of items in the cart.

Step #3: Checkout from Your Store

Once a customer has all the desired items in a shopping cart, she must then "check out" of your store, i.e., she needs to complete the purchase. To complete the checkout process, you need to collect the following information from the customer:

- Identifying information such as name, email address and company name (if applicable)
- Both the billing and shipping addresses as these might differ
- Shipping preferences, such as regular shipping or expedited shipping
- The method of payment and payment information (e.g., credit card number and expiration date)
- Whether the item is a gift, and, if so, whether a note or gift wrapping should be included

Do not collect unnecessary information for the purchase. If the customer feels you are collecting marketing or demographic information, she may think it unnecessary and abandon the purchase.

Once the customer provides all of the information, she should get an opportunity to confirm that the information is correct and to see the total price, including shipping, of the products she is purchasing. Once she completes the purchase, she should receive an email confirming the successful processing and shipping of the order. The confirmation email should also provide customer service contact information in case there are questions or changes to the order.

Getting Paid

A critical component of any thriving business is to move money from the account of the purchaser to you, the merchant. There are many complexities in getting paid through the Internet that do not exist in the physical marketplace, where you can interact directly with the customer. A customer cannot just hand you cash on the Internet. The money must move safely and quickly over great geographical distances. Conversion to a currency that you can use must take place so you can pay your own expenses and spend it wherever you live. Remember that putting your business on the Internet makes your products and services available worldwide, unless you specifically restrict where you do business. You may have potential buyers that use many different currencies and payment methods.

There are many payment options online, each with its advantages and disadvantages. You must choose which of the following payment options you are going to support before launching your online store:

Credit Cards

Once a customer provides a credit card number, you will need to use a secure online connection to verify the number's authenticity and approve the purchase. Therefore, you will need access to a Web server with secure connections (typically SSL or "Secure Socket Layer"), or you will have to find another company that will provide this service to you.

Merchant Services

Most payments occur using either credit or debit cards. However, online payment services are becoming more popular, especially in auction environments. Services such as Paypal (part of eBay) or Google Checkout allow payment through a third-party operation. This prevents the need to send sensitive information directly from the purchaser to you, the merchant. They also allow the customer to reduce their FUDs because they are providing their credit card information only to a reputable third-party company such as Google. However, these intermediaries charge your store to handle the money portion of your transactions.

Checks and Money Orders

Another means of receiving funds from a customer is mailing a check or a money order. Then you can use your bank to verify that the check is acceptable prior to shipping a product. This payment option requires the transmission and verification of less personal information. But you should remember that all of these activities take time and will delay the delivery of goods to a customer.

Bank Accounts

A final mechanism for getting paid involves collecting the bank information from the customer (i.e., the bank routing number and the customer's checking account number). While this method allows you to get paid very quickly, it also involves the transfer of very sensitive information and most customers are not willing to provide this information to an unknown entity.

Delivering Your Product or Service

Even the largest online stores utilize commercial shipping carriers. The most widely known carriers that offer shipping services to almost any country in the world include DHL (*www.dhl.com*), UPS (*www.ups.com*) and FedEx (*www.fedex.com*). Before shipping your first order, you should investigate the prices of the carriers and their availability in your local area and determine which carrier you will use to deliver your products to your online customers. You can set up a business account with each of these carriers that provides many services to you, such as package pickup and order tracking. You want to make sure that the shipping carrier that you choose can get your product to the customer quickly, reliably and at a reasonable price. If your product does not arrive on time or the customer faces a very large shipping cost, then he will feel discouraged about buying from your store again.

After determining the carrier that you will rely on to make successful deliveries, you will need to address who pays for shipping and the shipping options you will offer. You need to write a clear shipping policy. At the very least, your online store should offer no less than two shipping options to its customers—expedited and standard shipping. Expedited shipping will allow your customers to get their orders quickly (but at a higher cost), and standard shipping will provide a less costly (but slower) option. Next, you need to decide who will pay for the shipping costs. Many online stores now offer free shipping for the standard shipping option. However, the shipping is not entirely free as the online store typically adds the shipping costs (or at least a portion of them) to the actual price of the product.

Additionally, other questions to consider when deciding on your shipping policy include:

- ☛ Will you need to include special handing costs for packing and wrapping prior to shipping (e.g., for fragile items)?

☛ Will you offer an option to the customer to include gift wrapping when buying your products as a gift for someone else?

☛ Will you charge different prices for shipping domestically and internationally? Will you offer different shipping options for domestic and international shipping?

As soon as your product ships, you should notify the customer with an order tracking number. The shipping carrier that you choose will provide the tracking number. Upon its receipt (typically through an email message), the customer then can utilize the carrier's Website to determine when the order will arrive.

Responding to Questions and Issues

An online store should expect to have questions and issues arise from its customers. You must give quick and courteous replies if you expect to have repeat customers. Also, positive customer service experiences are vital to having your existing customers recommend your online store to other potential customers. Many Websites today, such as Shopzilla (*www.shopzilla.com*) and BizRate (*www.bizrate.com*), allow customers to publicly present reviews of their online shopping experiences. Negative reviews could be detrimental to your future business.

To ensure quality customer service you will first need to think about how you are going to respond to your customers and the policies you will have. You do not have the luxury of meeting your customers face-to-face, so you will need to use alternative means for responding. Methods that you can use to communicate with your customers include the following:

☛ *Email* is the most cost-effective and standard way of responding to customers. Email allows your customers to contact you twenty-four hours a day, seven days a week. You should have a dedicated customer service email address (e.g., customerservice@yourstoresname.com) that you must check frequently.

☛ Many customers prefer the telephone because it provides the most immediate and personal customer service. If you decide to provide customer service via the telephone, you will need to decide whether to set up a toll-free number or whether to require your customers to pay for any long-distance phone calls. You should also decide whether you will have a person always available to answer the phone or if you will just handle all calls via a voicemail system.

☛ *Mail* provides the most cost effective, but also the slowest, customer support. Customers will have to wait days or weeks to have their questions answered, so it should not be the only customer service method that you offer.

☛ *FAQs* (Frequently Asked Questions) or "self-service" is another convenient way (both for you and your customer!) of answering your customer's questions. FAQs are typically a page on your Website that lists questions previous customers have asked (or questions that you anticipate future customers might be asking), along with your answers to the questions. You must make sure to keep your FAQs up-to-date and add to them when new questions arise. You can answer a vast majority of customer service inquiries via the FAQs, but they should not be your only form of customer support in case the customer cannot find an answer to a question.

After you decide on the methods, you need to clearly describe your specific customer service policies: how quickly you will respond to inquiries, how to get support with any technical or product issues and what kind of warranties you will offer. Also, all of your customer service information should be accessible via a hyperlink on every page of your Website. You want to ensure that customers can get answers easily when they have questions or when issues arise.

Often, customers will decide that they do not want the product they bought. They will wish to return it for a refund. You must decide in advance, and include as part of your customer service policy, who pays for return shipping and whether you will always refund the entire amount. You could decide not to accept any returns or to accept all returns with no questions asked, but most return policies fall somewhere in between. For example, you might only accept returns for products within thirty days of delivery and that are in the same condition they were in when you sent them.

Also, before returning a product, a standard practice is to have the customer contact you to receive an authorization for a return. A return authorization allows you to anticipate the return and also to inquire about the reasons for the return. Perhaps your online store does not accurately describe the item and you do not want to have other customers repeatedly return the product for the same reason.

Protecting Your Property and Consumers

A security breach can bring negative publicity and destroy your business. You must make sure that only you or a person authorized by you has permission to change your Website and have access to other sensitive information, such as the payment and contact information provided by your customers.

First of all, you should make sure that you carefully select the passwords that you choose (i.e., use a mixture of characters, numbers and other symbols) and that you record them in a secure location. Also, you should be sure that you encrypt (code) any potentially sensitive information that you are transferring electronically, such as credit card numbers or passwords. We typically accomplish encryption online through the use of a Secure Sockets Layer certificate (or "SSL"). While we will not cover the details of how SSL works here, you should make sure that whenever you are transmitting sensitive information that you show *https://* at the beginning of the Web address (or URL) in the address bar of your Web browser.

Another critical need of all online stores is the protection of the data shared with you by your customers. Your customers must feel assured that you have protected any data you have in your files, whether electronic or hard copy, against intruders.

You should transmit any sensitive data securely over the Internet. Also, you should provide a secure authentication system for customers when they want to access or change their personal information. Online stores often allow customers to provide a username and password to log into the "My Account" section of the online store. Customers can store their credit card numbers for future use in this section. You can also store other information here, such as their billing and shipping addresses and other preferences. You should never give away the password of any customer via email. Your online store should allow customers to reset their own passwords. Typically, this takes place by first verifying the customer's identity by sending him an email message to the email address that he provided when setting up the account. The email message provides a link to a Web page that allows the customer to select a new password. Finally, you should never accept or send any sensitive information such as credit card numbers through email or by cell phone. It is easy to intercept these communications, especially if using a wireless connection.

Chapter Summary

By following the steps described in this chapter, you are more likely to succeed when launching an online store. However, the utility of the information discussed in this chapter is difficult to understand without a concrete example. Therefore, the Case Study on page 169 provides an example that follows a company called Unique Bicycles and discusses how this company used the information discussed in this chapter to create an online store that expanded its consumer base and sales.

Food for Thought/The World Wide Web and Internet Technology

- What is the distinguishing characteristic of Internet technologies?

- What is TCP/IP? Why are "open standards" essential to the independence of the Internet?

- Is there a central control point to the Internet? How do computers in different parts of the globe communicate with each other?

- Are the "Internet" and the "Web" the same thing?

- What are the differences between an intranet and an extranet? Can you think of how an intranet and/or an extranet can be useful in your future career or current job?

Food for Thought/E-Commerce

- What are the differences between e-business and e-commerce? Is the act of buying a book on Amazon.com considered e-commerce or e-business?

- What are the characteristics of hosting solutions that one should consider when selecting a host? What advantages do merchant solutions such as Yahoo! provide?

Have your experiences with stores hosted on Yahoo! and other merchant platforms been positive?

🖰 When trying to "get known" online, why are search engines so vital? How can online businesses improve their placement on search engine results?

🖰 What is meant by FUDs? Why is reducing FUDs so vital to successfully doing business online? What happens when your FUDs are not reduced when shopping online?

🖰 What are the advantages and disadvantages of the payment methods that you can use online? Are you comfortable with using all of these?

🖰 Have customer service experiences shaped your usage of certain e-commerce Websites? Can you think of very positive experiences that you had? Negative experiences?

References

Austin, Robert D. 2003. "The Worldwide Web and Internet technology," Harvard Business School case 90198-020, February 13, 2003.

Building Your Online Store

THE UNIQUE BICYCLES EXAMPLE

Chapter 10 provided you with background knowledge aimed at building your understanding of e-commerce. Now you will learn how to create an actual e-commerce Website that allows a business to sell products over the Internet. Make sure that you have read Chapter 10 and feel comfortable with the material. We now will put that knowledge to use.

Introducing the Unique Bicycles Store

To illustrate how to implement an e-commerce Website, we will focus on a fictional online store called "Unique Bicycles." Unique Bicycles has been selling unique used, new and antique bicycles in its local community (based in London in the United Kingdom) for more than ten years. Tina Owen owns the store and runs it with the help of five employees that work as customer representatives, maintenance technicians and cashiers. While the bicycle store has achieved success in the local community, Unique Bicycles has decided to start planning a new online store to potentially increase their revenues and to gain access to new customers across the European Union.

We will revisit the topics introduced in Chapter 10 in the following sections, which will show you how Unique Bicycles approached such specific activities as setting up a product catalog, getting known and building trust.

Prerequisites to Implementing the Unique Bicycles Online Store

The owner of Unique Bicycles has thought about and made decisions about the business model, the financial plan, the operations plan, the marketing plan and internationalization plans before even taking the first steps in the implementation of a new online store. While we will not discuss in detail how Unique Bicycles approached each of these topics, the key decisions made by the owner of Unique Bicycles follow:

- **Business model:** Unique Bicycles decided that they will not be able to compete on offering the lowest price for their bicycles due to the hundreds of other bicycle retailers already online. Instead, they believe that they offer bicycles that no other online store has, and therefore Unique Bicycles will be competing primarily on the novelty of their product. They hope to double their bicycle sales through the use of the online store.

- **Financial plan:** The owner has been putting aside a portion of the profits toward creating and funding the implementation of the online store. Hence, Unique Bicycles estimates that they will be able to pay for the effort involved in implementing their new online store without taking out a loan or seeking any additional financing. However, they cannot make a final decision until they fully explore the cost of the hosting options, which topic 3 of this module discusses.

- **Operations plan:** Unique Bicycles is doubling their bicycle orders from their suppliers prior to the launch of their online store, so that they can support the expected increase in sales.

- **Marketing plan:** The owner of Unique Bicycles has decided that she will write an online newsletter targeted towards her current customers, invest in search engine advertising and pay for banner advertisements on other bicycling Websites. Topic 5 of this module will discuss Unique Bicycles' marketing plan in more detail.

☞ **Internationalization plan:** Unique Bicycles decides that the high shipping costs of bicycles (due to their large size and heavy weight) will initially constrain the geographic area that they can ship their bicycles to. Also, Unique Bicycles currently does not have enough resources to support languages on their Website other than English, so they have decided to sell their products only in the European Union where English is the primary language of many businesses. They have also decided to use the Euro as their primary currency because most of the European Union countries use the Euro today. Unique Bicycles will explore expanding their online market in the future.

Designing the Unique Bicycles Store

As discussed in Chapter 10, a usable Website must have a properly designed structure, that is, a Website visitor must be able to easily and quickly find the information that he is seeking. Therefore, the first step in designing an online store is to think about the overall structure and how the visitor is going to navigate the Website.

To design the structure of their Website, Unique Bicycles uses a simple tool called a sitemap. A sitemap is a hierarchical representation of the structure of an entire Website; that is, it shows how a customer or visitor will navigate to every page that composes a single Website. As shown below in Figure 10.1 of Unique Bicycles' sitemap, the homepage is at the top because this is where a Website visitor typically starts when visiting a company's Web location. Below the homepage are the pages that the visitor can navigate to from the homepage (About Unique Bicycles, Shop Online, Customer Service,

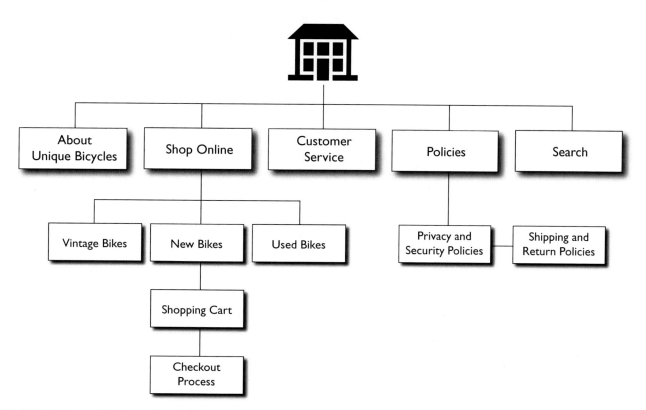

FIGURE 10.1—*Unique Bicycles' Sitemap*

Policies and Search). Below these pages are pages further down in the Website hierarchy that the visitor can navigate to. For example, from the Shop Online page, the sitemap shows that the visitor can navigate to the Vintage Bikes, New Bikes and Used Bikes pages. In addition to showing how the visitor can navigate to specific pages, the sitemap shows each page of the Website so that Unique Bicycles can determine whether any pages are missing.

As a first step in designing your Website, you should produce a sitemap that you think works best for your particular online store. You need to determine the structure that will make the most sense to your customers when they visit your Website. This means that you need to empathize, to think like your customers and to understand why they have come to your site. You can download popular software such as Microsoft Visio to create an electronic version of the sitemap, or you can simply draw a sitemap on a piece of paper.

After you define the structure of your Website with a sitemap, the next step is to design the individual pages that compose it. A very simple tool for thinking about how to design each page is a paper prototype. A paper prototype is a very rough representation of a Web page on a piece of paper. All you need to create paper prototypes are a few pieces of paper and a pen or a pencil—it is that simple! You need to sketch out the format and content of each page in a rough draft form.

To design every page within their sitemap, Unique Bicycles created paper prototypes of each of their pages. Figure 10.2 shows an example paper prototype that Unique Bicycles created for the homepage. The paper prototype determines the location of the navigation (top-right corner of the page), what the body of the page will include

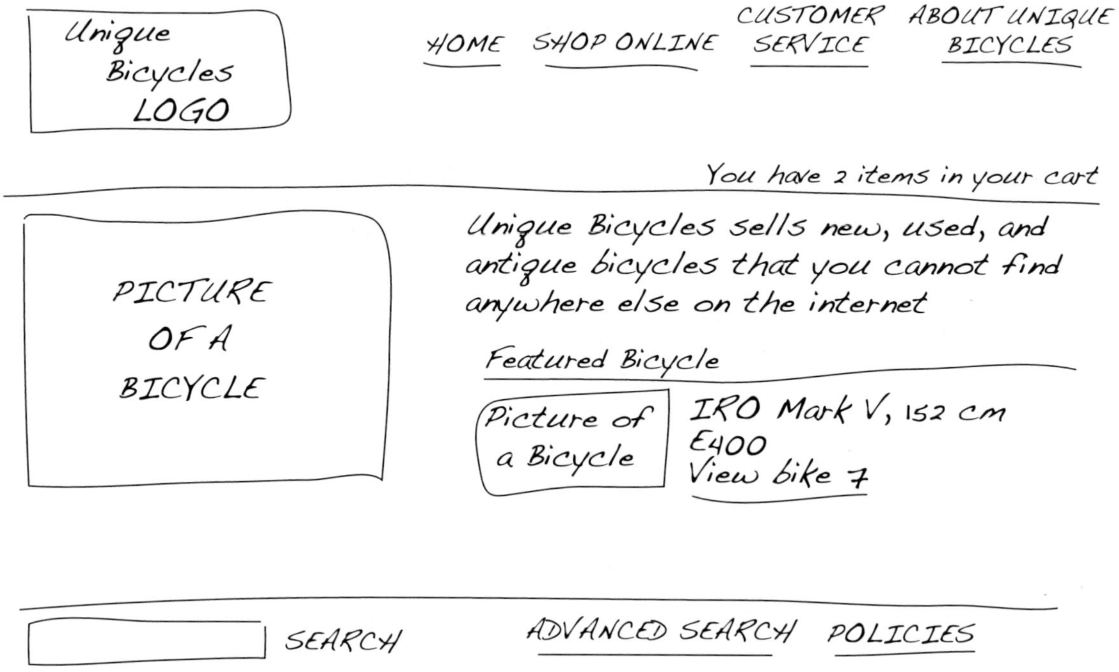

FIGURE 10.2—*Example Paper Prototype*

(i.e., a picture of a bicycle and information about the company) and the overall layout of the page. However, you will notice that words describe some of the contents (e.g., no bicycle picture is actually included, and a drawn box shows where to place the picture).

The overall prototype is very rough (e.g., lines are not straight, there is no color and so forth). The reason for not paying attention to these details is that the purpose of the paper prototype is for designing and testing the layout of a single page only and not other aspects such as color and image usage. Having a simple, consistent, navigable structure with relevant content is essential when designing a usable Website. You should draw paper prototypes for every page included within your sitemap. This process forces you to think about the structure of each page and what information you plan on including.

Once you have created paper prototypes for all of your pages, how will you know that they are usable? To determine whether your current design is in fact usable, you must test your paper prototypes with representative users.

To test their prototype, Unique Bicycles' employees first brainstorm a series of important tasks that customers on the Unique Bicycles Website can easily accomplish:

- The customer is looking for the email address of a customer service representative at Unique Bicycles. How would she go about finding it?

- A customer is looking to buy an "IRO" brand used bicycle. How would the customer go about finding the bicycle and then purchasing it online?

- A customer wants to review the return policy at Unique Bicycles before making an online purchase. How would the customer go about finding the return policy?

You must have empathy for the customer, what the person is feeling and his logical mental steps. Remember you are creating this site for your potential customer, not for yourself.

Next, Unique Bicycles recruits up to five individuals whom it believes are representative of customers who will be using the Unique Bicycles Website when it is available. Two employees meet with one of the persons in a quiet room and present the individual with the paper prototype of the homepage. Then they ask the individual to perform the first task. They ask the person to "talk out loud" while he explains where he would click on the homepage to start looking for the customer service information. After he states that he would click a specific link in the paper prototype (e.g., on "Customer Service" in the navigation), the employees show the next paper prototype to the individual (e.g., the "Customer Service" page). While he attempts to perform the task, one of the employees takes notes and pays careful attention to any problems identified (e.g., the individual cannot find the "Customer Service" link, which is a problem with the navigability of the Website), so that the company can revise the paper prototype to address these issues. Once the first task is accomplished, they use the same approach to verify that the user can perform the remaining two tasks.

If changes are necessary due to a significant problem, they should change the prototype pages prior to testing with the next individual. If there are just minor changes or if you believe it may be an idiosyncrasy of the individual, you should move ahead to the next test person and see if similar problems occur.

After completing the testing sessions, Unique Bicycles updates their paper prototypes and the site map to address the issues identified during the testing sessions. Since the sessions identified only a few minor usability issues, Unique Bicycles decided not to perform another round of usability testing. (However, if you find that you need to make significant changes after your initial usability testing, you should verify that the changes you made to your prototypes addressed the major usability issues.) The testing allows Unique Bicycles to determine any usability issues before creating their actual Website. This is less time consuming than addressing usability issues after creating the Website.

Hosting the Unique Bicycles Store

After conducting some research, the owner of Unique Bicycles decides to use the merchant services of Shopify (*www.shopify.com*) by signing up for the professional plan (*https://app.shopify.com/services/signup*). The owner made the decision by considering all of the hosting factors discussed in Chapter 10:

- **Advertising:** Shopify does not include any unwanted advertising on your pages.

- **Amount of disk space:** The professional plan offers 240 MBs.

- **Reliability:** Shopify guarantees that the Unique Bicycles store will be available at least 99 percent of the time.

- **Bandwidth:** Shopify provides unlimited bandwidth to support future growth.

- **Technical support:** Shopify provides an extensive FAQ section and a community area that allows other storeowners to interact and help each other. Shopify also offers email support; they generally answer emails within twenty-four hours (and usually within a few hours).

- **Security:** The professional plan includes SSL encryption, which protects all sensitive data.

Shopify is also more than a hosting company, and it offers other essential merchant services:

- An administrative area for creating pages such as customer service information and store policies, as well as for defining the navigation of the entire Website without any technical expertise

- An administrative area for creating and maintaining an online store without technical expertise

- Ability to control and offer multiple shipping options within the online store

- Inventory tracking and management

- Integration with other services such as PayPal and Google Checkout that provide credit card processing

- Support for over forty-five languages and multiple currencies, which allows Unique Bicycles to expand their business to non-English speaking countries in the future

However, the hosting and the other merchant services come at a price. Unique Bicycles must commit $59 a month and 1.0 percent of the price of each bicycle that it sells. Since the owner does not possess any technical expertise though, she views the services Shopify provides as essential and worth the fees—the benefits of Shopify outweigh the costs.

Next, Unique Bicycles sets up their account with Shopify. After providing login information, the store's name and other business information, such as the address and a credit card for the fees charged by Shopify, Unique Bicycles receives access to the administration area (accessed via a Web browser). The administration area is where the owner can set up and manage the Website and online store. It has links to the following essential features:

- **Orders:** Allows Unique Bicycles to keep track of online orders and communicate with customers (e.g., to provide a shipping tracking number when an order is sent)

- **Products:** Allows Unique Bicycles to add and delete products and to manage the online store

- **Blogs and pages:** Allows Unique Bicycles to add pages such as customer service information to their Website

- **Navigation:** Allows Unique Bicycles to set up their navigation (or "site architecture" shown on the sitemap)

- **Marketing:** Provides an ability to submit a site to popular search engines, so that potential customers are more likely to find it

- **Assets:** Provides an ability to upload pictures of products and other documents that can be distributed via the Website

- **Preferences:** Allows Unique Bicycles to set the currency of the products sold on their Website, add taxes, provide shipping options and set up their domain name

- **Account:** Allows the owner to give access to the administration area to other employees and to make changes to the information provided when the account was set up

We will discuss the administration features introduced here in detail during the following topics so that you can see how Unique Bicycles utilized them to create their Website and online store.

Now that Unique Bicycles has set up a hosting account that is right for their business, the final step in hosting their online store is to register a domain name that gives Unique Bicycles a distinct identity on the Internet. The owner goes to Network Solutions (*www.networksolutions.com*) to register a unique and memorable address for their online business. Unfortunately, someone else has already registered her preferred domain name, uniquebicycles.com (.com stands for "company"). However, her second choice, uniquebicycles.biz (.biz stands for "business"), is still available. Figure 10.3 provides a screenshot of the domain name selection process at Network Solutions.

The owner purchases the rights to the domain name from Network Solutions for $34.95 for a year. The final step is to "point" the uniquebicycles.biz domain name to the Unique Bicycles Website that Shopify is hosting. This takes place by providing Shopify's Domain Name System (DNS) information to Network Solutions. The DNS information is a "phone book" that tells the rest of the Internet the location of the Unique Bicycles online store. As shown in Figure 10.4, you can find the DNS information by clicking on the "DNS & Domains" link within the administration area at Shopify.

Creating and Maintaining the Unique Bicycles Store

The first step in creating the Unique Bicycles online store is building the navigation and pages that the sitemap in Figure 10.1 defined.

To accomplish this using the Shopify administration area, the owner first goes to the "Blogs & Pages" section to add all of the pages for that part of the sitemap. As Figure 10.5 shows below for the About Unique Bicycles page, you add the pages one at a time and then add the page's contents.

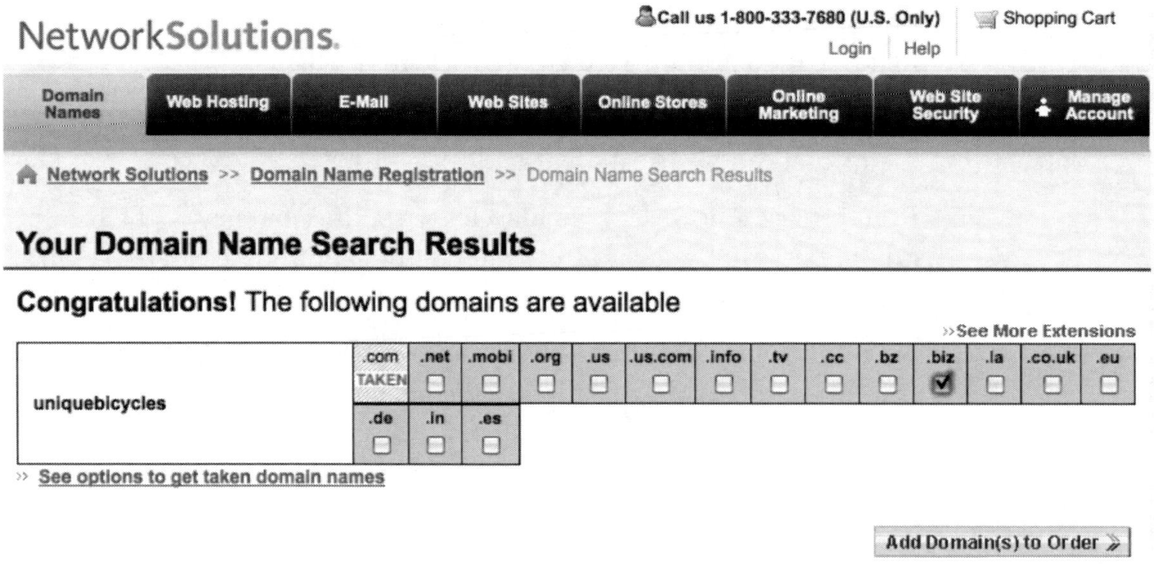

FIGURE 10.3—*Domain Name Selection at Network Solutions*

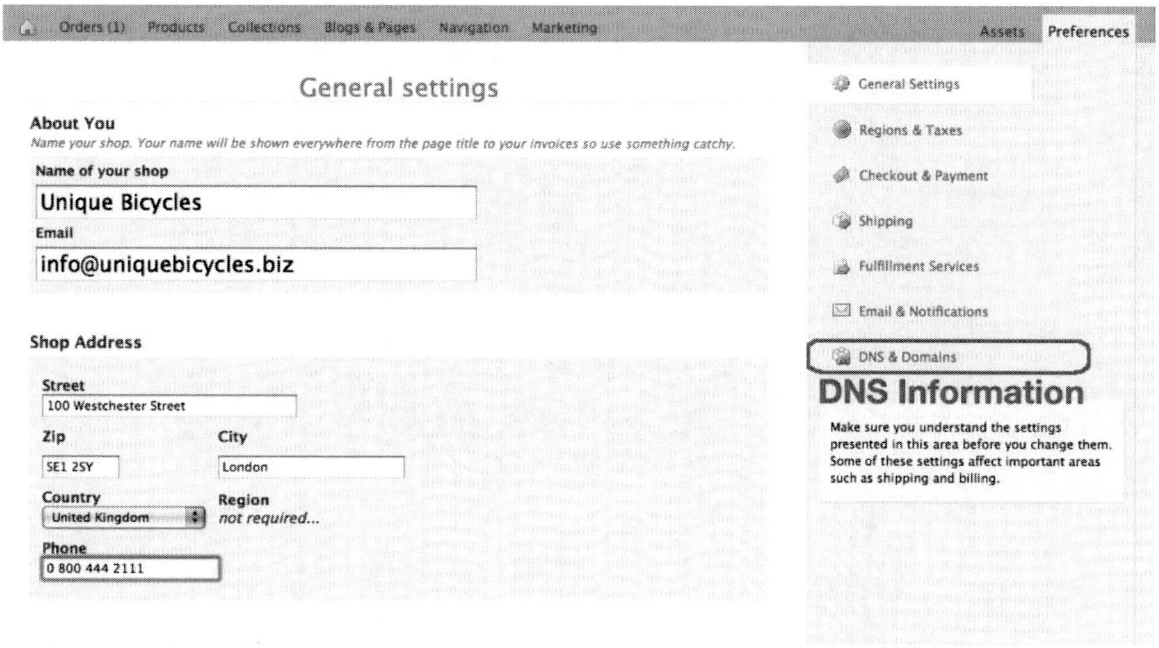

FIGURE 10.4—*Finding DNS Information (highlighting added by authors is not part of Website)*

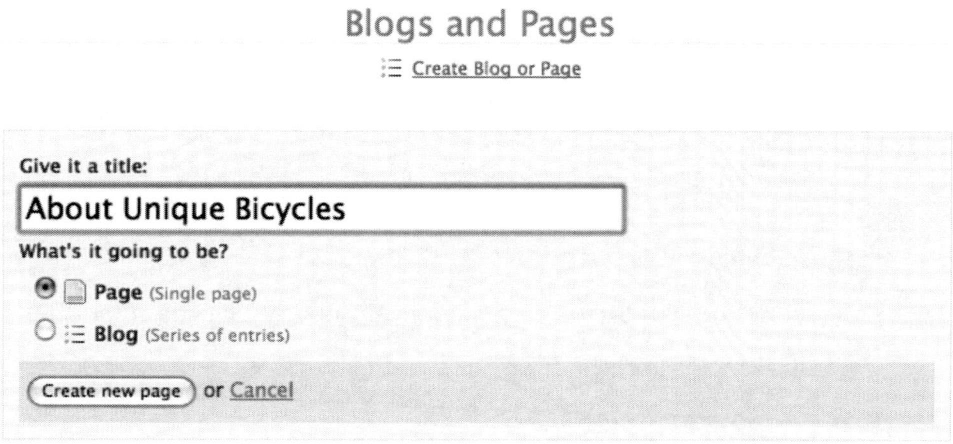

FIGURE 10.5—*Adding a Page Using Shopify*

Now that they have added the individual pages, Unique Bicycles must build the navigation structure that allows individuals to navigate to the pages. The owner uses the "Navigation" section within the administration area to add the navigation to the Website. As previously defined in the sitemap, there are five links that they need to include in the navigation from the homepage. Based on the results of the testing in topic 3, Unique Bicycles includes some links on the top of the page or the "main menu" (About Unique Bicycles, Shop Online, Customer Service, and a link back to the homepage), and they add the remaining links at the bottom of the page or the "footer." It is easy to add this navigation structure using Shopify. Figure 10.6 shows how the owner adds the About Unique Bicycles page to the navigation structure. She follows an identical process to add the remaining pages.

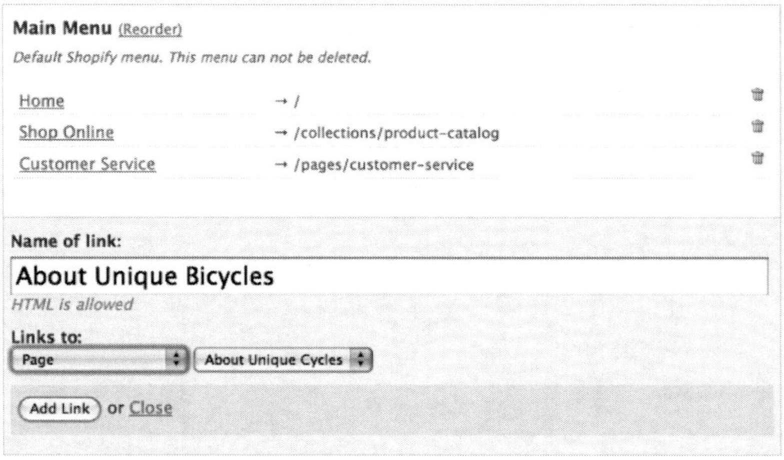

FIGURE 10.6—*Adding a Link to the Navigation*

Now that Unique Bicycles has set up their Website using Shopify, the owner turns her attention to gathering information for the online product catalog.

As defined in its sitemap, Unique Bicycles has organized their online product catalog into three categories: new bikes, used bikes and antique bikes. The shop's owner first creates an inventory of bicycles within each category by collecting each bicycle's name, the number of those bicycles in stock and the product number. Next, the owner decides that the following information is essential for describing each bicycle within the inventory:

- The name of the bicycle
- An extensive description of the bicycle
- The vendor of the bicycle (i.e., the company that manufactures the bicycle)
- The bicycle's price
- The weight of the bicycle
- The size of the bicycle's frame
- The color of the bicycle
- A picture of the bicycle

The owner believes that the above information will allow customers to effectively evaluate the bicycle within the online catalog. She also takes extra care to include at least one quality picture of each bicycle because any customer shopping online wants to see what the bicycle looks like before making a purchase.

Now that Unique Bicycles has gathered the necessary information about their bicycle inventory, they use Shopify to add the products to their online catalog.

To add each product, Unique Bicycles goes through the following process using the Shopify administration area:

1. They enter the title of the bicycle (the bicycle's name) and a description; then they select the type of bicycle (used, new or antique), and select the bicycle's manufacturer. Note: Putting <b></b> (referred to as tags) around the weight and color will cause highlighting of this information on the product page (Figure 10.7).

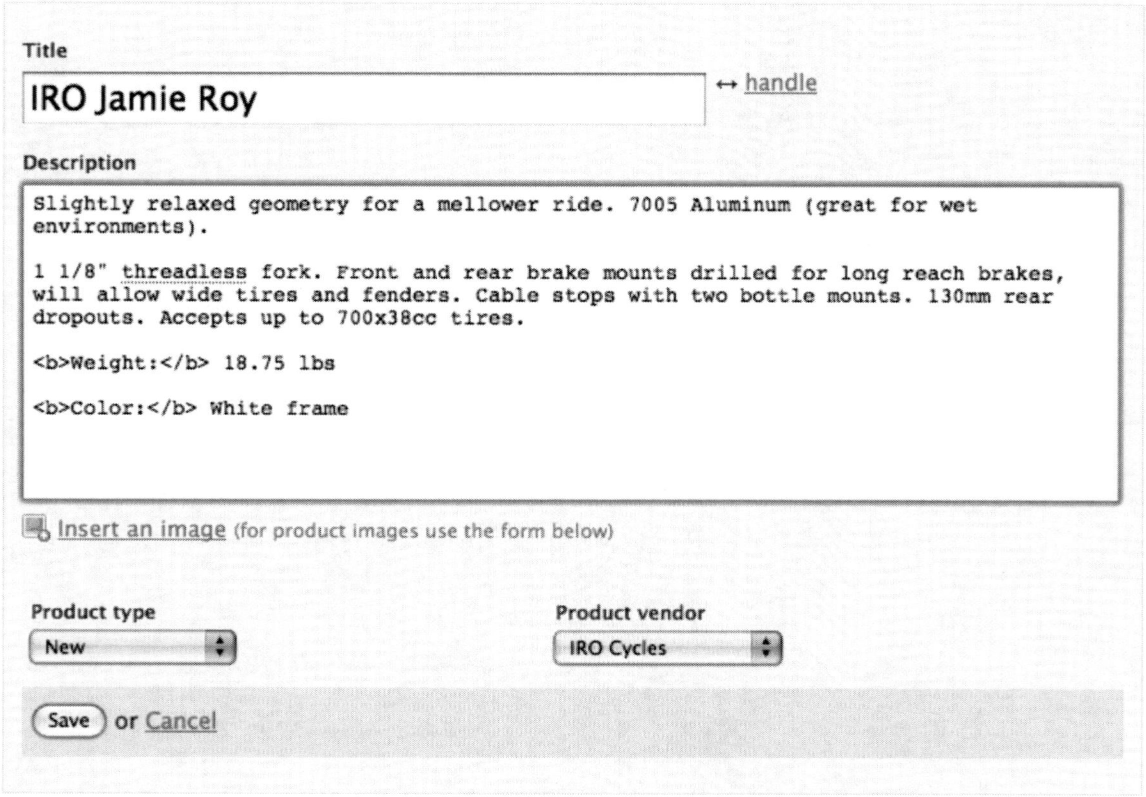

Title

IRO Jamie Roy   ↔ handle

Description

```
Slightly relaxed geometry for a mellower ride. 7005 Aluminum (great for wet
environments).

1 1/8" threadless fork. Front and rear brake mounts drilled for long reach brakes,
will allow wide tires and fenders. Cable stops with two bottle mounts. 130mm rear
dropouts. Accepts up to 700x38cc tires.

<b>Weight:</b> 18.75 lbs

<b>Color:</b> White frame
```

Insert an image (for product images use the form below)

Product type

New

Product vendor

IRO Cycles

Save or Cancel

FIGURE 10.7—*Addition of a New Product*

2. Next they provide the size of the bicycle, the selling price, the weight, the stock keeping unit (or the "product number") and the number of bicycles in stock (Figure 10.8). They do this for each bicycle size (i.e., a variation of a bicycle model), since each bicycle can come in multiple sizes (e.g., 152cm, 156cm).

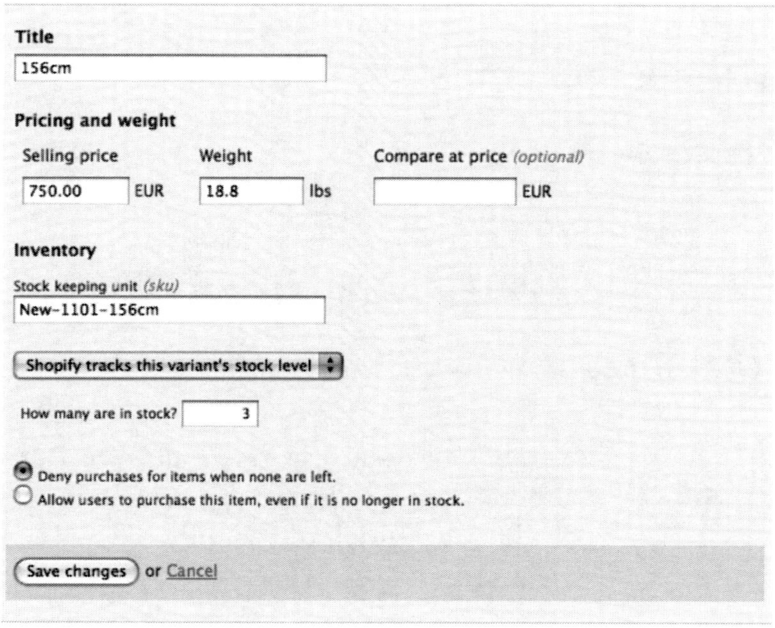

Title

156cm

Pricing and weight

Selling price	Weight	Compare at price *(optional)*
750.00 EUR	18.8 lbs	EUR

Inventory

Stock keeping unit *(sku)*

New-1101-156cm

Shopify tracks this variant's stock level

How many are in stock?   3

◉ Deny purchases for items when none are left.
○ Allow users to purchase this item, even if it is no longer in stock.

Save changes or Cancel

FIGURE 10.8—*Addition of a New Product*

3. They take a picture of the bicycle using a digital camera (making sure that the picture clearly and accurately depicts the bicycles) and upload the picture (in JPG format) (Figure 10.9).

Images

Drag these images to sort them. The first in the list will be the featured image and will be the most prominent one on its product page.

🗑 delete

Upload more images...

FIGURE 10.9—*Addition of a Product Picture*

4. Finally, the owner previews how the product would appear within the online catalog and verifies that all of the information is accurate (Figure 10.10).

IRO Jamie Roy

Slightly relaxed geometry for a mellower ride. 7005 Aluminum (great for wet environments).

1 1/8" threadless fork. Front and rear brake mounts drilled for long reach brakes, will allow wide tires and fenders. Cable stops with two bottle mounts. 130mm rear dropouts. Accepts up to 700×38cc tires.

Weight: 18.75 lbs

Color: White frame

Vendor: IRO Cycles
Type: New

⦿ 156cm for **€750.00 EUR**
◯ 152cm for **€750.00 EUR**

+ Add to Cart

FIGURE 10.10—*Previewing a Product Addition*

Shopify makes it easy for Unique Bicycles to keep track of the inventory. For each product that it adds, Unique Bicycles enters how many bicycles it has in stock. When the bicycles are all sold Shopify will automatically indicate that the bicycle is out of stock (Figure 10.11).

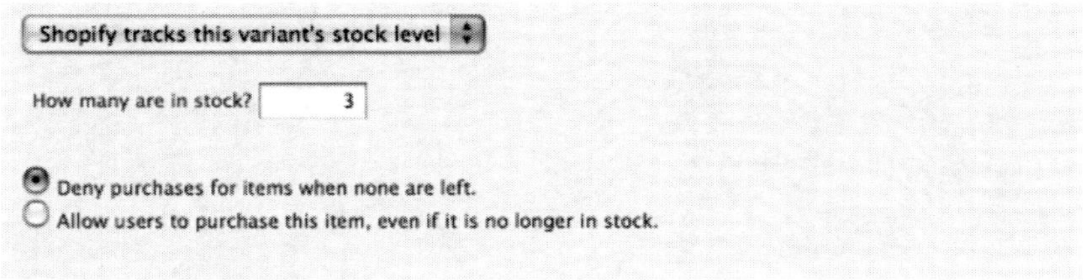

FIGURE 10.11—*Inventory Tracking of a Product*

However, if Unique Bicycles receives more bicycles from a manufacturer, or if it sells one of the bicycles in their physical store location, the owner needs to make sure to update their online inventory to accurately depict each bicycle's availability. You could lose future customers if someone wants to buy a bike that the catalog lists but it is not available.

Getting Unique Cycles Known

The first (and simplest) way to get the word out about an online store is to simply add specific keywords to your Web pages that accurately describe the store's contents. These keywords improve your chances to be in the top ten results when someone enters a relevant keyword in a popular search engine. Therefore, Unique Bicycles makes sure that it clearly describes every page's contents. For example, the homepage features a clear description of exactly what Unique Bicycles sells (i.e., used, new and antique bicycles). In addition to including keywords within a page's contents, any online business should also include hidden keywords called "META" data. Luckily, Shopify already does this automatically for the Unique Bicycles Website, and the owner does not need to learn any more technical skills to optimize their Website for search engines.

However, even though Unique Bicycles has optimized their Website for search engines, the Website will not show up within the search results of popular search engines until these search engines find the uniquebicycles.biz site. To speed up this process, Unique Bicycles submits their Website directly to Google and Yahoo! The owner first submits their Website to Google by going to the Google submission page at *http://www. google.com/addurl/,* and submitting their uniquebicycles.biz domain name. Next, they go to the Yahoo! submission page at *http://search.yahoo.com/info/submit.html* to submit the uniquebicycles.biz domain name to the Yahoo! search engine.

However, being included in a search engine's search results is often not enough to drive sufficient traffic to a new online store. Therefore, the owner of Unique Bicycles decides to devote some of her resources to a Google advertising campaign. As shown below in Figure 10.12, Unique Bicycles' goal is placement on the right side of Google's search results in the "Sponsored Links" area when potential buyers type relevant keyword(s).

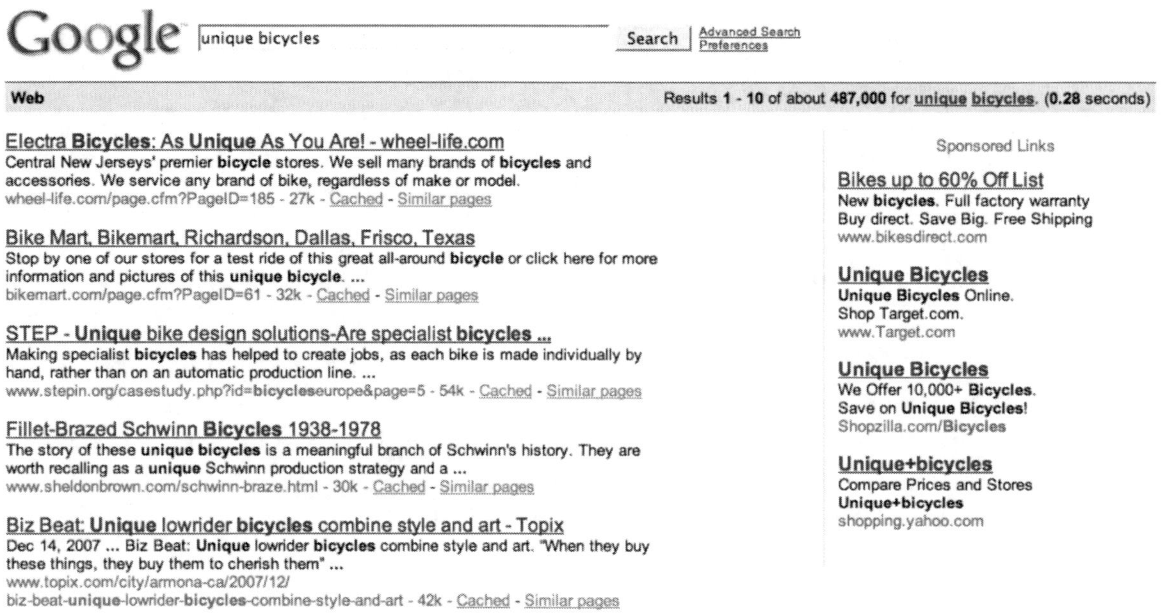

FIGURE 10.12—*An Example of How Google Links Results with the Sponsored Links Area*

Unique Bicycles decides to invest €100 a month using Google's advertising software called AdWords (*http://adwords.google.com/*). After paying a small setup fee, Unique Bicycles bids on specific keywords on AdWords, such as "antique bicycles," "unique bicycles" and "bicycle shop." Their bid amount and the bids of other businesses (typically between €0.01 and €1.00) determine how often their store information appears on the right side of the page. Unique Bicycles is charged their bid amount each time their advertisement shows up and a user clicks on the link. Thus, you should be careful with the size of your bid since you could run up a very large bill and not get commensurate sales. For example, if they bid €0.10 and a hundred Google visitors click on their advertisement, then Unique Bicycles would be charged €10.00.

Optimizing for and advertising on popular search engines helps to drive traffic to your online store. However, millions of people use search engines, and most of these individuals have no interest in your products. Therefore, to target their customer base more precisely, Unique Bicycles decides to employ two additional advertising strategies. First of all, they decide to buy advertising space in online magazines and on Websites for bicycle enthusiasts, such as Fixed Gear Gallery and Urban Velo. For a monthly fee (typically between €50 to €200), Unique Bicycles posts a small banner advertisement with the domain name of their online store, a picture of one of their bicycles and a short tagline. The banner advertisement is targeted directly to bicycle enthusiasts, and Unique Bicycles hopes that communicating directly with their target customer base will drive even more traffic to their Website.

Secondly, to stay in touch with and to drive their existing customers to making more purchases, Unique Bicycles decides to design an online newsletter (or "e-newsletter"). An e-newsletter provides interesting information and product announcements (e.g., items going on sale, new products, etc.) to remind individuals about a business. They then distribute their e-newsletters via an email message to customers who have already provided their email addresses (either by purchasing a product or signing up directly for the newsletter).

Online newsletters are only effective if they provide customers with interesting information and do not appear as a burden. Therefore, to make sure that their newsletter marketing is successful Unique Bicycles considers the following questions before sending out their first one:

- **What format should the newsletter be in?** A plain-text format allows Unique Bicycles just to send text via the email message, whereas a rich (or "HTML") format also provides the ability to add images, colors and other eye-catching formatting. The disadvantage of the rich newsletter format is that some email software cannot read the rich format. However, Unique Bicycles determines that they want to include pictures of their new bicycles and other rich content, and they decide to go with the rich newsletter format.

- **How often should they send the newsletter?** Unique Bicycles wants to actively stay in touch with their existing customers, but they also do not want to send so many email messages that customers become frustrated with the burden of increased email. They also need to be able to devote enough resources to create an interesting newsletter. They decide that a monthly newsletter is most appropriate for their business.

- **What information should they include so that customers get interesting information?** Unique Bicycles decides to include articles about their bicycles and how to best maintain them, special product offers (e.g., 10 percent off any used bicycle), special sweepstakes (e.g., a drawing for a free bicycle) and news updates about their business in the newsletter.

- **How will they design and manage the newsletter?** Unique Bicycles decides to use the Campaigner (*www.campaigner.com*) software (for $10 a month) to create their newsletter, to deliver the newsletter via an email message and to allow those customers who do not wish to receive it in the future to "opt out" of the newsletter.

Building Trust for Unique Bicycles

A vast majority of Unique Bicycles' online customers have never stepped inside their physical bicycle shop. The Unique Bicycles brand is not well known. Therefore, Unique Bicycles needs to develop a strategy for reducing the FUDs (Fears, Uncertainties and Doubts) of its online customers. We describe below the policies, customer service information and other strategies used to reduce FUDs at Unique:

Reducing Fears

Privacy and Security Policies

In the first paragraph of the policy, Unique Bicycles describes the information that they will collect from their customers when they purchase products from the company.

Unique Bicycles clearly states that it will require only absolutely necessary information, such as name, address, email address and payment information. It will not require any other sensitive information, such as a birthdates or driver license number.

Next, Unique Bicycles describes how they will be collecting the information from the customers. The owner decides that they will only collect the information via forms on their Website (the customers will not be able to phone in their personal information), protected via SSL (which Shopify automatically provides).

Then, Unique Bicycles describes how they will store the information that they collect about their customers. The policy states that they will store the information in a database at Shopify, and only the owner of Unique Bicycles (and no other employees) will be able to add, change, delete and distribute the information provided by customers.

Finally, Unique Bicycles clearly states that they will not be sharing any customer data with any other business or company. And if a customer has any questions or would like to be removed from the customer database, Unique Bicycles includes contact information (an email address and phone number) at the bottom of the policy.

Shipping and Return Policies

In the first paragraph, Unique Bicycles includes an estimate of how long it will take to send an order to a customer. The policy states that all orders will be shipped within two business days of being placed online. If they do not ship the order within two business days (or forty-eight hours) the shipping cost will be reduced to zero.

Next, the policy describes the shipping options available to customers. Unique Bicycles offers four domestic shipping options: free shipping for all domestic orders over €99 (10–14 business days), standard shipping (3–7 business days), expedited shipping (2–4 business days) and overweight shipping (for large orders over 100 lbs, 10–14 business days). For international orders (within the European Union but outside of the UK), they will offer only two shipping options: standard shipping and expedited shipping. Also, the policy states that they will ship all orders via the UPS shipping carrier, and that they will send a tracking number to the email address that the customer provided when the order shipped. Unique Bicycles' policy also explicitly states that they currently only will ship orders to countries that are part of the European Union.

Finally, the policy describes how Unique Bicycles handles returns. The policy states that Unique Bicycles will accept all returns within sixty days of the order received by the customer, but the customer must pay for return shipping. Also, Unique Bicycles' policy is to only accept bicycles that are in an unused condition (the customer cannot have ridden or damaged a bicycle). The customer must contact Unique Bicycles to get a return authorization. Also, Unique Bicycles decides not to charge a restocking fee (that typically covers the costs included in integrating the returned item back into an inventory) because the owner is worried that it would deter customers from making purchases from their online store.

Reducing Uncertainties

Contact Information

The owner of Unique Bicycles makes a commitment to a very high level of customer service because she believes that it will be essential to the online store's success. Therefore, she assigns one of her employees to answer phone calls and customer emails. The Unique Bicycles Website includes a toll-free number that customers can call during business hours and a dedicated email address (*customerservice@uniquebicycles.biz*). Also, Unique Bicycles writes a series of FAQs that discuss issues ranging from how to pick the right size of bicycle to questions about warranties of the bicycles sold by Unique Bicycles. The FAQs will be discussed in more detail later in this chapter.

Customer Service Policy

In addition to including multiple ways that customers can contact Unique Bicycles, the owner has written a clear customer service policy. First of all, the policy clearly states the contact options (i.e., email, toll-free phone number and mailing address) that Unique Bicycles offers, as well as the hours of operation. Also, Unique Bicycles promises that they will answer all inquiries via email within twenty-four hours on business days. The customer service policy will be discussed in more detail later in this chapter.

Next, the customer service policy explains the warranty offered for all of the bicycles sold at Unique Bicycles. All Bicycles sold receive a limited sixty-day warranty from all functional defects. The warranty excludes customer abuse such as crashing a bicycle.

Reducing Doubts

Third-Party Review

Unique Bicycles decide to submit their online store to apply for the Control Scan Seal (*https://www.controlscan.com/products_secure_seals.php*). Control scan reviews an online business's application, and if it passes certain security criteria, then the business Website can include a Control Scan "seal of approval." Unique Bicycles successfully applies for the seal of approval and includes it on their Website to reduce customer doubts about their businesses. The seal of approval shows that Unique Bicycles is a reputable business that has taken appropriate security and privacy precautions.

The policies and other information used by Unique Bicycles to reduce FUDs will be worthless unless their customers can find the information that they are looking for. If a customer is curious about the shipping policy of Unique Bicycles, she must find it quickly and without frustration to reduce FUDs.

As shown on the next page in Figure 10.13, there is a link to the policies included at the bottom of every page of the Website (i.e., the "footer"). It also includes a link to the customer service information (that includes contact information) at the top of every page in the main navigations. Unique Bicycles wants to make sure that customers are able to find this information very easily.

FIGURE 10.13—*Navigation Considerations to Reduce FUDs*

Make a Sale on the Unique Bicycles Website

Once Unique Bicycles builds sufficient trust, they must motivate visitors to make a purchase on the Unique Bicycles Website. By using the Shopify merchant account, the owners set up an intuitive online sales process that allows customers to find the bicycle that they are looking for and to check out of the store.

Step #1: Find Desired Products in Your Catalog

As discussed earlier, any online store must be able to support browsing and searching functions within the online product catalog. Unique Bicycles makes sure to support both of these functions in an intuitive manner. As shown in Figure 10.14, the product catalog provides a product search where customers can type certain keywords to help them locate a bicycle. Alternatively, the customer can "drill down" to the product that he is looking for by using the three categories of bicycles on the right side of the product catalog. The customer can select one of the categories of bicycles (e.g., used bikes), and the product catalog will only show this subset of bicycles.

Step #2: Use a Shopping Cart to Keep Track of Products

Once a customer either browses to or searches for a specific bicycle, he must be able to add the product to the shopping cart to keep track of it while continuing shopping. As shown in Figure 10.15, an "Add to Cart" button appears on each product page that allows the customer to add the specific bicycle to the shopping cart.

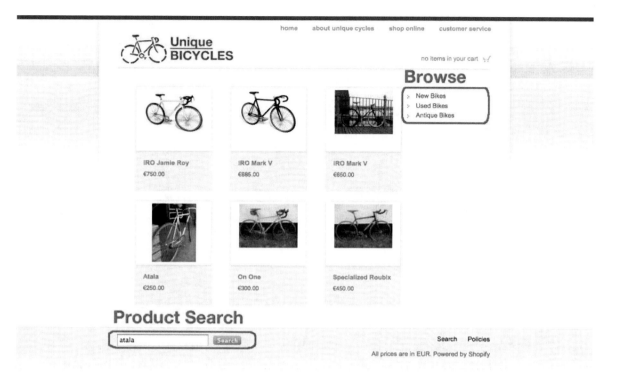

FIGURE 10.14—*Browsing and Searching Mechanisms in the Online Catalog*

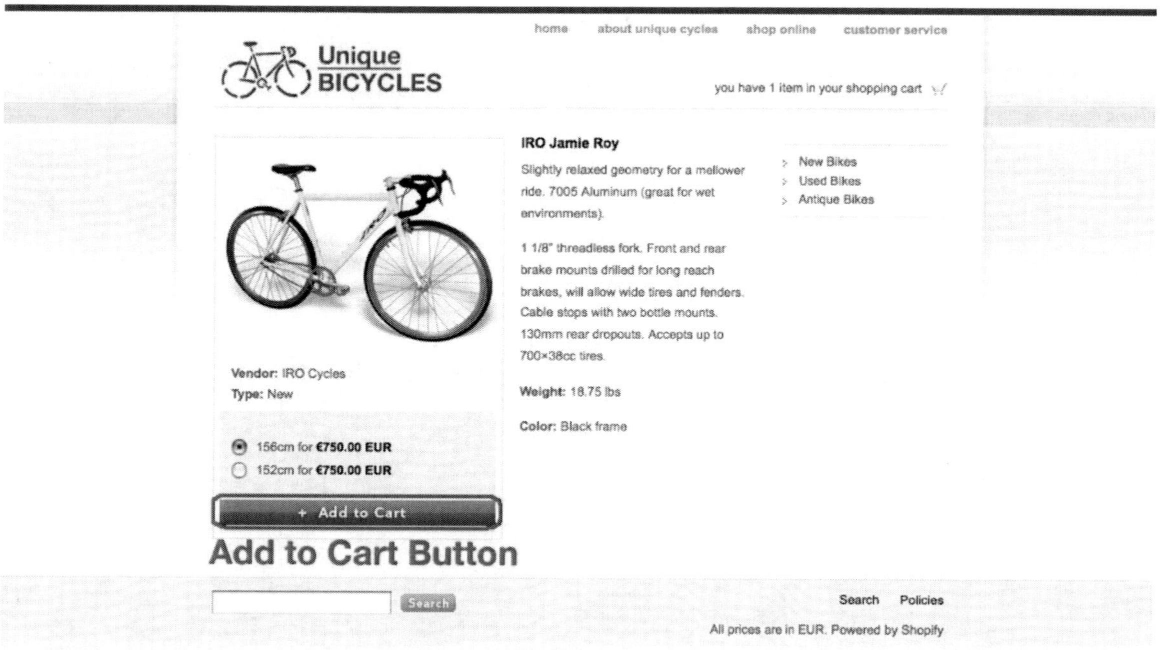

FIGURE 10.15—*Adding Products to the Shopping Cart*

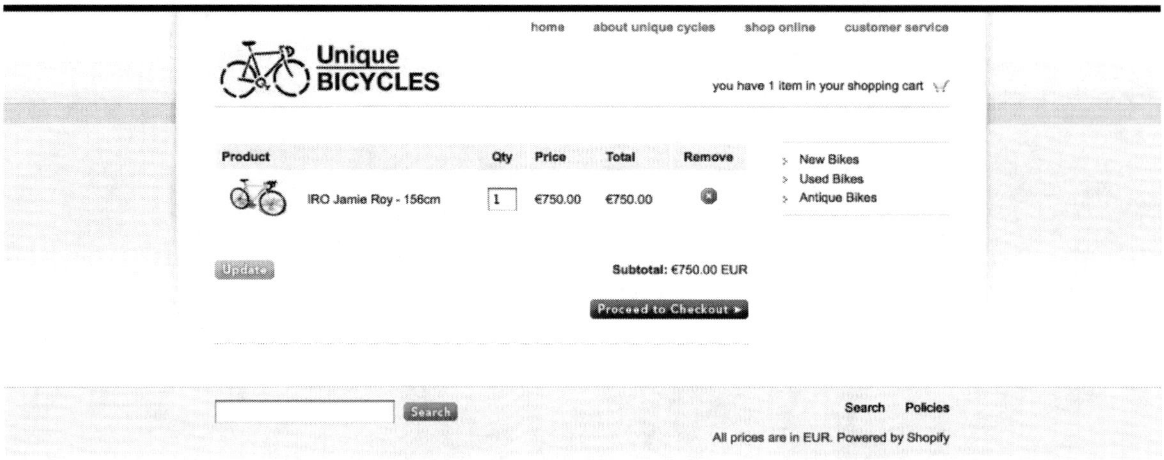

FIGURE 10.16—*Shopping Cart Provided by Shopify*

Once the customer clicks the "Add to Cart" button, the product is added to the shopping cart and the customer is redirected to his current shopping cart. As shown in Figure 10.16, the shopping cart allows the customer to update the quantity, to remove a product and to add additional bicycles to the shopping cart.

Step #3: Checkout of Your Store

After the customer has finalized the shopping cart, the Unique Bicycles Website provides an intuitive checkout process that collects information needed to make a successful sale. During the first step of the checkout process, Unique Bicycles collects essential contact information, including the customer's email address, telephone number, shipping address and billing address. It should also remind the customer what he is about to purchase; Unique Bicycles shows the details of the customer's shopping during each step of the checkout process (see Figure 10.17).

After the site collects the contact information, it must collect payment information from the customer, which is the focus of the next topic ("Getting Paid").

Getting Paid

Shopify offers numerous options for getting paid. Therefore, the Unique Bicycles' owner needs to select the options that work best for her specific business—more payment options offer greater flexibility for customers, but at the same time they require additional resources.

Unique Bicycles decides to offer three payment options: credit cards, merchant services (using PayPal) and money orders. The credit card and merchant service options satisfy customers who are comfortable sharing and using their credit card information online. The money order option satisfies customers who would rather not share any personal information via online transactions. The owner decides not to accept

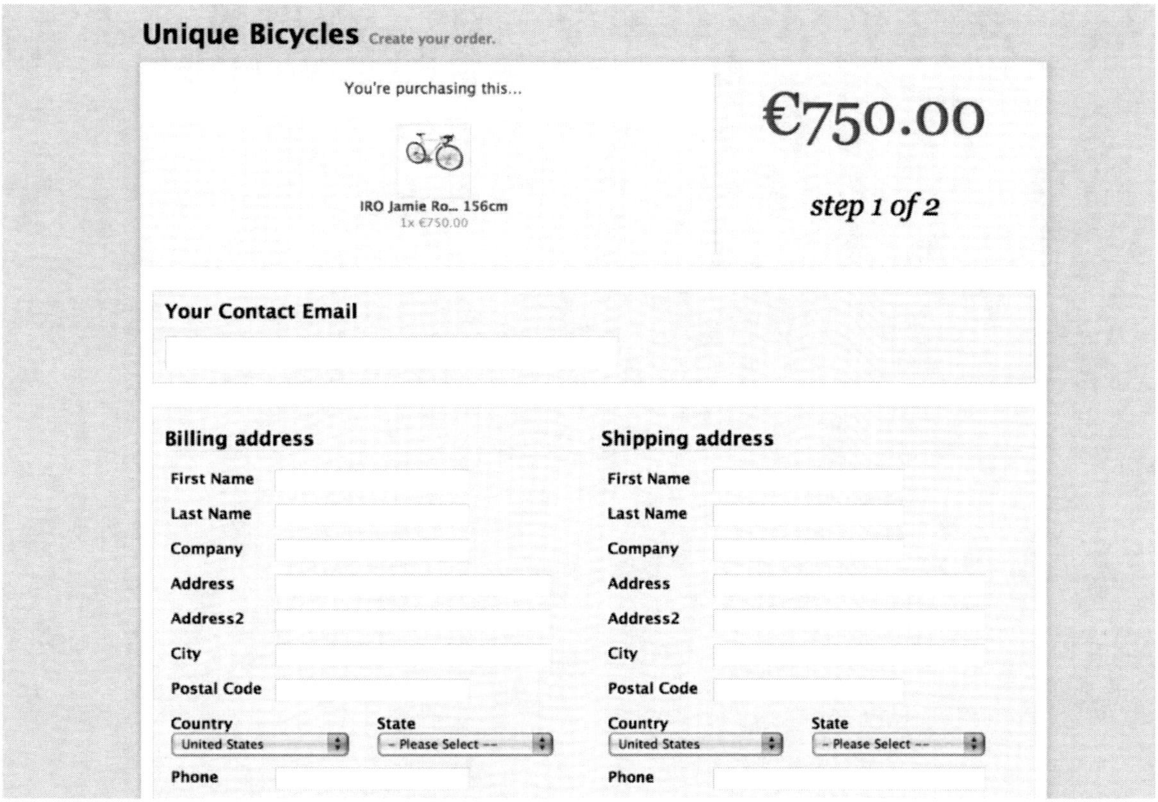

FIGURE 10.17—*First Step of the Checkout Process*

payments via bank accounts because she believes that most customers would be unwilling to share this extremely sensitive information with her business.

These three options are easily added to the Unique Bicycles Website in the "Preferences" section of the Shopify administration area.

Credit Cards/Merchant Services

Credit card processing and the use of the PayPal merchant services are set up at the same time on Shopify. As shown in Figure 10.18, Unique Bicycles first selects that they would like to accept credit cards and PayPal.

The owner then provides Unique Bicycle's PayPal username/password and selects the type of PayPal account. They must first set up the PayPal account directly at *www.paypal.com.*

Money Orders

After setting up the credit card processing, they can select other payment options. As discussed above, Unique Bicycles would also like to accept money orders as a payment option. The owner selects the money order option from the list below and provides instructions about how to pay by money orders.

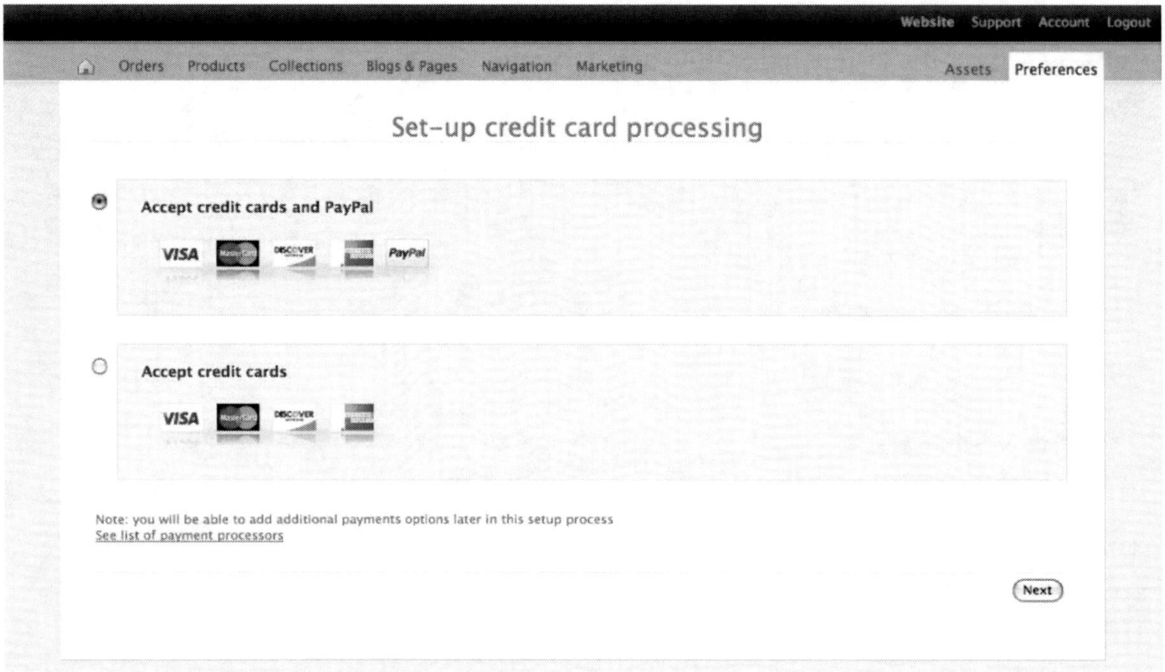

FIGURE 10.18—*Setting Up Credit Card Processing*

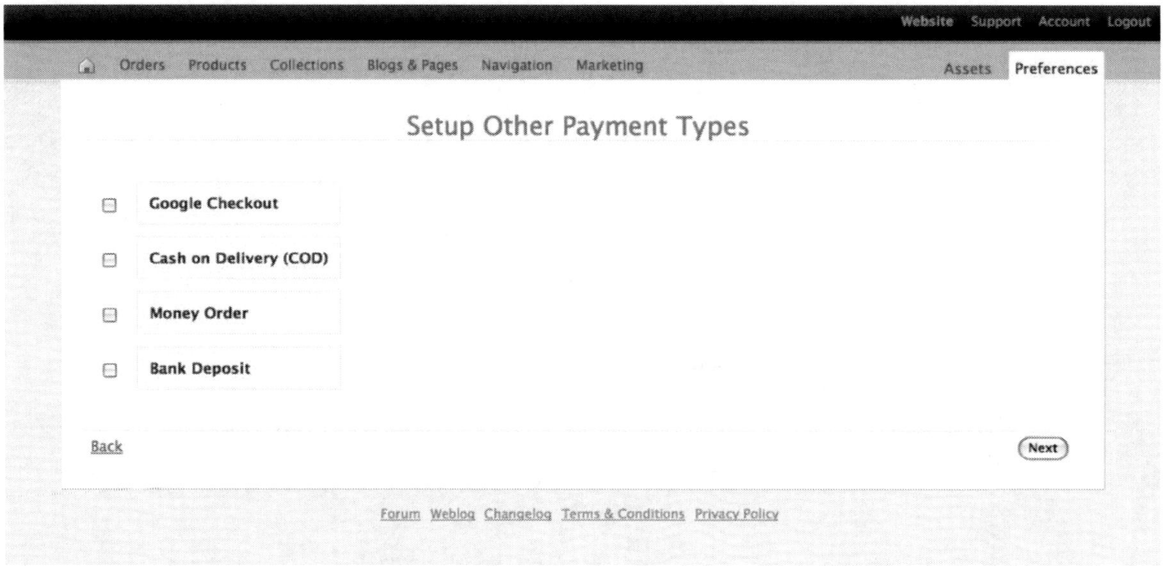

FIGURE 10.19—*Setting Up Other Payment Options*

Now that Unique Bicycles has added the payment options to the account, a customer is able to finish the checkout process discussed during the previous topic. After providing his contact information, the customer sees a screen that provides the payment options that the owner of Unique Bicycles added. As shown in Figure 10.20, the options appear before the customer on the last page of the checkout process. Once the customer selects the specific payment option (Credit Card, PayPal or Money Order) and provides the necessary payment information (e.g., credit card number and expiration date), he can

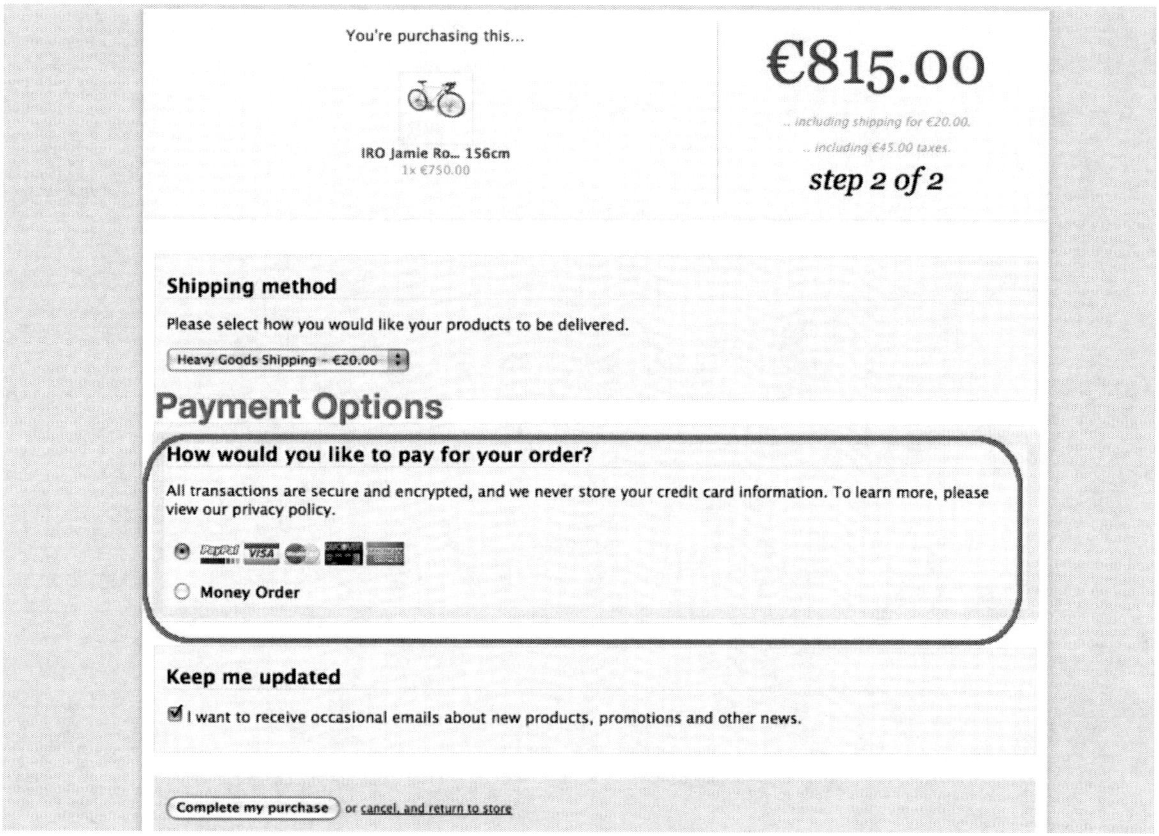

FIGURE 10.20—*Selecting a Payment Option During Checkout*

click the "Complete My Purchase" button at the bottom of the screen to finish the checkout process.

After the order is successfully processed, Shopify automatically sends a customer a confirmation email with the details of the order and the customer receives a confirmation screen, as seen in Figure 10.21. The sale has been successfully completed!

Delivering Unique Bicycle's Products

After researching other shipping carriers, the owner of Unique Bicycles decides to use UPS to fulfill her shipping needs. The owner sets up a business account on the *UPS.com* Website (for more information on the account setup process and requirements, please see the Small Business Guide on the UPS Website in your country). While we will not provide a step-by-step guide of what Unique Bicycles' owner did to set up her account (the process varies in each country), below is essential information provided to set up the business account:

- Business information, such as the business name, address and phone number

- The name and email address of the individual managing the account and a password for secure access

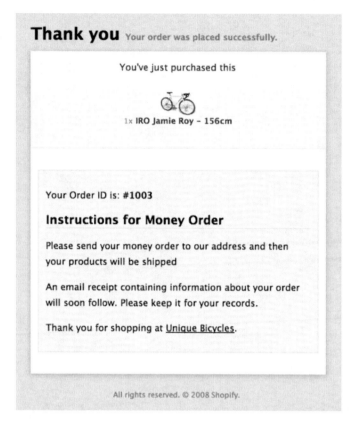

FIGURE 10.21—*Order Confirmation*

> ☞ Payment information (either a credit card number or an address where a weekly bill should be sent)

> ☞ Description of average shipping needs (e.g., how many packages per week will they ship)

Once Unique Bicycles provides this information, a new UPS account number is generated for them. With the account successfully set up, Unique Bicycles can now perform essential shipping functions by using the UPS business account. For example, Unique Bicycles can pay for the shipment of a package, print out a shipping label and send a shipment tracking number directly to the customer. Unique Bicycles also can request that UPS pick up the package directly from their business location (for a small fee), or they can drop the package off at any of the local UPS shipping centers.

After setting up their business account at UPS, Unique Bicycles adds the shipping options described in their shipping policy using the Shopify administration area. In the "Preferences" section, the owner clicks on the "Shipping" link in the menu on the right side. Within this section, Unique Bicycles can manage the countries that it ships to, the shipping options that each country offers and the prices for each shipping option.

The owner first adds the three domestic shipping options: free shipping (for orders € 99+), standard shipping and expedited shipping. Also, as mentioned in the policy, when an order exceeds 100 lbs, then a different shipping rate is charged. Shopify allows for offering shipping options based on weight and price. For example, when a customer's shopping cart contains bicycles that weigh more than 100 lbs, then Unique Bicycles will offer only the "Domestic Overweight" shipping option to the customer during the checkout process. Figure 10.22 shows a listing of the domestic shipping options once they are added using Shopify.

Once the domestic shipping options are added, the owner turns her attention to adding the international shipping options. As described in the shipping policy, Unique Bicycles only ships to other countries in the European Union, and they offer two international shipping options—standard and expedited shipping. For example, Figure 10.23 shows the shipping options for customers in Switzerland. Unique Bicycles adds identical shipping options for the rest of the countries that it ships to in the European Union.

After they add the shipping options, using the Shopify administration area, these become available during the checkout process. For example, for a domestic customer purchasing bicycles weighing less than 100 lbs, the options shown in Figure 10.24 are available during the checkout process.

⊞ United Kingdom			
Standard Shipping	0.0lbs – 100.0lbs	€25.00 EUR	🗑
Expedited Shipping	0.0lbs – 100.0lbs	€50.00 EUR	🗑
Domestic Overweight	100.1lbs – 250.0lbs	€75.00 EUR	🗑
Free Shipping	€100.00 minimum	€0.00 EUR	🗑
Add weight-based rate	Add price-based rate		

FIGURE 10.22—*Domestic Shipping Options*

⊡ Switzerland			
Standard International Shipping	0.0lbs – 100.0lbs	€30.00 EUR	🗑
Expedided International Shipping	0.0lbs – 100.0lbs	€65.00 EUR	🗑
Add weight-based rate	Add price-based rate		

FIGURE 10.23—*Shipping Options for Customers in Switzerland*

Shipping method

Please select how you would like your products to be delivered.

Free Shipping – €0.00
Free Shipping – €0.00
Standard Shipping – €25.00
Expedited Shipping – €50.00

FIGURE 10.24—*Selecting Shipping Methods*

As soon as UPS picks up the order, or Unique Bicycles drops it off at a UPS location, it needs to send a shipment tracking number to the customer. The tracking number tells the customer where the package is and when UPS will deliver it. Customers shopping online now expect this information.

Unique Bicycles accomplishes this by logging into their UPS business account and creating a new shipment. After selecting certain shipping options (e.g., shipping speed, insurance, etc.), they generate a tracking number and send an email to the customer who is receiving the package. The tracking number is sent to the customer via an email automatically generated as soon as UPS scans the shipping label. By clicking a link within the email message, the customer is redirected to a UPS online system called "QuantuumView," where he can track the progress of his shipment.

Responding to Questions and Issues

As already discussed, a link to the customer service information is included on each of the pages that are part of the Unique Bicycles Website. We already discussed the details of the customer service policy, but now the company must add the information to its Website. Also, as part of the customer service page, Unique Bicycles wants to include some answers to frequently asked questions (FAQs), customer service contact information for when FAQs do not answer a question and a description of how to return bicycles.

To add the information, the owner goes to the "Blogs & Pages" section in the administration area and clicks on the Customer Service page. Then the owner clicks the "edit this page" link and adds the necessary information to the Customer Service page as shown in Figure 10.25. Once the information is saved, it becomes available on the Unique Bicycles Website as shown in Figure 10.26.

In addition to including a clear customer service policy and contact information, the Customer Service page includes a series of Frequently Asked Questions (FAQs). Whenever a customer contacts Unique Bicycles, the employees have instructions to add the customer's question and the answer given to the FAQ page. This process allows for Unique Bicycles to more efficiently communicate with customers; they do not have to answer the same questions via phone, email or mail more than once. For example, Figure 10.27 shows some FAQs included on the customer service page.

Returning an Item

A customer must first contact Unique Bicycles before returning her purchased bicycle, and she must specify a reason for the return. Then, if approved, Unique Bicycles provides a Return Authorization number to the customer that she must write on the package that contains the returned bicycle. The Return Authorization number allows Unique Bicycles to match a returned bicycle to a specific customer. Also, since the customer must contact Unique Bicycles prior to making a return, the owners can anticipate a return in advance, so they have the necessary personnel available to handle processing the returns.

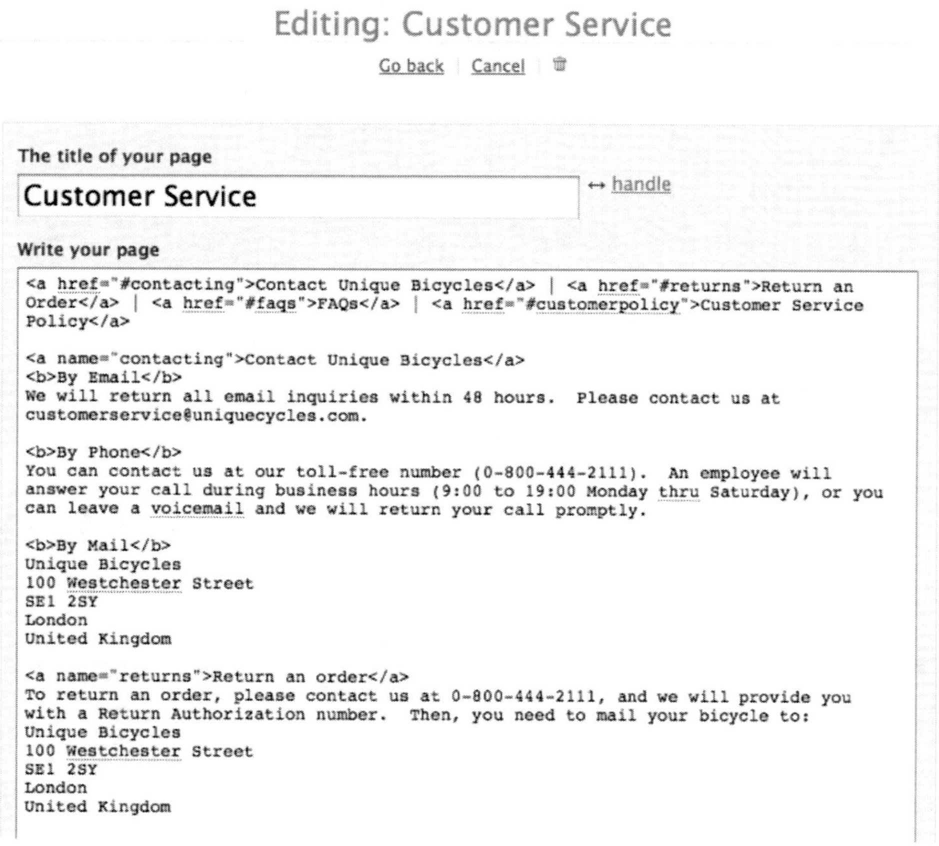

Editing: Customer Service

Go back | Cancel | 🗑

The title of your page

Customer Service   ↔ handle

Write your page

```
<a href="#contacting">Contact Unique Bicycles</a>  |  <a href="#returns">Return an
Order</a>  |  <a href="#faqs">FAQs</a>  |  <a href="#customerpolicy">Customer Service
Policy</a>

<a name="contacting">Contact Unique Bicycles</a>
<b>By Email</b>
We will return all email inquiries within 48 hours.  Please contact us at
customerservice@uniquecycles.com.

<b>By Phone</b>
You can contact us at our toll-free number (0-800-444-2111).  An employee will
answer your call during business hours (9:00 to 19:00 Monday thru Saturday), or you
can leave a voicemail and we will return your call promptly.

<b>By Mail</b>
Unique Bicycles
100 Westchester Street
SE1 2SY
London
United Kingdom

<a name="returns">Return an order</a>
To return an order, please contact us at 0-800-444-2111, and we will provide you
with a Return Authorization number.  Then, you need to mail your bicycle to:
Unique Bicycles
100 Westchester Street
SE1 2SY
London
United Kingdom
```

FIGURE 10.25—*Addition of Information to Customer Service Page*

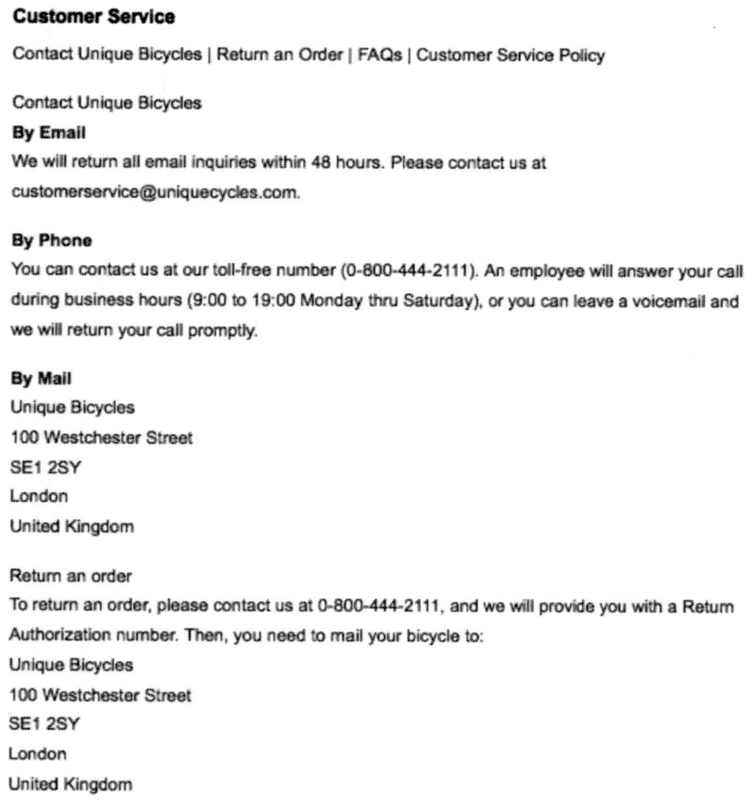

Customer Service

Contact Unique Bicycles | Return an Order | FAQs | Customer Service Policy

Contact Unique Bicycles

By Email

We will return all email inquiries within 48 hours. Please contact us at
customerservice@uniquecycles.com.

By Phone

You can contact us at our toll-free number (0-800-444-2111). An employee will answer your call
during business hours (9:00 to 19:00 Monday thru Saturday), or you can leave a voicemail and
we will return your call promptly.

By Mail

Unique Bicycles

100 Westchester Street

SE1 2SY

London

United Kingdom

Return an order

To return an order, please contact us at 0-800-444-2111, and we will provide you with a Return
Authorization number. Then, you need to mail your bicycle to:

Unique Bicycles

100 Westchester Street

SE1 2SY

London

United Kingdom

FIGURE 10.26—*Customer Service Information on the Unique Bicycles Website*

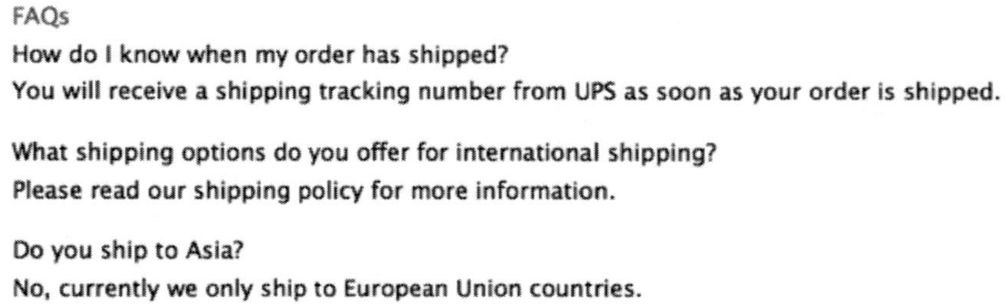

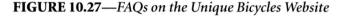

FAQs

How do I know when my order has shipped?
You will receive a shipping tracking number from UPS as soon as your order is shipped.

What shipping options do you offer for international shipping?
Please read our shipping policy for more information.

Do you ship to Asia?
No, currently we only ship to European Union countries.

FIGURE 10.27—*FAQs on the Unique Bicycles Website*

Also, shipping a returned bicycle is not easy. It must be disassembled and packaged in a way that keeps it from being damaged during the shipping process. Therefore, the Unique Bicycles Website includes detailed instructions about how to disassemble bicycles and their packing materials. The Website also specifies that the customer is responsible for all damages that occur during the shipping process due to poor packaging.

Protecting Unique Bicycles' Property and Customers

Employee Policy

The first step in successfully protecting the property of Unique Bicycles is to implement a clear employee policy. The owner of Unique Bicycles often will need help from employees to successfully fulfill orders. Therefore, any employee allowed to administer the Unique Bicycles Website who has access to customer and order information must have a clear understanding of what she should and should not do. The employee policy also clearly defines how to respond to certain customer requests where potentially sensitive data might need sharing (through the phone and via email).

SSL

Another important mechanism for protecting the property of Unique Bicycles and its customers is to use encrypted communication whenever they transmit any sensitive data. The Web address used to log into the administration interface at Shopify starts with *https://,* which signifies the use of SSL encryption. Also, whenever customers are providing any personal information, the site needs to encrypt this data. Shopify also provides SSL encryption protection. In addition, the owner verifies that PayPal provides SSL encryption and finds out that PayPal uses the strongest available level of encryption.

Privacy Policy

Finally, the owner verifies that Unique Bicycles is in compliance with the privacy policy included on its Website mentioned earlier ("Building Trust"). The owner verifies that Unique Bicycles (1) is collecting customer information described in the privacy policy, (2) is only collecting information via Web forms with SSL encryption, (3) is not allowing access to customers' financial information to its employees and (4) is not sharing the customer information with any other companies or organizations.

Launching the Online Bicycles Store

After completing the steps discussed earlier, Unique Bicycles is ready to do business online. However, launching an online store is not the end of the story. The owner must adjust and make changes as the company gathers consumer feedback and makes sales. Consumers might demand new products, additional shipping options or new payment options. However, due to the methodological approach to building the e-commerce storefront that the owner undertook, Unique Bicycles is unlikely to have to make major changes to their online store in the future.

Exercise

Review the Shopify Website mentioned in this chapter and record your discoveries. What would be the hardest part of establishing your own online store? Why?

chapter 11

The People Part of Operations and Information Management

Change! The Greatest Hurdle to Get Over

System Usability

Wrap Rage?

Some History of Meeting User Needs and Desires

What Is "Usability"?

Why Is Usability Important?

What Can Be Done to Improve Usability?

Usability Can't Be Ignored

Chapter Summary

Although we have mentioned that people in organizations are important, this chapter dwells on both people inside and outside the organization that assist in leading the organization to success. With regard to Operations and Information Management, people must perform business tactics, people must use systems provided to fully take advantage of the leverage provided, and people must be customers for both products and services. Human behavior and reactions to a changed system can make or break a revised process, a different Website or human-technology interface and how well accepted a change is. This chapter focuses on the considerations that must be made in the people side of systems.

Change! The Greatest Hurdle to Get Over

Whenever a system or process is changed, people must change what they currently are doing and do something different. This is a huge challenge for most people. They want to continue to do what is familiar and comfortable and avoid the unknown. Maintaining the status quo is the easiest path to take. The rational side of systems may get put aside and the emotional side can take over. Change could affect perceived power, status in the organization, social groups and ability to communicate with others, ego and even job security. Change is difficult. But, as the world and the environment change, people must adapt and ensure that the systems they are using fit with and can thrive in the changed environment.

One major factor that we must address is to ensure that people understand why change is necessary and that they have contributed their viewpoints and feelings regarding the change. Without participation in the change process, we can expect resistance to the change. The change should be perceived as "our" idea and not someone else's idea forced on them. They must understand that individual and organizational survival depends on change. Change is necessary to adapt to changes in the world surrounding the organization. They must believe that there is value in changing and that some kind of reward will come to them for any changes they make. An old adage is that "you get the behavior you reward" and "what gets rewarded gets repeated." Rewards often shape our behavior. A simplistic view of change and motivation occurs to anyone who has trained their pet. They will understand that "treats" of some kind are the reward that motivates behavior.

Some behaviorists such as Elizabeth Kubler-Ross have described various stages of death and dying. Tannenbaum believes that we can view change as requiring someone to "die a little death." The dying person goes through various stages before accepting his or her fate. He stated that people having to go through a change may also go through a series of "little death" stages as they have to give up something they currently know about to accept something they know little about. Change creates a fear of the unknown. A modification of the Kubler-Ross stages applied to change might include the following stages:

- **Surprise**—"Are you sure I have to change?"

- **Denial**—"No, not me. You must mean someone else."

- ☞ **Anger**—"This makes me mad. Can't we just leave good enough alone?"

- ☞ **Resentment and Envy**—"Why not someone else? Why me?"

- ☞ **Bargaining**—"Can I have more time? I know I can make the old way work better."

- ☞ **Grief with the Past**—"I should have done things differently and I wouldn't be in this situation where change is necessary."

- ☞ **Grief with Future Losses**—"If I had more time in the future, I would do some things differently and I could still be in control."

- ☞ **Acceptance**—"I should have realized it was inevitable and I need to make the best of the situation."

As change agents, we must realize the stages that people we are asking to change are in and attempt to address their concerns. Those who become surprised need assurance by verification and clarity about why the change truly is necessary. We should help the changed understand why change is necessary. Those in denial need help addressing the question and the issue and assurance that change really is necessary and that they cannot avoid it. We can address anger with empathy and the understanding that change is never easy for anyone. The change agent must help the changers with "letting go" of the past as well as dealing with the future. We must address resentment and envy with both facts and a belief that the persons advocating the change have studied the issue and are familiar with the processes and activities that need changing. Bargaining often requires detailing the consequences of not making the change and why the situation will get worse. We can deal with grief about the past and the future by assisting the people who face the change to experience some future state thinking and describing how things will be in the future. Hopefully, the persons having to change can see new opportunities and a chance for excitement and advancement. Often, this requires dealing with the uncertainty of what life will be like and a fear of the unknown. All of these stages can lead to an acceptance of change, but the change agent should be observant of what stage persons are at that need to change.

Along with the promoted change come some other concerns. Consider the rewards that you find necessary upon introducing change. Following from the above premise of "you get the behavior you reward" is the fact that we must analyze current and future reward systems. If someone's job changes and he or she has added responsibility, a need may exist to adjust the pay for the position. Another consideration is that change might bring a need for training to perform the business tactics and use the results from the changed operations process models or the changed information provided to the decision makers. Finally, if the job has changed and requires hiring new people, there is a need to change job hiring descriptions and entry qualifications. The organization must manage all of this change and not just force it on the members. Human resource specialists often can provide assistance in putting all of these pieces together.

Communication is critical to managing change. Some essential basic concepts and values accompany change management. We can summarize them with the TRECF concept:

- **T for Trust** that must be earned so that management trusts the workers and the workers trust management. As with the information cycle in Chapter 3, trust is the foundation of change management.

- **R for Respect** for each other. Workers must have respect for the ability of management to lead the organizational effort at all levels. Likewise, management must have respect for the workers' skills and knowledge. Without respect, it is very difficult to work with each other and to build synergistic team efforts. Some persons have stated that TEAM really summarizes **T**ogether **E**veryone **A**ccomplishes **M**ore.

- **E for Empathy** means that all people must try to "walk a mile in someone else's shoes." This means that there is true understanding of others and their fears and anxieties.

- **C for Communication** requires that we allow a true exchange of ideas and motivations. Without communication, there is little trust, respect and empathy.

- **F for Fairness** is the effort put forth to assure people that they are receiving treatment as though others truly care for them and their needs.

All of the TRECF concepts are necessary to assure people that they are valued members of the organizational team and that their contributions make the organization a better place for other workers and customers. Change requires conscious and conscientious thought and care since it can have an effect on the individual (psychological) as well as on the team (sociological). It may take less power to prevent a change than it takes to institute a change.

In summary, the organization must understand the need for change; the persons required to change must participate in planning the change; both psychological and sociological factors must be considered; and there must be concern shown for fear of the unknown. The important concepts of empathy and understanding, which we will discuss later in the chapter, are critical in addressing resistance to change.

System Usability

Along with change, another human issue that we must address is system usability. Often change brings on new and enhanced systems. And change may be better accepted if newly introduced systems are truly usable. You want the people who are changing to say "this is so much easier than what we did before." Then the change will become a reality.

Part of the design of the systems includes consideration of how the human and computer-based systems will interact. Often we refer to this as the human-computer interface. But the issue of usability goes far beyond interfaces between humans and the computer. Even everyday objects must be usable. We will introduce the idea of interaction by looking at some everyday objects that should be usable.

Wrap Rage?

When we think about a typical day, we find many things that are hard to understand and hard to use. Often when we buy a new product, our first struggle is to get it out of its packaging. This has led to a term called "wrap rage." Many electronic devices come in hard plastic containers. Getting them out of these packages can lead to anger and frustration. We often resort to using knives and sharp objects to cut and saw through a package. Removing something as simple as the cellophane from recorded media such as a compact disk (CD) often is a challenge. The packaging simply is not usable.

Zapping Wrap Rage?

The Zibra Open It multitool is a ten-inch-long device to help reduce wrap rage. The steel sheers can cut through plastic clamshell packaging. It also includes a retractable utility knife that can cut through cardboard or cellophane packages. It probably is not best to try to carry this through airport security. (See Figure 11.1)

FIGURE 11.1—*The Zibra Open It Multitool*

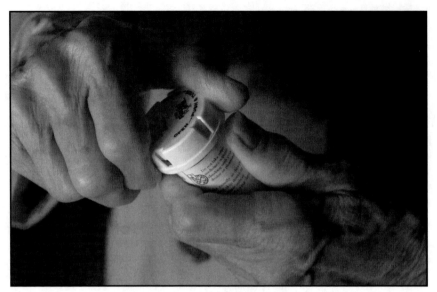

© Carsten Reisinger. Used under license from

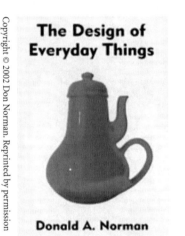

FIGURE 11.2—*An Unusable Teapot*

Another package that often is hard to open is a simple condiment wrapper. We all have seen a person struggling with a mustard or ketchup packet and trying to tear off a piece of a side to get at the contents. Frustration can get so great that people will go without the condiment or resort to using a sharp tool or even biting on the package. We can often say the same for factory sealed pill bottles. The foil or cellophane bottle sealer needs puncturing and then scraping off to have a clean lip on the bottle. Usability starts with unwrapping or accessing the purchased products.

A classic book called *The Design of Everyday Things* by Donald Norman reviews many objects fraught with usability issues. Norman examines doors that are difficult for people to determine whether to pull or push or which side to push. Pushing on the hinged side could result in physical injury. He has a photo of an elegant tea pot with the handle and spout on the same side (Figure 11.2). He also reviews computer systems that are difficult to use.

So why do users of products and systems have such difficulty? Much of the reason lies in the lack of a user-centered design. The designers simply did not consider the user and the actions needed to use the product or device. Then they did not test the product in a real situation.

Some History of Meeting User Needs and Desires

Technically skilled engineers often design computer-based systems and even modern electronics. These engineers do have an end user in their minds. But, the end user they think of is themselves, not the everyday user. And many would argue that most people do not think like engineers. This is the basis of the popular Dilbert cartoon series.

A 1982 book by Paul Heckel entitled *The Elements of Friendly Software Design* introduced a historic perspective on design by engineers. Heckel reviews the art form of presenting and communicating images and looks back in history at filmmaking. He recalls that engineers, including the great inventor Thomas Edison, controlled the original filmmaking industry. Theatres in Edison's age would show films that were eight minutes long. Edison believed that each of the eight-minute segments should cover four or five subjects. He believed that people liked variety. His influence hindered innovation in the film industry for many years.

Finally, Edwin S. Porter took Edison to task and argued for a new art form view of films and filmmaking. Porter wanted films to tell a story, not just report some facts in a visual fashion. According to Heckel, early filmmakers produced films by having a stationary camera and actors and actresses that would perform some action in front of the camera. The camera did not move.

In 1903, Porter staged a film that attempted to tell a story, *The Great Train Robbery*. But the big breakthrough in film came in 1914 in a film by D. W. Griffith entitled *Birth of a Nation* that changed the filmmaking business. The film truly communicated a story to an audience. The epic film introduced the basic techniques of filmmaking that are still in use today. The techniques included moving cameras and incorporated the close-up, the moving shot, the fade, the cutaway and the dissolve.

These innovative techniques caused quite a stir in theaters. According to Heckel, the first close-up used in the film caused "panic when shown because the audience mistook it for a 'severed head.'" Remember that the audience was used to stationary cameras. We could compare the phenomenon to you sitting in a stationary car, losing your frame of reference and feeling you are moving when the car next to you actually is moving.

Griffith used a montage of images to create action and excitement in the film. He cut from one action sequence to another, reducing each time segment to create a crescendo effect. Griffith was communicating with his audience, his "users."

The innovative film *Birth of a Nation* was not eight minutes long, but it lasted two and a half hours. Millions of people paid the huge amount at the time of $2 each to see the film. In previous times, the lower classes typically viewed short films, but the new film appealed to even the middle and upper classes. It was the first film shown to President Woodrow Wilson in the White House. Moving from an engineering perspective to an art form created a revolution. The user truly was recognized as an audience that needed a new form of communication, something needed in the technology industry today.

Not to pick on Thomas Edison, but he also was the subject of a discussion by Donald A. Norman in a 1998 book entitled *The Invisible Computer*. Edison invented the phonograph and told early users to be persistent in learning how to use it as it only would take two weeks to fully understand how to operate the device. Norman claimed Edison was a great inventor but a poor businessperson since he thought like an engineer, not like a user-centric marketer. Edison believed everyone thought and behaved like he did. He took the engineering viewpoint where technology for technology's sake was the rule. Other companies that considered the needs and wants of the customer usurped Edison's phonograph business.

Finally, Alan Cooper in his book *The Inmates are Running the Asylum: Why High-Tech Products Drive Us Crazy and How to Restore the Sanity* claimed that engineers were truly the inmates running the technology design process. This led to unused features on new products and systems that engineers thought were "cool," but that did not serve the needs of the customers and made products and systems more complex. Cooper believes that empathy for the end user is necessary and achievable through the use of an approach called "personas," which we will describe later in this chapter.

The point to keep in mind is that we desire simplicity and usability that get the job done for the customer, not complexity and technologic superiority that makes the engineers happy.

What Is "Usability"?

Usability is the ease of using products and systems without having to think. A book by Steve Krug entitled *Don't Make Me Think* referred to designing usable Websites. If a site is truly usable, it should be natural and the first-time visitor should easily understand what the Website is representing and where each link leads. It should be written in a clear and understandable language. The visitor should not have to think and wonder.

The same is true of other things that people use. If two adjacent light switches controlled a left bank of lights and a right bank, then the left switch should control the left lights and the right switch should control the right lights. This is natural and what people expect.

Good usability means good flow through a set of processes. Users should anticipate what is coming next. For example, a usable form for a customer to complete would have the name with the first name first and then the last name, the address with the street first and then the city, state and zip code; then would come the phone number with the area code first and then the number. This is the order that users expect. Any deviation from this expected or natural order causes confusion and anxiety.

Usability has become a huge issue in using computer systems and Websites. As the audience for using technology has grown, frustration with difficult to use systems also has grown. Although usability has improved over time as evidenced by the simple change of moving a personal computer on/off switch from the back of the device where one could not see it to the front, we still are confronted with difficult to use technology. For example, one area of concern that still exists is the formatting of documents where changing a margin or pasting in text with a different font size or type can cause an entire document to reformat. Another area of concern is receiving an error message that does not tell you what you can do next.

A truly usable system, Website or product does not require a detailed user manual or require training to use it. The function and purpose should be intuitively obvious and not require some complex act such as holding down multiple buttons in a certain order.

FRANK WOODWARD

AGE: 48
PROFESSION: Police Officer
LOCATION: Boulder, CO

A Persona of a Police Officer
in Need of a Web Portal

Frank Woodward is a 48-year-old police officer in Boulder, Colorado. Frank took up police duty because he liked the authority it offered him. He is known for being a tough cop with an uncontrollable temper—recently, he was put on probation for a physical altercation with a CU student. In particular, Frank is known for his aggressive questioning of popular environmental and community outreach programs at the police department. Frank is a staunch conservative who tries to push his views onto other police officers through aggressive questioning of their liberal views and environmental concerns.

Frank enthusiastically uses My Yahoo! to help him make a stand against the propaganda of his own community and police department. Frank believes that a new recycling program at the police department is a terrible idea that infuriates him since he feels it wastes, not saves, energy. He uses My Yahoo! to find information about recycling so he can put an end to the recycling program. Frank also recently verbally assaulted his supervisor for assigning him to lead the police department's involvement in a community garden project because now he has to interact with

Boulder's citizens that he characterizes as "liberal freaks," and he angrily uses My Yahoo! to find information on sustainable farming practices and organic gardening. Frank also is boycotting the police department's effort to replace their old police cars with hybrid cars because he doesn't want to ever be seen in a tree hugger hybrid, so he finds the hybrid-related news on My Yahoo! an essential resource for finding stories that he perceives as biased in favor of hybrid technologies.

Frank also uses My Yahoo! to access conservative viewpoints and to find information that he then uses as a basis for his angry attacks that shock other police officers and community members. He thinks that most media is biased and spreads lies, and he uses his My Yahoo! page to access news stories that he passionately agrees with from Fox News and Rush Limbaugh (a popular conservative commentator). Also, according to Frank, the liberals made up global warming just to sell more windfarms, and he actively uses My Yahoo! to read the content about the Republican perspective on the environment and content that argues that global warming is just a hoax.

Why Is Usability Important?

Usability is important since simplicity and ease of use make a product or system more desirable to the user. In fact, usability can be a system feature or even a corporate strategy, such as that pursued by Apple Computer. The Apple Macintosh started much of the concern by others with usability. Usability can impact the organization's bottom line since revenues can grow from increased sales due to usability. Usability also can reduce costs since fewer customers will place help calls; they will figure things out for themselves. Usable systems allow self service since the users can avoid having their hands held.

Good usability also can reduce product returns. Customers return many electronic consumer products because they simply can't figure out how to operate them. Testimony to this fact is the number of electronic devices with clocks that are incorrect or are sitting there blinking "12:00" "12:00" "12:00." Auto dealers have reported that complex dashboard clock settings have resulted in service appointments to reset the clock when daylight saving time changes. All of this results in unhappy users and added costs.

Poor Website usability also can impact the organization's bottom line. Website abandonment can occur if the e-commerce site is not usable. If a potential customer on an e-commerce site becomes confused, he or she will leave the site and go to one that is less confusing. Revenue will be lost. As mentioned in the chapter on e-commerce, the site visitor is only one click away from another store. Usability also can increase costs when a site visitor gets confused and requests information from your customer service group.

Finally, bad usability can become fatal. When driving a car, the ability to easily turn on windshield wipers when needed could help avoid an accident. As reported in the chapter exercise, bad design may have contributed to the death of singer John Denver. Allan Cooper also reports in *The Inmates are Running the Asylum* that an American Airlines flight from Miami, Florida, to Cali, Columbia crashed into the side of a mountain, killing 152 passengers and eight crew members. The National Traffic Safety Board determined that the pilot was responsible. The pilot had selected "ROMEO" rather than "ROZO" from a list of possible navigation fixes. The gauges on the plane indicated the same pattern before landing as it did before crashing. Was this pilot error or a system with an uninformative interaction?

What Can Be Done to Improve Usability?

There are several factors that can assist designers when attempting to achieve usability. Although these factors are simple, designers who assume too much about their target audience often ignore them. These factors are empathy, action-orientation and testing.

Empathy

The first area where we can improve design processes is to truly understand the end user. As mentioned above, if the designers do not consciously think about and identify with the ultimate user of the designed object, they will design it for themselves. Often the designer will have a very different set of skills and different knowledge from the ultimate user. The result is a design that does not work for the end user. The designer needs to understand and empathize with the persons who will receive the design.

One means of understanding the end user is to interview some actual end users and then to create a fictional representation called a *persona*. The persona should have a name, a face represented by a picture, a background description including personal items such as family member or friends' names and ages, a typical day where the persona might use the designed object and some emotional descriptions such as fears, uncertainties and doubts of the persona. The persona should become real in the designers' minds and assist them in understanding the end users' needs and concerns. Then the designers are more likely to design for the persona and not for themselves. A sample persona is shown on the next page.

Action-Orientation

The designers must focus on the persona's goals and what the persona wants to accomplish. Then they must turn to what tasks or activities need doing to accomplish the goals. If the persona or end user needs to do something, then the designers should specify the action. In essence, action-orientation we can be summarized by the simple statement "Just tell me what to do."

An example of an action–orientation weakness in systems is the terse nature of error messages. If a person is using a system and a problem occurs, a message stating "ERROR TYPE 41" is not very helpful. Anxiety can exist if the error message asks you if you want to "shut down" or some other action without telling you the consequences of the action. The user will wonder if he or she will lose unsaved work. Thus a usable system that is action oriented will not only tell the user "what to do" and any options available but also will be informative.

Often the "HELP" function within a system is not very helpful since it informs you about some topic, but it does not give you a step-by-step action sequence that you can follow in order to do something. If you had a personal tutor, the tutor would lead you through the steps needed to accomplish your activity. A well designed action-orientation approach for getting something accomplished will be similar to a recipe for creating a fine dish.

Testing

Designers will have tested a truly usable system with representative users. This means that personas similar to the end user in skills and knowledge have performed the action sequences. Testing with technical persons or engineers is not satisfactory. Designers should improve any weaknesses in the system until they achieve a natural flow and have removed frustrating confusion points.

Usability Can't Be Ignored

Usability does matter in an organization. It makes good business sense to consider usability whether you are a developer of such products as software or are a user of systems that are dependent upon usable systems to do your job. Developers of systems want their products bought to ensure that their organization will remain competitive in the marketplace. With usable systems, business workers can more efficiently perform the business tactics that allow their organization to achieve its business objectives.

Usability does affect the bottom line of an organization. Organization members who are productive in performing business tactics can best achieve business objectives of increasing revenues or reducing costs. Better information supports the tactics. But unless the information is accessible by easy-to-use systems, people will ignore it at the peril of the organization. The organization will operate without the business intelligence to make it competitive in the marketplace.

Usability exists all around us. Significant organizational systems such as enterprise resource planning, supply chain or customer relationship management systems can become valued tools if they are simple, straight-forward and easy to use. Otherwise, the benefits from the utilization of business intelligence will not offset the cost of the system tactics used to increase revenues and reduce costs.

Chapter Summary

People are important when examining organizational systems. People must develop systems to provide information to assist in the functioning of the organization. People use systems to run the operations of the organization. People use information from the systems to obtain business intelligence to effectively and efficiently manage the processes and to make decisions in the organization. Unless organizations consider people when developing or introducing organizational systems, they will resist change, build their own alternative systems and ignore system outputs. As mentioned in Chapter 3, the information cycle continues to operate because of people. Technology is not enough.

References

Cooper, Alan. 2004. *The inmates are running the asylum: Why high tech products drive us crazy and what we can do to restore the sanity.* Indianapolis, IN: Sams Publishing.

Heckel, Paul. 1991. *The elements of friendly software design.* San Francisco: Sybex, The New Edition. (Orig. pub. 1982. New York: Warner Books.)

Krug, Steve. 2005. *Don't make me think: A common sense approach to Web usability.* Indianapolis, IN: New Riders Press, Second Edition.

Norman, Donald A. 1998. *The invisible computer.* Cambridge, MA: MIT Press.

Norman, Donald. 2002. *The design of everyday things.* New York: Perseus Books Group, Basic Books.

Tannenbaum, Robert. 1976. "Some Matters of Life and Death." Working Paper #76-2, Human Systems Development Study Center, University of California, Los Angeles, April 1976.

Exercise

Pilot Error or Bad Design?

Singer John Denver crashed and died in his homemade experimental Long E-Z aircraft on October 12, 1997. The National Transportation Safety Board investigated the crash and concluded that lack of training and pilot error contributed to the crash. But a usability expert might view the situation differently. The airplane had run low on fuel and the pilot had difficulty switching to his backup tank. The location of the fuel tank selector handle that switches fuel flow from one tank to the other was behind the pilot's left shoulder rather than in a conventional location between the pilot's legs. The pilot had to remove his shoulder harness and turn around to switch tanks. Denver and a maintenance person even tried to extend the handle with Vise Grip pliers, but this did not work. Investigators believed that when the pilot tried to reach behind and switch tanks, he pressed on the right rudder pedal, which put the aircraft in a roll and resulted in a crash. Was this pilot error or bad design? Do you feel testing would have found such an error and potentially prevented such a crash?

Exercise

Finding a Bad Design

Find an everyday thing you encounter that you feel has a bad design that you could improve. This could range from something on your car to a small appliance to the location of something in your home or workplace. Describe the current situation and tell how you would change the design to improve usability.

Exercise

Confronting Change

Describe a situation where you encountered change that you resisted. This could range from having to move to a new location, having to take a different or new job, having to attend a different school or doing something different and unfamiliar at work. Why was the change difficult for you? Why did you resist the change? Did you follow any of the stages of change described in this chapter?

chapter 12

The Future? Where Are We Going?

Throughout this book you have learned about a diverse set of topics, including viewing and studying organizations as systems, the alignment of systems and business strategy, the information cycle, business intelligence, making and delivering products/services, business processes, enterprise resource planning, project management, electronic commerce and the people side of systems. At the core of these topics are a variety of information systems (IS) and information technologies (IT). Many of these topics support business operations. For example, in order to perform e-commerce transactions we require such information technologies as Web servers, relational databases, fiber optic wires and so forth. From project management activities to managing businesses processes, information technologies/information systems (IT/IS) provide the essential infrastructure that allow real-time access to information, business intelligence and knowledge, quicker decision making and more responsive organizations that operate on something more than intuition and gut feel.

However, there is disagreement on the importance of technology in modern organizations. Many questions arise. For example, is IT/IS simply the infrastructure that modern organizations depend on? Is the infrastructure any different from any other infrastructure, such as the highway system or the electric grid? Do IT/IS add strategic value or are they merely a commodity that gives little or no competitive advantage? Do investments in expensive systems and technologies simply provide a transaction processing service?

In this chapter, we will address these provocative questions by examining the views presented by two respected authors and researchers, Nicholas Carr and Thomas Friedman. We will provide and build on their views to discuss the future role of IT/IS in organizations and how they will affect your individual future. This book is an attempt to provide you with some views and information so that you can make your own judgments about their impact on your future.

IT Doesn't Matter? Or Does It?

Nicholas Carr's article, "IT Doesn't Matter," published in May 2003 in the *Harvard Business Review,* sent shockwaves throughout the business community. In this often referenced article, Carr presented a stimulating and controversial argument. He stated that IT has now become a commodity and organizations should cut back or at least not increase their IT spending. This view raised eyebrows because the predominant view at the time was that IT/IS is capable of producing strategic value and that organizations could use it to differentiate themselves from their competitors. However, was Carr really arguing that "IT Doesn't Matter"? To critically consider this question, it is necessary to examine Carr's characterization and definition of IT/IS.

This book's view is that the primary issue with Carr's argument is his extremely narrow definition of IT/IS. According to Carr, the primary functions of IT are data storage, data processing and data transport. He views IT/IS as what we have called system tactics: the software, hardware and networking technologies. Carr also argues that IT is most comparable to infrastructural technologies such as the electric grid, the telephone system and the railroad. Infrastructural technologies are costs that organizations need to incur to keep businesses running. We agree that infrastructural technologies such as the telephone no longer help an organization gain a competitive advantage. Today almost every business has access to telephones at a very low cost. However, we do not agree with Carr that IT/IS is directly comparable to these infrastructural technologies. As we discussed at the beginning of this book, Information Technology or IT is a narrow definition of something that we have expanded in this book in the belief that Information Systems(IS) is a more appropriate term when taking a business intelligence perspective.

Think back to the model showing the alignment of business and systems strategy (BSOT) discussed at the beginning of this book. Systems tactics are where the Chief Information Officers and technologists challenged by other organizational managers spent most of their time. The primary question examined when considering system tactics is "How could the (information) system do it?" If we think of IT/IS as system tactics, then the question becomes "Do the tactics produce any strategic value?" According to the BSOT model, both system and business tactics consume organization resources and have a cost associated with them. System tactics, or the infrastructure, do not have any inherent or direct value. They only produce value to an organization when they help meet system objectives to provide better information, which assists in performing business tactics that eventually help meet the business objectives. Only then can we say that we have achieved value with information technology. System tactics can assist in producing value only when business objectives are met and benefits (in either increased revenues or reduced costs) outweigh the costs of performing the tactics.

We have introduced a series of examples in this book of how to use specific technologies and systems to influence business objectives. For example, in a previous chapter we discussed how an e-commerce storefront can radically transform a local business and open its doors to millions of potential consumers. The chapter did not focus on the information technology that enables e-commerce transactions, such as Web servers, relational databases and Web services. It did not focus on these concepts because that would present too narrow of a view of e-commerce. The technologies that make e-commerce work are only valuable if used to influence the overarching business objectives that impact the bottom line.

We provided another example in Chapter 6 how information technologies not only influence typical revenues and costs expressed as business objectives, but can transform an entire supply chain. In the e-Choupal case, a company introduced computers, printers and other technologies into the villages of the soybean farmers. They then used these e-Choupals to fundamentally transform the soybean supply chain through better information dissemination. The farmers received real-time access to soybean prices, weather conditions and industry best practices. Instead of being removed from the information flows of the supply chain, the farmers became informed members. They improved their crop yields, profit margins and their daily way of life. Their standard of living increased to the point where they were able to become consumers of other products. This in turn increased the gross national product and the economy in general. The e-Choupal technologies did not have any inherent value by themselves, but how the company used the technologies influenced the supply chain and the bottom lines of the various stakeholders.

An overall concept from this book is that IT "matters" less than IS. Second, many technology vendors only sell technology while some vendors sell solutions that assist in increasing revenue and reducing costs. Finally, risks can come from the extremes of being too aggressive or from falling behind competition in technology usage. Value and innovations from technology can increase efficiency and allow doing things not previously possible.

We must also consider systems concepts. An organization might consider system boundary expansion to include suppliers or customers and alliances to cross-sell. Organizations can expand the enterprise systems discussed in Chapter 8 to include entities often considered external to the business system. Information can be provided to gain business intelligence. Overall, technology can assist in amplifying intellect through the use of better business intelligence. We should not forget the *Moneyball* story from an earlier chapter where the use of better information transformed the entire baseball industry. This requires moving from the world of Online Transaction Processing to Online Analytic Processing.

Thus, we can conclude that information technology can matter when seen as an enabler. Mere existence of the technology is not enough. It is how the technology is leveraged to become more effective by being able to do things not previously possible and becoming more efficient by doing them with the best ratio of outputs to inputs.

Is the World Flat or Round?

We can further examine Carr's provocative proposition of whether information technologies matter by taking a broader view of the role of technology in the global society. In his 2005 book titled *The World is Flat: A Brief History of the Twenty-First Century*, Thomas Friedman examines how information technology has reshaped and transformed our world. Unlike Carr, Friedman argues that we are closer to the beginning than to the end of the technologic revolution, and that information technology is still having a profound, "flattening" impact on how business takes place today.

In a synopsis of his book in the *New York Times* (see References), Thomas Friedman begins by explaining:

> *In 1492 Christopher Columbus set sail for India, going west. He had the Nina, the Pinta, and Santa Maria. He never did find India, but he called the people he met "Indians" and came home and reported to his king and queen: "The world is round." I set off for India 512 years later. I knew just which direction I was going. I went east. I had Lufthansa business class, and I came home and reported only to my wife and only in a whisper: "The world is flat."*[1]

---

[1] Excerpt from "It's a Flat World, After All" by Thomas L. Friedman appeared in *The New York Times Magazine*, April 3, 2005 and was adapted by the author from his book, *THE WORLD IS FLAT* by Thomas L. Friedman. Copyright © 2005 by Thomas L. Friedman. Reprinted by permission of Farrar, Straus and Giroux, LLC.

Thomas Friedman came to the conclusion that the competitive environment had flattened after visiting with entrepreneurs in Bangalore, India. The entrepreneurs explained that the playing field had leveled. Companies in countries such as China and India were now competing with (and sometimes suppressing) Western companies that have traditionally dominated and controlled knowledge and knowledge work.

Friedman's travel to India led to an awakening. He found many United States personal income tax forms were completed in India after sending input data using communications technology; that radiologists in India were reading U.S. medical x-rays; that airline luggage was traced from India; and that huge banks of persons in India were offering software help from Bangalore. He also found that operations is a global activity and that information technology was enabling both the building of products in India and China and the offering of services such as problem solving from around the world. Closer investigation found that another part of the world could deliver marketing, finance, human resource and even accounting services. "Chindia" (China/India) was grooming skills and knowledge and offering them to the rest of the world, many times at a lower cost. Friedman explained that during a visit to the campus of Infosys Technologies with CEO Nandan Nilekani, the CEO exhibited a global videoconference room with a huge flat-screen TV where they could "hold a virtual meeting of the key players from its entire global supply chain." Clocks on the wall in the room were labeled U.S. West, U.S. East, G.M.T. (Greenwich Mean Time), India, Singapore, Hong Kong, Japan and Australia. The world was shrinking due to the use of information technology and virtual appearances at meetings through cameras and screens.

Many of the changes to knowledge work resembled the way the Internet operated. Recall the chapter on electronic commerce that discussed how messages are broken into packets, sent to their destination and reassembled. Now, in a flat world, work is split up. Nilekani described it as ". . . intellectual work, intellectual capital, could be delivered from anywhere. It could be disaggregated, delivered, distributed, produced and put back together . . ." The global supply chain is now turning into a global enterprise resource planning (ERP) system where work becomes distributed around the world. The playing field is leveled across the world—a flat world. Globalization is progressing from phase 1.0 where *countries* operated globally in acquiring resources to phase 2.0 where *companies* operated globally for markets and labor and now to phase 3.0 where today *individuals* must consider where they fit globally. This means you and me! We will need to communicate and compete globally, not just in our own country.

Friedman explains that much of what is happening in the world today is based on ten events and forces. These include the following: the falling of the Berlin Wall, which had symbolized confinement and closed viewpoints; Windows 3.0, which provided a global interface; Netscape and browsers allowing global search; fiber optic communication overinvestment providing infrastructure; outsourcing by allowing seamless software connections; offshoring, including moving entire factories to sources of inexpensive labor; open-sourcing, which is reducing proprietary software; and in sourcing, which is allowing others to come into your company and run your operations. This includes such things as UPS logistics managing your inventory, supply chaining or understanding and managing your supplier to customer channels globally, and informing through searching, which such activities as "Googling" make possible. Note that many of these forces relate to information technology and its ability to amplify organizational activities. Advances in technology, such as wireless operations, global positioning systems and radio frequency identification, have provided even more opportunities to excel.

Much of what we have discussed in this book emphasized this flattened world. We have moved from the old method of online transaction processing to the use of analytics. But we still need to abide by basic principles, such as cleaning bad/dirty data that could lead to incorrect results. We need to understand managers' decision-making needs. We need to take advantage of new organizational structures and processes. As we discussed in Chapter 7, Friedman mentions that a process view is replacing hierarchical/silo views. He states that "hierarchies are being flattened and value is being created less and less within vertical silos and more and more through horizontal collaboration within companies, between companies and among individuals."

Note that the forces enabling the flattening of the world are the same information technologies that according to Carr no longer matter! The massive investment in technology during the dot-com boom provided developed and developing nations alike with cheap access to broadband telecommunication capabilities, software and desktop computers. Companies in countries such as India are now using these technologies to fundamentally transform the business environment. Thus, we are going beyond the infrastructure that Carr mentions to innovative uses of these system tactics.

All kinds of work can now be off-shored and outsourced to places that can do it quicker, cheaper and possibly better. Even the United States Internal Revenue Service (IRS) outsources some of its auditing work to individuals and companies in India. This seamless transfer of work from one location to other work units around the world can only occur with the support of and the information provided by technology. Companies can work on many problems around the clock by transferring work in progress to other parts of the world. When a work shift ends in one location, they can move the work to a work group or an individual that may be just starting their work shift. Again, the technologies themselves are not flattening our world, but they certainly are enabling this rapid change.

According to Friedman, we are much closer to the beginning than the end of the technology revolution. The dot-com boom and subsequent bust was just the "warm-up act." In other words, information technologies will have a profound influence on our everyday lives, on how business is done and on how governments function. Formerly impoverished countries are just now realizing the positive influences that technology can have on their economies. Recall the impact of the e-Choupal effort and its influence on both the companies and the lives of many workers. Most companies and governments are still playing catch up. Processing power is still growing exponentially. In the near future, technology can provide more than just infrastructure; it can influence the way we compete.

So, Who Is Right?

As you probably sensed, we agree more with Thomas Friedman's assessment of the current state and future of information technology and operations management. However, it is more important for you to make an individual assessment. You are the future CEOs, CIOs and CFOs that will ultimately influence what role information technologies will play in our society.

If you agree with Carr's assessment then information technology is something that you should understand as a manager. This includes the following: (1) Spend less on information technology, (2) follow and not lead others in your technology purchases, and (3) focus on your technology vulnerabilities (e.g., security or privacy threats) instead of opportunities. In essence, this is a defensive stance. In sports, it is difficult to "score" while on defense.

On the other hand, if you think that Friedman is providing a more accurate assessment, then you need to prepare yourself to be the technology savvy business manager or the business savvy technology manager of tomorrow. You will need to either have a deep understanding of information technologies and how to use them to influence business objectives or possess a strategic focus with an appreciation of how to leverage information technologies to have an impact on your specific line of business.

In summary, Friedman and Carr have differences, but some differences depend upon definitions and some depend upon pessimism versus optimism. But both Friedman and Carr believe the future must be managed. Technology can facilitate communication, but it must be planned and managed. Cooperation between business functions is necessary and alignment is necessary. Business intelligence forces an organization to focus on customers and costs. You need to know whom you are selling to and where you will get your materials, machines and labor. This is all part of operations and information management, and if you work in business you won't be able to ignore this subject area. You can't avoid OPIM! It is a critical part of business.

The challenge that you will face is an increasingly competitive job environment. There are dozens of people who have the technology skills that you do. Countries such as China and India are infusing the workforce with talent. You will need to raise the bar to stand out. You not only will need to understand a broad range of technologies, you must have the creativity and insights to put them to use to impact the business objectives.

What Else?

Friedman's message about the flat world should serve as a warning in your career. Your competition for jobs and careers also is global. Now we see "Made in China," but the objective of developing countries also is "Designed in China." There is a need for innovation in your own career management. You should keep in mind what some refer to as the law of large numbers. There are over three billion people in China. A statement from Microsoft Corporation reminds us: "Remember, in China, when you are one in a million, there are 1,300 other people just like you." For other challenges you will face, view the video called "Shift Happens." (See References)

You cannot avoid information systems and you cannot avoid operations management. If you are the one starting a business that produces a product or a service, you will need to forecast and schedule, to manage projects and to understand and design processes, and you will need to do it using the best business intelligence in order to make better decisions faster. It will be difficult to avoid data warehouses and data mining. We live in an information focused world. You will be making decisions, and the best decisions will be made using a decision process that allows you to be the best and information that informs you and doesn't confuse you.

The rest of your world may be changing as well. Our cars and houses may become smarter, taking advantage of modern technology. Smart grids may manage our energy systems right down to the individual home level. We may even be living in a smart home. What does this mean?

Imagine a scenario where you link and "wire" your home to monitor and even control it. For example, you may have a repair person coming to your home to repair your dishwasher. A future scenario might include your watching the repair person pull into your driveway on a video camera that transmits an image to your portable computing device. You then greet the repair person from your distant location by speaking to your computer, give the repair person directions to the front door, unlock the door, watch him on other cameras in your home and guide him to the dishwasher. You then monitor and communicate with him as he does the repair. You let him out of the house and lock up again. He sends you an electronic bill, which you approve and pay, and you don't even have to be there. The future is coming faster than we believe. We should be ready for it.

Chapter Summary

Although there are arguments about the impact of information in our future, we believe it is good preparation to understand how our future will change. We can best confront our global competition at the country, company and individual levels by knowing about business and about how operations and information management can allow us to be better business people to enhance our own future. May you live in abundance and excitement. Happy trails.

Food for Thought/IT Doesn't Matter

- ☛ Carr claims that IT's potency and ubiquity has increased, but he believes its strategic value has not increased. Do you agree with this?

- ☛ Carr talks about infrastructural technologies. Is this an appropriate level of thinking or is it too wide or too narrow?

- Try to imagine a discussion between Nicholas Carr and Thomas Friedman regarding overinvestment in technology infrastructure. What do you think each would say?

- Do you believe that IT is just a commodity? Do you believe that IS and BI are commodities as well?

- Jim Collins in his book *Good to Great* found that technology is an accelerator rather than a driver of greatness. Does this align with Carr's argument? Explain.

Food for Thought/It's a Flat World After All

- So who is right? Is it Thomas Friedman or Christopher Columbus? Why?

- Why might you receive very different answers if you were to ask workers in many companies the simple question: "What time do you go to work?"

- Why is intellectual work best suited for a flattened world?

- If Globalization 1.0 defines countries globalizing for resources and imperial conquest, and Globalization 2.0 defines companies globalizing for markets and labor, what is Globalization 3.0 all about?

- Why can "crazy overinvestment be good"? Has this happened before in history?

- What role can a company like UPS play in world flattening?

- Which of the ten "flatteners" do you think is most important? Least important?

- Some believe that the last twenty years have been a warm-up act for the future. How are you preparing to play in the real game, the main event?

- What does it mean when someone says, "You are one in a million," in China?

- Do you think businesses in the U.S. and North America are in peril? Why or why not?

References

Carr, Nicholas G. 2003. IT doesn't matter. *Harvard Business Review* (May 2003), pp. 41–49.

Carr, Nicholas G. 2004. *Does IT matter? Information technology and the corrosion of competitive advantage.* Boston, MA: Harvard Business School Press.

Does IT matter? An HBR debate. *Harvard Business Review* (June 2003, pp. 2–17. Also found at: *harvardbusinessonline.hbsp.harvard.edu/b01/en/files/topic/Web_Letters.pdf*

Friedman, Tom. 2005. "It's a Flat World After All" (a summary of his book published in the *New York Times*), *http://www.nytimes.com/2005/04/03/magazine/03DOMINANCE.html*

Shift Happens. A compelling look at globalization with a strong IT emphasis: *http://www.youtube.com/watch?v=ljbI-363A2Q*

Exercise

Developing Your Analysis Skills: Our Future

Do you believe Carr that "IT Doesn't Matter"? Explain why you think it does or doesn't manner.

Exercise

Is there a business job or a career you can pursue where you would not need to know about operations and information management? Be prepared to defend your argument and to share it with others.

Exercise

Conduct a search on the Internet to find out what careers are predicted to be in most demand in the future. Do information systems fit into such careers? How about operations management? Explain how and why.

Exercise

As part of a team, brainstorm examples of businesses in your country that could be susceptible to global challenges. Relate this to your functional area, such as accounting, finance, human resources or marketing. Could global competition also challenge entrepreneurs? What can we do to react to such challenges?